WILLIAM OF ORANGE
AND THE
ENGLISH OPPOSITION
1672–4

WILLIAM OF ORANGE
AND THE
ENGLISH OPPOSITION
1672–4

BY

K. H. D. HALEY

LECTURER IN HISTORY IN THE
UNIVERSITY OF SHEFFIELD

GREENWOOD PRESS, PUBLISHERS
WESTPORT, CONNECTICUT

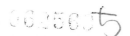

Library of Congress Cataloging in Publication Data

Haley, Kenneth Harold Dobson.
    William of Orange and the English opposition,
1672-4.

    Reprint of the 1953 ed. published at the Clarendon
Press, Oxford.
    Bibliography: p.
    Includes index.
    1. Dutch War, 1672-1678. 2. William III, King of
Great Britain, 1650-1702. 3. DuMoulin, Pierre, d. 1676.
I. Title.
[DJ193.H3 1975]   949.2'04   74-30846
ISBN 0-8371-7934-3

Originally published in 1953 at the Clarendon Press, Oxford

This reprint has been authorized by the Clarendon Press,
Oxford

Reprinted in 1975 by Greenwood Press,
a division of Williamhouse-Regency Inc.

Library of Congress Catalog Card Number 74-30846

ISBN 0-8371-7934-3

Printed in the United States of America

ACKNOWLEDGEMENTS

THE researcher in foreign archives is even more than usually dependent on the kindness of those in charge of them, and I wish to acknowledge the help received from de Heer H. Hardenberg at the Algemeen Rijksarchief in The Hague. I also have to express my gratitude to Professor Violet Barbour for sending me references to Peter Du Moulin which she collected when working on her biography of Arlington. Professor Caroline Robbins wrote two helpful letters, and Professor S. T. Bindoff provided me with some valuable assistance when I was first contemplating searching Dutch sources for this period. Miss Dorothy Kirkland devoted much of her spare time to deciphering my manuscript; and last, but by no means least, I gladly acknowledge grants received from the Sheffield University Research Fund to assist my expedition to Holland.

K.H.D.H.

SHEFFIELD
October 1952

CONTENTS

DATES

THE year has invariably been given in the New Style, i.e. in accordance with the modern practice of beginning it on 1 January. With regard to the day of the month, however, it has been felt that the most convenient method for reference is to date all events in England in Old Style, but to allude to all events on the Continent, all letters written from the Continent, and all dispatches from foreign ambassadors in London in both styles, e.g. 9/19 August.

I

INTRODUCTION: THE CRISIS OF 1672

THE year 1672 was a year of crisis both for Europe and for England. In that year Louis XIV attacked the United Provinces of the Netherlands, and his troops, under the generalship of Turenne, outmanœuvred the scanty Dutch forces and established themselves in the heart of Dutch territory at Utrecht. Most of five out of the seven provinces was overrun, and the remaining two, Holland and Zeeland, seemed to be at Louis's mercy.

Louis was to win many more battles and to make more territorial acquisitions, but it was probably at this point in 1672 that he stood at the zenith of his power. France was by far the strongest power in Europe. Her population may not have been far short of that of Spain, the hereditary Austrian dominions, Holland, and England, together. Thanks to the work of Richelieu and Mazarin her king was in far more effective control of the national resources than any other European monarch: there was no sign of opposition to Louis's will. Thanks to France's natural fertility and the work of Louis's Controller General of Finances, Colbert, he had also a greater revenue on which to draw than any other European monarch. And thanks to the organization of Le Tellier, Louvois, and Vauban, and the leadership of Turenne and Condé, he had by far the most powerful army to enforce his aggressive foreign policy.

At the same time, each of his rivals was under a cloud. The Austrian Hapsburgs, exhausted and their Imperial authority reduced almost to vanishing point by the Thirty Years War, had also to contend with a threatening revival of the Turkish power. Spain, weakened by a mistaken economic policy and a century of almost continuous warfare, had rapidly declined and, under a diseased and half-witted child, Charles II, with his mother nominally in control as Regent, was now no match for France. Sweden, which Gustavus Adolphus had placed in the forefront of European Powers, had also declined to some extent, and in any case was usually a French ally, in return for subsidies. Only Holland remained as an obstacle on the Continent, to hinder Louis from advancing his north-eastern frontier towards the Rhine at the expense of the Spanish Netherlands and acquiring a dominating position in Europe generally; and now, in 1672, it seeemd that Holland must surrender to him.

The consequences of a Bourbon domination of Europe may be difficult to assess precisely, but there can be no doubt that they would have been considerable. It may be argued that such a domination could not have been permanent; but still there was at the least a considerable danger that Europe's development would be shaped by Louis XIV from Versailles. The attraction, not merely of French manners and French literature, but of French ideals of government, was sufficiently great in any case; if Louis had been successful in all his aims, it would have been supreme everywhere in the West. And Louis was the principal exponent in his day of a political absolutism, combined with religious intolerance, and based on military power. Though he probably never uttered the famous boast of *L'état, c'est moi* attributed to him, he would certainly have been justified in doing so, since there were no substantial checks on his authority; and religious uniformity was part of his political creed. In 1672 the Revocation of the Edict of Nantes was still thirteen years in the future, but already the policy had begun of whittling down the rights given to the Huguenots by an excessively literal application of its provisions. The independence of other states, and such political and Protestant liberties as existed in the late seventeenth century, were alike threatened by Louis XIV, and were fundamentally at stake when he threatened to overwhelm the Dutch.

There remained one other important power concerned by the 'new order' which Louis was seeking to establish. This was the England of Charles II. Charles had the usual choice in such circumstances: he could either join a coalition to resist the 'new order', or he could co-operate with it. It is generally regarded as a traditional factor in English foreign policy that no single power should be allowed to dominate Europe, and especially that the strongest continental power should not be allowed to dominate the Low Countries; and

Charles to this extent shared this traditional preoccupation that in 1668 he joined in a Triple Alliance with Holland and Sweden to limit Louis's conquests in the Spanish Netherlands in that year in the Treaty of Aix-la-Chapelle. Even this, however, had been done partly in order to enhance his value as a possible ally in Louis's eyes, and Charles wrote to Louis to explain away his action. Fundamentally Charles saw little to fear in French expansion on the Continent, and from it something valuable might be gained, namely, the destruction of England's greatest naval and commercial competitor, and the wiping out, by a joint attack on Holland, of the disgrace incurred in the previous Second Anglo-Dutch War when in 1667 De Ruyter had sailed into the Medway, burning English shipping and towing off the English flagship, the *Royal Charles*. And Louis's absolutism, his Roman Catholicism, and his powerful army, so far from being a disadvantage in Charles's eyes, were rather a recommendation.

In the famous Secret Treaty of Dover of 1670, between Charles II and Louis XIV, English foreign policy and domestic policy were both involved. Charles undertook to join Louis in his attack on Holland in return for Walcheren, Sluys, and Cadzand from the spoils, and for French financial assistance during the war; but in addition he was to receive further assistance, in men as well as money, to enable him to declare himself Catholic at an appropriate moment and to strengthen the royal authority against possible opposition. Quite how seriously Charles ever intended these 'Catholic clauses' may well be doubted. He had first communicated his intention to declare himself a Catholic to his brother James and a few intimates on the anniversary of the Conversion of St. Paul (25 Jan. 1669), but his own conversion was not so drastic in character. Temperamentally he certainly did not possess the zeal of a missionary, and though he probably appreciated the political support which Catholicism could give to the royal authority, he also had a shrewd sense of what was and what was not practical politics, and he had no inclination to endanger his throne by any excessive devotion to principle. Still, he did sign the 'Catholic clauses', which were his own idea and not that of Louis XIV; and however serious his own intentions were, there can be no doubt of those of his brother, James, Duke of York, who by 1670 was generally expected to be the next king, since Queen Catherine was most unlikely to bear children. James was already a fervent Catholic, though his Catholicism was not yet public property, and on his devotion to the great design and to the French alliance, Colbert, the French ambassador in London, could rely.

When Louis's troops invaded Holland in 1672, they had an English contingent under the Duke of Monmouth with them, and they had the help of Charles II's fleet at sea. On the Continent, to judge by the terms offered by Louis at Utrecht, a victory for the two monarchs would have meant that Holland would be reduced to little more than a French protectorate, and that in turn would have meant that the Spanish Netherlands would have been at Louis's mercy. It is true that the Treaty of Dover contained a clause in which Louis undertook not to break the Treaty of Aix-la-Chapelle, but this would not have meant much in practice, certainly not when (as was annually expected) Charles II of Spain died childless, and Louis could demand the Spanish Netherlands as part of his claim for the entire Spanish succession. At sea a victory for the two kings would have meant that England would win naval and commercial supremacy—at least until Colbert's schemes matured sufficiently to enable France to challenge it. Inside England the consequences of an Anglo-French victory in the war are more difficult to assess; but the prestige of a successful war would certainly have strengthened the royal authority and might have modified English constitutional development. The Declaration of Indulgence suspending the operation of the laws restricting Catholic and Dissenting freedom of worship, which was issued by Charles simultaneously with the beginning of the war, represented the first stage of the attempt to impose the royal religious policy on the country, with French assistance.

Much therefore depended on the resistance which the Dutch could put up against the French and English forces. The story is well known how the dikes were opened to flood the country in front of the French armies, so that, while the Dutch 'are fain to drive up and down in such boats as they can go, just as Noah drave upon the flood of the universe',[1] the French could make no further progress; how Louis XIV insisted on impossible terms; how there was a revulsion of popular feeling against the great Republican Pensionary, John de Witt, which put the young William of Orange into power and led to the lynching of de Witt and his brother by the mob of The Hague; and how under William a European coalition against Louis XIV was gradually built up and the Dutch armies began to make headway. These events have been related, for instance, in Miss Trevelyan's book on *William III and the Defence of Holland*, and were sufficiently stirring in character to attract the attention of historical novelists from Dumas to the present day. But there is another important side to these events, equally picturesque since it tells of the activities of spies, secret agents, and fifth-columnists, which has not been previously described. An essential part of William's policy was the detaching of England from the French alliance, finally achieved in the Treaty of Westminster in February 1674. This book is concerned with the secret intrigues by which this result was brought about.

In 1672 William was a young man of twenty-two, of poor physique, asthmatical, and without political experience save that education acquired in the process of being brought up under a highly suspicious Republican administration anxious to exclude him from power. The situation which faced him might have daunted statesmen who were more experienced and more securely in power than he; for though many Republicans rallied to him in the national emergency, the old Republican-Orange feuds were not entirely healed. His uncle, Charles II, professed to be fighting partly in his interests against the Republicans, and would no doubt have been prepared to patronize him and help him to establish his authority over what was left of the United Provinces after partition; and it might have been in William's personal interests to accept the position of Charles's protégé. But this was far from his intention. From the beginning he devoted himself to the task of repelling the French invasion and forming a coalition to resist French expansion, and this aim he

[1] J. T., letter of 17 Jan. 1673, R.A. Fagel 244.

pursued with a single-minded sense of duty to the end of his life. If in the process he lost no opportunity of improving his own position in Holland and in England, it was the better to enable him to achieve this purpose. He was indeed prepared to consider every means for this purpose. He appraised every man and every circumstance to see how each could be turned to account.

His aptitude for calculating, and readiness to use every weapon that came to hand, are well illustrated in his endeavour to break the alliance between England and France. Having decided to try to detach England, he tried first to use his relationship with his uncle Charles II, not to secure his patronage, but to persuade him to make a separate peace. William would certainly have liked to detach England from the French alliance by convincing Charles that French power was a danger to England and Holland alike; probably from the beginning he hoped eventually to include England in a European coalition against Louis XIV to free Europe from the French danger. Of course William knew nothing of the Secret Treaty of Dover; he could not realize that by it Charles was almost bound hand and foot to Louis. Even if Charles had wanted to repudiate his obligations to Louis when he became tired of the war, he could hardly risk doing so; for a slight indiscretion, whether inadvertent or deliberate, on the part of Louis could be extremely dangerous—as was shown when the revelation of subsidy negotiations in 1678 brought about the fall of Danby. The series of attempts which were made to persuade Charles *of his own free will* to change his foreign policy were therefore all abortive, though William never altogether abandoned hope even when he was trying other methods. Charles could, and would, only make a separate peace when he was forced to do so and when he could show Louis that there was no alternative.

There were other men and other circumstances which William could use. Those five principal ministers of Charles, generally known to history as the Cabal, were not all on good terms with one another. Only Clifford and Arlington were in the secret of the Treaty of Dover; and of these the impetuous Clifford, after his rapid rise from an ordinary Devon squire to Lord Treasurer, was a much more zealous advocate of the Catholic clauses. Converted to Catholicism, he adopted his new religion with a characteristic vehemence which commended him to James, Duke of York, though, like James, he kept his faith a secret until the auspicious moment should come. Arlington's religious views were closer to those of his master Charles; there were complaints of his 'favouring Popery', and perhaps a slight personal preference for it, but no proof of any conversion until, on his death-bed, political considerations became insignificant. As the principal Secretary of State from 1662 to 1674, he was the person on whom Charles chiefly relied to carry out his foreign policy. The black plaster covering the scar on his nose was a constant reminder of his Cavalier service on the battlefield and in exile; and for most of his life he remained essentially a courtier, anxious to make himself useful and acceptable to his King and to retain as much influence as possible with him. Although he was originally supposed to hold 'pro-Spanish' views, and had married into a Dutch family descended illegitimately from Maurice of Nassau, in 1669 he fell in with Charles's policy of a French alliance against Holland and was his principal agent in the negotiations leading up to the Treaty of Dover.

The other three members of the Cabal, Buckingham, Ashley, and Lauderdale, were not in the secret of the Catholic clauses of the Treaty of Dover. For their benefit, a special *traité simulé* of 21 December 1670 was concocted, binding England and France simply to war against Holland; the subsidy which Louis XIV had previously promised to pay to enable Charles to declare himself a Catholic was now added to the subsidy for the war. The three 'Protestant' counsellors were taken in by this deception, and threw themselves wholeheartedly into the new policy. Buckingham, the Zimri of one of Dryden's most convincing portraits, was the only member of the Cabal without administrative responsibilities other than those of Master of the Horse; and his erratic nature and restless desire for power led him to take up the new course of foreign policy. Round the name of Ashley, the subject of an even more famous but perhaps less accurate caricature by Dryden, mysterious rumours of intrigue and conspiracy cling more freely even than to most Restoration politicians;

but his interest in foreign affairs was always limited, and his motive for joining in the attack on Holland may certainly be described as commercial, pure and simple. As for the brutal Lauderdale, who in a classic phrase 'governed or rather misgoverned Scotland', he had so few friends, in Scotland or in England, that the loss of Charles's favour would mean ruin; and so he too supported the French alliance.

The motives of the five ministers were therefore very dissimilar, and there was considerable rivalry between them. Arlington was resentful when the coveted office of Lord Treasurer was given not to him but to his former client, Clifford; but more serious was the perpetual rivalry between him and Buckingham for influence with the King. Ashley was playing for his own hand. Lauderdale still retained Ashley's friendship in 1672 but had very few other friends at Court. There were, in fact, rivalries and disagreements between them from which William might draw profit; but here also, as in his attempts to persuade his uncle Charles, he failed in 1672. If they were united in nothing else, and if they were united from different motives, they all backed the war so long as it had any hope of success. Some powerful means was needed of bringing pressure to bear on Charles, and dissolving the ties which kept the Cabal in its uneasy alliance; and this means could only be found in Parliament, when Charles had to call it to ask for money. The House of Commons could grant or withhold taxes; the House of Commons had also in its possession the threat of impeachment, at which the King's ministers might well tremble. Some of them, including Arlington, had played their part in stirring up the anger of the House in 1667 against Clarendon when that statesman had been forced to spend his last days in exile; they knew how serious it could be to fall foul of the Commons, and they knew that if Charles would not protect the man who had been his great adviser for nearly twenty years they could not count on the royal favour themselves. Montpellier, or worse, was a possibility to be reckoned with. It is not surprising that Arlington, courtier though he was, always showed great prudence (which some have gone so far as to describe as timidity) in considering the possible reactions of the House; and both Buckingham and Shaftesbury were also very sensitive to the trend of its debates. A parliamentary attack on the King's ministers might lead to a general *sauve qui peut* among them.

When the House of Commons of 1661 had been elected it had seemed that at last a Stuart king had found a Parliament with which he could work in harmony: indeed, the difficulty in its early years was that it showed itself more Royalist than the King. This honeymoon, however, soon came to an end, and dissatisfaction and disillusionment grew. Even the Cavalier Parliament had a small body of members with Puritan antecedents, which increased in numbers as by-elections took place to fill vacancies made by death or succession to the peerage. Moreover, many of the Cavaliers themselves became discontented as their hopes of the Utopia which they had associated with a Restoration faded; many considered themselves insufficiently rewarded for their exertions and sacrifices in civil war and exile, and envied others more fortunate than they in getting pensions and places in Court. Reluctance to increase taxation would have been extreme in any House of Commons; and criticisms of extravagance at Court and wasteful administration (whether justified or not) grew in volume, particularly after the Medway disaster in 1667. Religious fears also played their part; the suspicion arose that Catholic influence at Court was becoming too strong, particularly as the rumour spread that the heir to the throne was inclining towards Catholicism. Lastly, there are always those who seek to serve their own interest by opposition to the government, just as there are also those who make their way by supporting it; and the Restoration was no exception to this rule, though this element in it is often exaggerated.

Clarendon had fallen, a scapegoat to the growing discontent, in 1667, but even after his fall no parliamentary session was productive of much money, and, though each member of the Cabal took care to organize a small following in the House of Commons, this did not mean that any of them could be described as popular in it. There was much discontent, and even signs of the development of something like a critical Country Party, of which William might take advantage.

It would not, however, be easy to do this. It was acknowledged that foreign affairs were a matter on which the royal prerogative was supreme. The Dutch 'butterboxes', England's commercial rivals against whom two wars had already been fought in the twenty years before 1672, still seemed to be England's natural enemies. Yet there were also some ties of friendship between the two peoples. In religion both were Protestant, in contrast to France, and the Nonconformist sects had connexions of long standing with Holland. Politically both were strongly opposed to absolutism of the French type. These feelings to some extent influenced many Englishmen, but they naturally appealed most to those survivors from the Commonwealth period who had never wholeheartedly been converted to the Restoration; and Holland did indeed contain many English exiles whose radical religious and political views had attracted the attention of Charles II's government. Also, as is often the case with two great commercial nations, they were competitors over a wide field, but there were, too, considerable commercial connexions between them, and both alike were threatened by the protectionist policy recently introduced by Colbert in France. For all these reasons, there was a section at least of English public opinion which might be brought by suitable propaganda to consider itself more endangered by Louis XIV than by Holland; and the arguments of this propaganda might appeal to those who were already inclined to be critical of Charles II's administration for the reasons already given.

It became, therefore, the aim of William and his Grand Pensionary Fagel (who substantially controlled Dutch policy so long as the national emergency lasted) to work on these potential allies in England, and particularly in the House of Commons, by means of what can only be called a kind of 'political warfare'. It is with this 'political warfare' that this book proposes to deal. It was carried on mainly by a small group of Englishmen who combined the trades of spy, smuggler, and secret political agent in a manner more associated with historical adventure fiction than with history proper. One feels that some of the incidents to be related would not be out of place in a novel by Dumas.

William's principal agent in organizing this 'fifth column', indeed the principal advocate of this policy, the man on whom he relied for much of his information of English conditions and much of his pamphlet literature, was one Peter Du Moulin. As much of the story is derived from the papers left behind by him (now in the Rijksarchief at The Hague), a chapter may well be devoted to the previous career of this remarkable man and to his family background.

II

THE PRINCIPAL CONSPIRATOR

IT is curious that, in spite of the international importance of what Du Moulin did, references to him in histories of the period are only occasional, and often confined to footnotes. He is in fact a striking example of the man who is important behind the scenes in his own day, and yet falls into oblivion as soon as his activities are over. The *Dictionary of National Biography* does, however, give an account of three other distinguished members of the same family, who earn their place in it, not for their political activities, but for their eminence in the field of international Protestant scholarship.

Peter Du Moulin was no doubt named after his grandfather Pierre (1568–1658), a great Huguenot scholar whose large output of books was known to the learned of three states at least, namely, France, Holland, and England. The family from which Pierre came were early converts to Protestantism, and indeed Pierre's autobiography gives a picturesque account of how, as a boy of four, he narrowly escaped being involved in the Massacre of Saint Bartholomew by being hidden under a mattress while his nurse rattled pots and pans and his seven-year-old sister put her hand over his mouth to stop him from crying. Pierre was brought up a zealous Protestant, and as a young man went over to England, where from 1588 to 1592 he spent some time at Cambridge, acting as tutor to the son of the Countess of Rutland and at the same time completing his own education. In 1592 he crossed to Holland and became Professor of Philosophy at the new university of Leyden, where he had Scaliger as one of his colleagues and Grotius as one of his pupils; but in 1598 he returned to France to become a Huguenot minister there for the next twenty years, even acting as chaplain to Henry IV's sister.

The position of a Huguenot minister in the suburbs of Paris, which was strongly Catholic, was by no means free from danger, and on two occasions his house was pillaged and he had narrow escapes from violence at the hands of the mob;

and, finally, fear that the French government too might take a hand against him, forced him to flee the country in 1620. Five years previously he had spent a few months in England where James I had consulted him on some schemes for a union of the Protestant churches and had patronized him to the extent of a D.D. at Cambridge, a Welsh benefice, and a Canterbury prebend worth £200 per annum; and in 1620, presuming on this, Pierre Du Moulin was unwise enough to write to James, urging him to intervene in the Thirty Years War to help the Elector Palatine and justify the hopes placed in him by continental Protestants. This letter was intercepted by the French government and interpreted as treasonable, and Du Moulin fled from France to the then independent principality of Sedan, where he remained as Professor of Theology at the Protestant Academy until he died at the age of ninety, respected as the author of more than eighty works, most of them controversial.

Two of the uncles of our Peter Du Moulin also receive a mention in the *Dictionary of National Biography*. The eldest, another Pierre (1601–84), also studied for some years in each of the same three great Protestant educational centres, Sedan, Leyden, and Cambridge, but it was in England that he finally settled, with livings in turn in Leicestershire, Yorkshire, and Kent. During the Civil War he was a zealous Royalist, and he published a vehement reply to Milton's defence of the execution of Charles I, entitled *Regii Sanguinis Clamor ad Caelum*, with the title-page appropriately printed in red. As a reward for this, on the Restoration of Charles II in 1660, he was granted his father's former Canterbury prebend, in conjunction with his living as Rector of Adisham in Kent.[1]

The career of his brother Louis (1606–80) was quite the reverse. He studied medicine at Leyden, Cambridge, and Oxford, and like his brother finally settled in England, becoming a licentiate of the London College of Physicians in 1640; but during the Civil War he was not a Royalist, but 'a fiery, violent and hot-headed Independent, a cross and ill-natured man' in the words of Antony à Wood.[2] His piety,

---

[1] Petition of Pierre du Moulin, Jan. 1668 (?), S.P. Dom. Charles II, 232, f. 19.
[2] *Athenae Oxonienses* (1691), ii. 753.

his learning, and his Independency earned him in 1648 the promotion, remarkable for a medical man, to the position of Camden Professor of Ancient History at Oxford in place of an evicted Royalist. From the fact that Antony à Wood makes no attack on the way he filled this chair it may be inferred that his classical knowledge was at least adequate, but at the Restoration he was naturally ousted and had to spend the rest of his life as a noted Nonconformist controversialist. Though the careers of these two brothers differed in this way, however, and though one was Anglican and the other Independent, they shared a common hatred of 'Popery' which was reflected in the writings of both and was expressed with considerable vehemence.

Such vehemently expressed anti-Catholic views were a characteristic of the whole Du Moulin family, which was inherited by the Peter Du Moulin who is the subject of this chapter. They were a numerous family with relatives, friends, and correspondents among all the Protestant communities of western Europe. An aunt of Peter's married another Huguenot minister named Jurieu and gave birth to another of the most noted Huguenot writers of the century. Peter's own father, Cyrus Du Moulin (born 1608) did not achieve such eminence as a scholar but he too entered the Huguenot ministry. Of Peter's sisters one, Hélène, later married her cousin Jurieu, and another, Suzanne, married in 1684 Jacques Basnage, another Huguenot writer and author of one of the earliest histories of the United Provinces of the Netherlands.

It is clear, therefore, that Peter came from a family which had behind it a century of uncompromising Protestantism, and which was well known among the Protestant scholars at least of France, England, and Holland. This was the family tradition which Peter inherited, however much his uncles might differ on the form of Protestantism to be adopted; and in his own way too, he was to devote his life to a struggle against Catholicism in the person of Louis XIV. He was born, so we learn from the Act of Parliament which made him a naturalized Englishman,[1] in the county of Dunois in France, the son of Cyrus Du Moulin and Marie de Marbois. Dunois

[1] Publications of the Huguenot Society, xviii. 94.

was a small area to the north-west of Orleans, whose principal town was Châteaudun, where his father was a minister. This was also close to the area from which the family had originally come, and Cyrus perhaps combined with his pastorate the possession of some of the family patrimony. The Act of Parliament referred to gives him the title of 'Esquire'. It is clear from Peter's later writings that he acquired as part of his education the usual knowledge of the classics, and he also showed aptitude for the English, Dutch, and Spanish languages in addition to his native French; but nothing else is known or can be inferred about his early years. We do not even know how old he was or in what circumstances he crossed to England, probably shortly after the Restoration. He cannot, however, have been much more than thirty, and may have been younger.[1]

When the time came for Peter to choose his career, he did not follow the example of so many of his relatives and enter the ministry. Instead, he decided to enter the service of Charles II and seek for diplomatic employment of some kind. For this he was well qualified, since he knew something of conditions on the Continent and had a much greater knowledge of foreign languages than most Englishmen, but he needed an influential patron at Court. Somehow he was able to attract the attention of the more important of the two Secretaries of State, Arlington, who after his appointment in 1662 gradually proved to be Charles's most useful instrument in matters of foreign policy, and was consequently as useful a patron as Du Moulin could have won. How the connexion between them was formed is not known; it can hardly have been the outcome of religious sympathy, for Arlington's Protestantism was already suspect. But somehow Du Moulin was able to convince his patron of his ability and after he had become a naturalized English subject in May 1664, he was eligible for his first post.

This was on the staff of Sir Gilbert Talbot, who went as ambassador to Denmark towards the end of 1664. The second

---

[1] The statement made by the *Dictionary of National Biography* that Cyrus Du Moulin later became pastor of the Huguenot church at Canterbury seems to be incorrect: F. W. Cross, *History of the Walloon and Huguenot Church at Canterbury* (Canterbury, 1898), in the publications of the Huguenot Society, ignores him.

Anglo-Dutch war (1664–7) was by that time impending, and the English government wanted to obtain the alliance, or at least the neutrality of the two Baltic Powers, Denmark and Sweden, which could cut off from the Dutch a valuable carrying trade and important sources of naval stores.[1] After promising well at first, the embassy eventually failed not only to reconcile the two Baltic rivals in an alliance with England (an almost impossible task), but even to win the friendship of Denmark alone, and negotiations were finally broken off in March 1666. Du Moulin's position in the negotiation seems to have been that of secretary to the embassy, for which his linguistic abilities fitted him. It was not a position which gave him much opportunity for initiative, though on one occasion he received a visit from the Danish chancellor, Hannibal Sehested, at eleven o'clock at night when the ambassador was in bed, and made bold to express the English view with some downrightness, without troubling to awaken Sir Gilbert.[2] We hear also of another incident, when a letter addressed to the King of Denmark in French contained 'an incongruous expression' which led to a protest from him. Sir Gilbert excused himself to his friend Arlington by admitting that 'I have no skill in the French and therefore trusted another who is confident to be able to defend and justify it'.[3] It is natural to suppose that 'another' was his secretary, and in fact a long justification of the language used appears to be in Du Moulin's writing, and from his later career it may easily be seen that it was fully in character for him both to use language more forceful than that permitted by diplomatic convention, and also to justify himself at considerable length. It is not easy to imagine either Du Moulin, or for that matter any other member of his family, admitting himself to be in the wrong.

He certainly did not lose Sir Gilbert's confidence as a result, for later in the same year, when the old ambassador wrote home expressing the hope that he would be allowed to return, 'for it is time for me to look out my grave', he went on:

---

[1] See the article on diplomatic relations between England and Denmark at this time, by Schoolcraft in *E.H.R.*, vol. xxv.

[2] His own report, of 1 Oct. 1665, is in S.P. 75/17, ff. 427–8.

[3] Letter of 20 May 1665, ibid., f. 332.

'I conceive it may be necessary for His Majesty to have a minister here. . . . It will likewise be expected that somebody should be left in Sweden. Sir Thos. Clifford will likewise join with me to your Lordship in the recommendation of my Secretary Du Moulin, a naturalised Englishman, and a man of very good parts, and perfect honesty. I believe the Duke of York will move for him. . . .'[1] And again a month later, when Talbot was in two minds whether or not to obey a letter of recall, he suggested returning home himself and leaving Du Moulin behind in Copenhagen.[2] This would have meant a position of some responsibility for the young man, but Talbot received instructions to stay in Copenhagen himself, and when he finally left for home at the end of March 1666 with his mission a failure, he left no one behind him.

Du Moulin, however, had acquired valuable experience on this embassy; he could clearly expect that his master Sir Gilbert would give him a strong recommendation to Arlington back in London; and it also appears that at this time he could expect the patronage, not only of Arlington, but of the Duke of York himself (whose Catholic leanings were not yet pronounced). He could therefore look forward to further diplomatic employment, and in fact when the time came for peace negotiations with Holland to be opened at Breda, he accompanied the English ambassadors. His duties were not this time wholly diplomatic, for he seems to have been commissioned by Arlington to supply him with naval and political intelligence, reports on the state of Dutch public opinion with regard to the war, and the like. His first letter, written from Amsterdam on 31 May/10 June 1667, reports that he had absented himself from Breda on some unspecified private business, and goes on to give a curious account of a visit paid to the Texel, where the Dutch fleet then was. After some particulars about the fleet, he relates an encounter with two Englishmen, who declared that it was in the power of the Dutch to avenge themselves on England for their attacks on Dutch shipping in the Vlie by a similar attack on English shipping. These two men 'were recommended from very good hands to De Ruyter. I was resolved to watch them there

---

[1] Talbot to Arlington, 31 Oct. 1665, ibid., f. 461.
[2] Talbot to Arlington, 25 Nov. 1665, ibid., f. 480.

if I could have come on board, for I was myself going to De Ruyter's ship as a traveller to give a visit to his secretary, one of my old acquaintances and friends; but being not able to come up to him I was forced to take leave of these fellows who were put on board a galliot which was to follow the fleet.'[1] The destination of the Dutch fleet was the mouth of the River Thames, and it was by the aid of English pilots with a Commonwealth background that Admiral De Ruyter was able to sail up the Medway, destroying shipping, towing off the English flagship from her anchorage, and inflicting on England her greatest naval humiliation. It is interesting to find Du Moulin at this time acquainted both with Dutchmen of the standing of De Ruyter's secretary and with discontented Englishmen in Dutch pay, and to see him stumbling very near such an important naval plan as this, but there is nothing to indicate that he knew more of the plan than he admitted, or should have known as a loyal Englishman. He was probably sincere in continuing to subscribe himself Arlington's 'most humble and most faithful servant'.

For his services, a warrant had been issued in the spring of 1665 for the payment of £120 to Du Moulin, but at some time after his return from Holland he considered himself entitled to apply for further reward. He joined in the general hunt for some place at Charles's Court which carried with it useful perquisites but not very onerous duties. He discovered that there had formerly been an Assistant Master of Ceremonies to aid the Master, Sir Charles Cotterell, in his duties of introducing foreign ambassadors and supervising other such ceremonial occasions at Court; and promptly petitioned for the vacancy. In support of his case he cited the services of his grandfather to Protestantism and the writings of his uncle Pierre against Milton (his Puritan uncle Louis was of course passed over) before mentioning his own services in Denmark and Holland: the petition was similar to many others pleading the services of Cavalier families with which Charles was importuned. Sir Charles objected on the ground that he held the posts both of Master and of Assistant Master, and Peter had to point out that this was in its nature inconsistent, as a man cannot assist himself; and in any case the words of Sir

[1] S.P. 84/182, f. 131.

Charles's patent ruled it out. A draft order exists for a warrant appointing Peter to the office of Assistant Master of Ceremonies, with a fee of 6*s*. 8*d*. a day on condition that he acted only when Sir Charles was unable to attend personally.[1]

Further employment followed, as Secretary to Sir John Trevor, who was sent on a special mission to Paris in February 1668. On this occasion the French ambassador in London thought Du Moulin's appointment to the embassy important enough to be mentioned in his dispatch home, and described him as highly intelligent and a great confidant of Arlington's.[2] This was the time of the formation of the Triple Alliance between England, Holland, and Sweden to restrict the conquests of Louis XIV from Spain, and of the Treaty of Aix-la-Chapelle between France and Spain at which Louis pretended to give way to it.[3] Du Moulin was therefore able to note with some satisfaction, and in terms which leave little doubt of his antipathy for Louis XIV, the poor welcome which the French Court gave to the news of the signing of the Treaty of Aix-la-Chapelle. We do not possess many details of Du Moulin's own activities on this embassy, but we do know that he once travelled to Brussels, apparently on Trevor's behalf, and we also know that in order to report details of the extent of French demobilization, he was able to use his acquaintance with members of Turenne's household, which still contained several Huguenots. It is characteristic of Peter that wherever he was he always had such sources of accurate 'inside' information.[4]

[1] S.P. Car. II, 232, ff. 19, 20, 21. Peter's first petition mentioned that he was 'once taken prisoner' in the course of his missions, but it has not been possible to discover any further details of this. *Skippon's Travels*, in the *Collection of Voyages and Travels*, ed. A. and J. Churchill (1744–7), vi. 737, 746–7, refers to a meeting with a Dr. Du Moulin of Aberdeen at Nîmes on 16/26 Feb. 1666, and to the later arrest of this Du Moulin at Paris on 28 Mar./7 Apr. 1666, on the ground that he had at one time approached Cromwell on behalf of the Huguenots of Nîmes. This is, however, inconsistent with Peter's age, his English naturalization, and his presence at Copenhagen: though it is not unlikely that this was another member of the same family and that his fate supplied another reason for their hatred of Louis XIV.   [2] Ruvigny to Lionne, 10/20 Feb. 1668.

[3] He had in fact signed a partition treaty with the Emperor, providing for the partition of Spanish territories between them on the death of the child Charles II of Spain, and thus making it unnecessary to continue his war with Spain. Cf. Feiling, *Foreign Policy*, chap. vi.

[4] See Du Moulin's own letters from Paris in S.P. 78/124, ff. 74, 78, 80.

His conduct on this mission was so satisfactory that it greatly strengthened Arlington's liking for such a useful protégé, and Arlington's patronage was valuable. This was shown when in October 1668 the time came to appoint a secretary to the newly reconstituted Council of Trade. Arlington secured Peter's nomination in the face of strong opposition from the Duke of York, who had a candidate of his own. 'The debate and the heat lasted all the afternoon . . . it is not to be imagined how high this business was carried on both sides.'[1] Through Arlington's influence, Peter secured a permanent post bringing him into contact with influential people in politics and in trade.

Peter was interested in trading and colonial matters, but his principal concern was with international politics, and his position on the Council of Trade did not prevent him going on a last diplomatic mission to Paris with the new English ambassador Montagu in March 1669. This mission, however, turned out disastrously for him. This was partly because he contrived to get on very poor terms with Montagu from the outset. He made the necessary arrangements for the ambassador's lodgings in Paris and took it upon himself to give a pass to a French friend authorizing him to come over from England as a member of the ambassador's train. This Frenchman was stopped by the Customs authorities at Montreuil, his baggage was searched, and his 'pockets, drawers, and portmantell' found to be full of contraband silk stockings. Montagu felt himself in honour bound to get the man released, but he was not too pleased about it, and then, when he finally reached Paris, he found that the house which Du Moulin had taken for him was, to use his own words, 'not fit for a dog to lie in, and yet with the time I have paid for it already and am to pay, it will cost me a year's rent'.[2] Peter himself did not arrive in Paris for several days. When he did arrive, within three or four days Montagu was writing home about him. The details of the unedifying dispute which followed are quite unimportant in themselves, but some quotation from the correspondence is useful for the light which is

[1] L. Conway to Sir G. Rawdon, 24 Oct. 1668, in *Rawdon Papers* (1819), pp. 237-8.
[2] Montagu to Arlington, 17/27 Mar. 1669, in S.P. 78/126, f. 63.

thrown on Du Moulin's character, and incidentally on the mentality of the age.

Montagu wrote:

I spoke with him myself, to know what it was he desired. . . . He told me that his pretensions were these, that in the first place at my entrée and audience, whatsoever other persons there were with me, that he was to be one of those that were to go in the King's coach with me, as a right that belongs to him as he is Secretary of the Ambassade, that then I was to present him to the King by the name of Secretary of the Ambassade, and so afterwards to all the ministers, without which character he says he cannot have that free admittance to them as is necessary for him in order to those businesses which he has order from the King and your Lordship to treat of; and for all other envoys and residents of other princes that are in this Court, as he shall often have occasion to resort to them about treaties and business without this character, they will not give him the hand in their houses, which will hinder him visiting them. I confess, my Lord, I dare not venture of my own head to entitle him to all this that he desires, especially when your Lordship yourself, upon my asking you whether he was Secretary of the Ambassade, told me no, but that I should do well for his credit to let it pass so, which I have never contradicted, but since it extends itself so far and to so many things, I desire some further and some more positive directions from your Lordship, before I do what he desires. Mr. du Moulin, I find, apprehends that I am jealous lest his parts should eclipse mine. I confess, my Lord, I am extreme jealous of him, but it is of his folly and indiscretion; but for anything that may do him credit or good, I wish it as much as he. I shall always desire him to let the ministers of this Court alone for all businesses till he has first acquainted me with them, for this is a place where his pragmatical ill-bred way will not be at all acceptable. . . ."[1]

Du Moulin knew that the ambassador had written to Arlington, and also to the other Secretary of State, Trevor, but had to wait some time for his patron's reply, in the meantime writing short notes, first of all excusing himself on the ground that he had fever, and then referring to his 'anguish of mind'. When the replies did arrive from Arlington and Trevor, they proved to be severe rebukes for him, from which Montagu read aloud suitable extracts. Du Moulin would have done well to let matters rest here, but he was not the

---

[1] Montagu to Arlington, 27 Mar./6 Apr. 1669, ibid., f. 89. It is not known what the 'businesses' were of which Du Moulin was to treat save that he was commissioned to obtain copies of various books, manuscripts, and government ordinances.

man to rest under real or fancied injustice, and there followed a long letter to his patron, some 3,000 words in length, giving in great detail his own side of the case. It is in many ways a skilful composition, scoring many good debating points, well written and well argued, and possibly giving a truer version of events than the ambassador's letter, but far too long, protesting far too much, and lacking in tact. It was not without expressions of a desire for reconciliation with Montagu, but the best way of achieving it was not to try to make trouble between Montagu and Arlington by quoting remarks of the ambassador's reflecting on Arlington; it was not necessary to give a long account of an incident in which Du Moulin, owing to the sudden alteration of the weather, was 'struck with a violent cold accompanied with a fever and cruel fits of vomiting', and therefore kept his hat on to prevent his chill getting worse, when at the far end of the room in which the ambassador was working—an innocent transgression of the etiquette of the day for which, so Du Moulin argued, he had been unduly rebuked. One feels that Du Moulin may have been right in saying that his request for the title of Secretary to the Embassy was more respectfully phrased than Montagu had represented it, and yet that his manner in making the request may well have been unfortunate. The letter, in fact, is the work of a man with a genius for polemical pamphleteering rather than for patching up disputes.[1]

The days of Du Moulin's stay in Paris were now numbered. At the ambassador's official entry on 15/25 April 1669 it was he who read out Montagu's credentials, and he who was commissioned to write home a full account of all the formal ceremonial;[2] but only three days later Montagu was writing home also to the effect that 'Mr. du Moulin that is with me, I believe, will return shortly into England', and asking for someone to be sent out as his secretary.[3] Unaware of this, Du Moulin wrote next day to say that:

I acquainted Mr. Secretary Trevor the last week with the likelihood there was of our coming here to a better understanding, and I may assure your Lordship now, that I have so far overcome my passion

[1] The letter, dated 7/17 Apr. 1669, is in S.P. 78/126, ff. 132 et seq.
[2] Ibid., ff. 144 et seq.
[3] Montagu to Williamson, 20/30 Apr., ibid., f. 158.

and laid aside any petty interest or *point d'honneur*, wholly to devote myself to His Majesty's and your Lordship's service, without any interruption, that no unkindness from my Lord Ambassador of almost what nature soever shall lessen my respect to him, or make me more remiss in my attendance and the obeying of his commands. . . .[1]

In fact, he sought to reingratiate himself by exceptionally zealous application to his duties, and by supplying Arlington with exceptionally valuable and authoritative information—not realizing that in this way he was sealing his own fate.

He began by supplying a full list of the French fleet, with well-informed comment on its strength, and followed this up by promising a report on the state of the ports, and an account of 'the expense of the Navy both as to the building and setting out of their ships'.[2] But his real interests lay not in naval espionage, but in discovering the aims of French diplomacy all over Europe, and he supplied well-informed news and comment, of far greater quality than that given in the news letters of his colleague Perwich,[3] and showing greater ability than any indicated in the dispatches of his superior Montagu. Montagu has already been quoted as saying that 'Mr. Du Moulin . . . apprehends that I am jealous lest his parts should eclipse mine', and there would probably have been scope for such jealousy. Du Moulin's reports, for instance on French policy in regard to the vacant throne of Poland, show a remarkable knowledge and understanding of European politics in general. Even when his guesses (like those of so many other ambassadors) prove to be wrong, they are clearly the work of a man of keen intellect, ever ready to see the broad European significance of the smallest incident and to discuss the widest aspects of French and English policy, and incidentally able to pull strings in various French governmental circles to secure information and even copies of official letters. But his very ability and intelligence, perhaps, redounded to his disadvantage, since his outlook no longer coincided with official English policy.

---

[1] Du Moulin to Arlington, 21 Apr./1 May, ibid., f. 159.
[2] Letters of 24 Apr./4 May and 1/11 May, ibid., ff. 168–9, 180–7, and 189.
[3] A selection of Perwich's letters has been edited by M. Beryl Curran (Royal Historical Society, 3rd series, v, 1903).

In one of his letters he analysed the choice before Charles II in 1669 thus:

For to sum all up in few words, either His Majesty's intentions are to close with France, and hearken to their proposals, or to stick to the league he is entered into for the peace of Christendom and for the safety of his own kingdoms [i.e. the Triple Alliance]; if the first, as they give out here and with such a confidence as might be able to seduce if it were possible even the elect, there is nothing to be said, and new measures in that case must be taken as to all particulars.

But if His Majesty will still keep the foundation laid at The Hague and continued at Aix (as I am sure your Lordship will always advise His Majesty to 't) . . . &c.[1]

He made no secret of his own predilection for the policy of the Triple Alliance of The Hague and the Treaty of Aix-la-Chapelle, aiming at co-operation between England, Holland, and Sweden to prevent Louis XIV making extensive conquests from Spain and so coming to dominate Europe. But, in fact, Charles had chosen the other alternative in the previous six months: he was now negotiating his alliance with Louis, and Arlington, perhaps sacrificing his true opinions to his loyalty to his master, was prepared to act as his agent. In these circumstances it would not do to maintain at Paris a man so able, so dangerous, and so intractable as Du Moulin, whose 'pragmatical, ill-bred way' and uncontrolled tampering with French civil servants might endanger the success of the new negotiations with Louis XIV. It is impossible to assess how far Du Moulin's loss of Arlington's favour was due to this factor and how far it was more personal; but it is significant that in his later memoranda to William of Orange he dated the turn in English foreign policy in the same month as the turn in his own personal fortunes, namely, in April 1669.[2]

At all events, on 10/20 May, Du Moulin had to write a letter, at the ambassador's order, requesting Arlington to allow him to return. He supplemented it with another private letter two days later, in which he said:

[1] Du Moulin to Arlington, 1/11 May, 1669, S.P. 78/126, f. 189.
[2] Cf. Temple, i. 257, for the view that Du Moulin's disgrace was the result of the change in official policy.

I was very earnest with him [Montagu] to know of him what my miscarriages had been, and wherein I could be so guilty: but he told me he would not come to an *éclaircissement*, and that in few words we should never agree; expressing only his discontent that I had complained of him in England, as he pretended to be certainly informed, and saying withal that I would have been glad to be his master and was come hither to do your Lordship's, Mr. Secretary's and His Majesty's business, not his own. . . .

He went on to deny Montagu's suspicion that he and the merchant Papillon had cheated him by arranging disadvantageous bills of exchange for him in Paris, and used this suspicion as evidence of the ambassador's ill will to him.[1]

Montagu must have been aware what Arlington's reply would be, and the letter of recall duly arrived at the beginning of June: Perwich, Montagu's clerk, noted with some satisfaction, 'At length we have found the Triple Alliance [presumably of Montagu, Arlington, and Trevor, the other Secretary of State] in Monsr. du Moulin's retirement.'[2] The journey was delayed for some time while he negotiated for the purchase of some books and manuscripts for Arlington and Williamson, but on 26 June/6 July Perwich again reported, with considerable sarcasm, 'Yesterday Mr. du Moulin went hence, and for the ease of his person has left his equipage and baggage to follow him, but cannot tell how he has disposed of the present (which indeed proves to be in the future tense) the Court made him for his good services as His Majesty's Minister Extraordinary, &c.'[3] Neither now nor later was he popular with his colleagues, perhaps because they disliked his manner and the fact that he pretended to be, and was, their superior. Perwich also noted another of his characteristics when he added, 'He will be apt to do everybody here ill offices in England.' He never lost an opportunity of paying off an old score, and indeed in later life he boasted (admittedly in after-dinner conversation), 'entre autres discours à sa mode, que la vengeance était une passion des belles âmes, et qu'il s'y était laissé aller bien souvent, et que même il pouvait dire

[1] Du Moulin to Arlington, 12/22 May 1669, S.P. 78/126, ff. 213–14.
[2] Perwich to Williamson, 12/22 June, Curran, op. cit., p. 16.
[3] Ibid., p. 22.

qu'il n'avait jamais manqué de se venger de ses ennemis de quelque qualité qu'ils eussent été'.[1]

Foremost among these enemies came to be Arlington himself. Hitherto Du Moulin had striven to keep his patron's favour, and his letters are full of expressions of loyalty and zeal. Indeed, the Secretary of State was too valuable a patron to lose if it could possibly be avoided, and the breach probably came from the other side. Arlington had had several occasions to warn and rebuke his protégé for indiscretions, including one warning before the beginning of the Montagu embassy for some reason we do not know; and it may well be that Arlington no longer cared to encourage a man so awkward and with such pronounced anti-French sentiments. There was also something else, arising from the Paris embassy of 1669, which helped to set the two men at odds. In May of that year Du Moulin had had a conversation with P. Puffendorf, the Swedish resident in Paris, who had repeated something which the Swedish ambassador Koningsmark had heard from a 'person of quality' at the French Court, to the effect that in his latest dispatch from London the French ambassador Colbert de Croissy had reported his success in winning over Arlington to the French cause. At that time (according to Puffendorf) Du Moulin had loudly protested his disbelief, saying that Arlington could not possibly have changed his opinions in that way; but in the autumn of 1669 he not only began to repeat the story in England, but (or so it was alleged) he attributed Arlington's change of views to a sense of Louis XIV's liberality. Such hints of bribery completed Du Moulin's ruin in Arlington's estimation. It was probably this incident which Du Moulin later mentioned as common knowledge, and for which he asserted that Arlington persecuted him for three years until an opportunity came in 1672.[2]

After this, his career in the English diplomatic service was at an end. He remained, however, Secretary to the Council of Trade which had been formed in 1668. The little that is

---

[1] *Journaal van Constantijn Huyghens, den zoon*, in *Werken van het Historisch Genootschap*, Utrecht, 1881, p. 50.

[2] H.M.C. (45), *Buccleuch MSS. at Montagu House*, i. 443, 446–7; Du Moulin to Halifax, undated, R.A. Fagel 253.

known about the activities of this Council at this time does not indicate that the secretaryship was a very important post, until in 1672 the Councils of Trade and Plantations were amalgamated.[1] But it did serve a valuable purpose in that it kept him on the fringe of governmental circles and brought him into contact with important politicians, M.P.s, and City merchants. By 1672, indeed, seven years of employment in these various minor capacities had given him the opportunity to form a good knowledge of personalities and problems in English politics on which he was able to draw to William's advantage. His acquaintances included Lord Halifax, the great Trimmer, as yet only at the beginning of his career but even now fearing French power and for that reason alone sharing some of Du Moulin's outlook. No doubt it was not possible for their relationship to be intimate: yet a member of Du Moulin's family was later tutor to Halifax's son.[2] Another important personage connected with the Council of Trade on whose acquaintance he later tried to draw was Lord Ashley (elevated in 1672 to the earldom of Shaftesbury). Later developments will show that he had no great liking for the statesman whom Dryden has pilloried so effectively as Achitophel that it is difficult for us to escape from his partisan description: but the mere fact that Du Moulin's duties involved dealings with such an important member of the Cabal is evidence that he was well placed to study political developments at close quarters. Apart from these exalted persons, however, it is clear that he knew many merchants and M.P.s whose friendship enabled him to study the public opinion of classes which were becoming influential; and no doubt he also had connexions with important Dissenting congregations in London. In many people such as M. Papillon, all these three strains were represented, for he was at once another Huguenot like Du Moulin himself, a merchant of the City, and in 1673 a candidate for Parliament. All these three strains, too, were tending to become anti-French in opposition to the Catholicism, the strong protectionism, and the absolutism of Louis XIV and the most powerful state in Europe.

[1] Cf. C. M. Andrews, *British Committees, Commissions and Councils of Trade and Plantations*, 1622–75 (Baltimore, 1908), pp. 93–95.   [2] Foxcroft, i. 116.

Lastly, after those acquaintanceships which gave him insight into government policy and those which gave him insight into the state of public opinion, came those friendships which Du Moulin was directly to use in his 'fifth column', if that term may be used. More will be said about some of these agents in Chapter IV, but it is convenient here to refer to his friendship with William Howard. Howard is better known to history by the title to which he later succeeded, that of third Lord Howard of Escrick. In the days of the Popish Plot he acquired great notoriety by taking part in the plans of the Whig leaders, and then, in order to save his own skin, turning King's evidence and betraying Russell and Sidney at the time of the Rye House Plot in 1683. That was only the culmination of a long career of political intrigue, dating back to the period of the Commonwealth, and most of it in opposition to the established government, whether that of Cromwell or that of Charles II. He was of noble birth, related to the Duke of Buckingham, and, in the words of Burnet, 'a man of wit and learning, bold and poor'.[1] He has always been regarded as a selfish and unprincipled adventurer, and there can be no doubt that he never neglected an opportunity for his own profit nor was restrained by any considerations of loyalty when he found himself in danger. Yet the possibility cannot be altogether excluded that with these important qualifications there was a certain consistency in his association with the religious and political opposition to the English government after the first ecstasy of the Restoration had died down. At all events, when the war with Holland broke out in 1672, he chose to attempt to enter the Dutch service and to associate with his friend Du Moulin in working against the Anglo-French alliance.

These were the people with whom Du Moulin associated during the years 1669–72. At the same time he could observe the changes which were taking place in government policy. He could see that his former patron Arlington and the Duke of York, who had been bitter opponents at the time of his own appointment as Secretary to the Council of Trade, were now co-operating and appeared to be enjoying the King's favour; like most well-informed people, he now suspected

[1] Burnet, ii. 63.

that the Duke of York had been converted to Roman Catholicism and knew that his temperament was autocratic and his sympathies pro-French; he noted Buckingham's journey to France and the journey of Charles's favourite sister, Henrietta, Duchess of Orleans, to Dover in the summer of 1670. Only those few who were allowed into the secret could know that on that occasion a secret treaty was signed; yet in the next two years it became increasingly clear that the policy of co-operation with Holland to restrict French ambitions was giving way to a policy of *rapprochement* with France. One may conjecture that the declaration of war on Holland in March 1672 and the announcement of a French alliance for the purpose did not come as a complete surprise to so able and keen an observer as Du Moulin, and one can be certain that the change of policy was not one of which he approved. Within a few months he was definitely devoting his attention to an attempt to break this new Anglo-French alliance.

That was to be his work, and a work for which he was well fitted. Family tradition and personal outlook weighed heavily in giving him a feeling of hostility to Louis XIV and the power of France, and a sense of the dangers to European Protestantism which were bound up with French predominance. As a good European and a good Protestant, and a naturalized Englishman who even after his flight to Holland described himself as a 'lover of his country', he did what he could to ruin Charles II's foreign policy, and the rancour with which Charles's government pursued him after the signing of the Treaty of Westminster is ample evidence of the importance of the work which he did. William of Orange could have found no better agent combining such ability with such knowledge of English conditions and such powers of controversy.

III

THE OUTBREAK OF WAR

URING the winter of 1671–2 Charles and the Cabal completed their preparations for the attack on Holland. As always with Charles, the principal difficulty was that of money, since the French subsidies available under the terms of the Secret Treaty of Dover, useful as they undoubtedly were, of themselves fell far short of the sum needed for a year's campaign at sea. However, the proclamation generally known as the Stop of the Exchequer secured that the proceeds of taxation, as they came in, should not be applied to paying off money owing to the banker creditors to whom they were assigned, but should be available for current war expenditure. The government's immediate financial needs were therefore met, at the cost of some loss of credit in the future, and the campaign of 1672 was financed without having recourse to Parliament. On the last occasion Parliament had met, in 1670–1, the House of Commons had been called upon to vote money in support of the Triple Alliance against France; it was impossible to tell what its attitude would be to the new French alliance, and still less to the Declaration of Indulgence which was planned; and of recent years it had shown itself increasingly critical of the government and reluctant to vote taxes. So for the time being it was a relief to Charles and his ministers that they would not have to cope with Parliament (though Buckingham later declared that he and Shaftesbury had wanted to do so), and they could hope that when they had finally to face a Parliament again they would be much stronger as the result of a victorious war.

During the same winter pretexts for the projected aggression against Holland were carefully husbanded. That they were only pretexts is quite clear, and so a detailed discussion of the rights and wrongs of the issues raised is unnecessary here, but some brief mention of them must be made, because without it many of the later negotiations would not be intelligible.[1] The Treaty of Breda which had concluded the previous

[1] Cf. Feiling, *Foreign Policy, passim.*

Anglo-Dutch war in 1667 had not finally settled many of the disputes outstanding between the two countries. There had been no satisfactory agreement on matters of trade in the Indian Ocean and the East Indies, where the English East India Company was constantly trying to break into the Dutch monopoly; and the English government had not finally abandoned its claim that the Dutch fishing fleet should pay for the right to fish off the east coast of England. In some respects also the treaty supplied matter for further dispute. It laid down that, in return for New Amsterdam (now re-christened New York), the Dutch should receive possession of the English colony of Surinam in Guiana. Prolonged negotiations had failed to secure an agreement on the conditions under which English planters in Surinam should be able to leave the colony, and in 1670 the French ambassador reported that the English negotiators were deliberately raising difficulties in order to keep Surinam as a pretext of war.[1] In the Treaty of Breda the Dutch had conceded the English claim that Dutch ships should acknowledge English supremacy in home waters by striking sail to English warships they met, but this 'right of the flag' was not sufficiently closely defined, and early in 1672 the English deliberately manu-factured a further pretext of war by sending a yacht through the Dutch fleet and complaining when the Dutch refused to strike sail. To these four points—the East India trade, the fishery, Surinam, and the flag—were added complaints of offensive Dutch medals and pamphlets referring to the Med-way disaster of 1667 and abusing Charles II, and after war began these grievances were made the basis of a demand for 'cautionary towns', or in other words for the annexation of part of the Dutch province of Zeeland, which would be a security that in future English complaints would be promptly satisfied and not allowed to drag on. For the same reason a war indemnity was also included in the English demands after war had begun. The effect of these demands and those of Louis XIV would have been to put the United Provinces permanently at the mercy of the two kings.

The war did not, however, begin as the result of any break-down in negotiations; indeed, a Dutch extraordinary ambas-

---

[1] Colbert to Louis XIV, 22 Sept./2 Oct. 1670.

sador, Meerman, was in London in March 1672 offering a
complete settlement of all England's just grievances, not
realizing that Charles had determined on war in any case. In
the discussions in the Foreign Committee of the Council,
Arlington pointed out that 'our business is to break with
them and yet lay the breach at their door', and it was agreed
that the ambassador was to be referred from the King to
Lords Buckingham, Lauderdale and Arlington, and they were
then to refer each point to the King, so gaining time.[1] But
this careful manœuvring was abandoned when news arrived
that a Dutch merchant fleet from Smyrna was sailing up the
Channel, and the prospect of obtaining from these rich prizes
extra revenue for the government, and possible pickings for
many of those concerned, excited the greed of Charles and
his ministers. Sir Robert Holmes was instructed to attack
them off the Isle of Wight and capture as many as possible.
Some have been found to say that in the seventeenth century
a formal declaration of war was not obligatory, but in any case
the attack was unprovoked. It was a rather ignominious
failure, but although neither Louis nor Charles was ready to
begin serious operations so early in the year, it left the English
government little option but to follow immediately with a
formal declaration of war. At the same time the Declaration
of Indulgence was issued, suspending the action of the penal
laws against Nonconformists—and incidentally against
Roman Catholics. The fact that the two declarations were
issued almost simultaneously is significant. The Declaration
of Indulgence could be represented as an attempt to prevent
Nonconformist disaffection and the possibility of plots in
co-operation with the Dutch, and also it fitted in with appeals
to Zeelanders and to other Dutch to transfer themselves to
English protection and become English citizens; while for
those in the secret of the Treaty of Dover, both declarations
were stages towards the 'Catholic design'.

Charles followed this up by bestowing honours on several
of his ministers. Arlington received an earldom, as did Ashley
as Earl of Shaftesbury; Clifford received a peerage, and
Lauderdale, already an earl, became a duke. In this way he
hoped to bind the quarrelling members of the Cabal together

[1] 8 Mar. 1672, in For. Ent. Bk. 177.

and induce them to sink their differences in his service. Much
was staked in a desperate cause. At first, however, all promised well. The naval battle of 28 May was indecisive,
but on land the troops of Louis XIV carried all before them.
Turenne's great march and crossing of the Rhine took a French
army, far superior in numbers to that of the young William
of Orange, right into the heart of the United Provinces, and
by 13/23 June he had established his headquarters at Utrecht
and Holland appeared to be at his mercy. It looked as though
the campaign might well be brought to a speedy conclusion.

The very speed and comprehensiveness of the French
successes naturally aroused some jealousy among Englishmen. It is clear from the dispatches of the French ambassador
that even before the campaign started there were some people
distrustful of the new Anglo-French alliance, for he reported
first that the Duke of Ormond was opposed to the declaration
of war, and then that Bab May (the King's pander) and lords
Suffolk, Newport, and Darcy, and others of his own household
were spreading the opinion that the war was being undertaken solely for the extirpation of the Protestant religion.[1]
But as yet such misgivings were not sufficiently widespread
or powerful to be of much use to the Dutch, particularly
as the English government was well aware of the danger
of its disaffected subjects getting in touch with them, and
took steps to prevent it. The extraordinary Dutch ambassador, Meerman, soon left for Holland, but the ordinary
ambassador, Boreel, delayed winding up his affairs in London. On 28 March the Foreign Committee of the Privy
Council had decided that he should be asked to leave 'for the
ill offices he may do', and on the following day Boreel
reported to his government that he had been urged by
Arlington and by the Master of Ceremonies to leave as soon
as possible, and, in the meantime, to curtail his conversations
with, and visits to, certain Englishmen. On 21 April a spy
was set to watch Boreel's activities.[2] These precautions were
all the more necessary when, with the naval battle impending,
it was decided that the lesser evil was to keep Boreel in England until it was all over.

[1] Colbert to Louis, 1/11 and 11/21 Apr. 1672.
[2] For. Ent. Bk. 177; R.A. St. Gen. 7332; S.P. Chas. II, 319A, dates given.

They were well justified, for Boreel was doing his best to send home any intelligence, naval or political, which he thought might be valuable, and he was postponing his departure as long as possible for this purpose. His previous dispatches give no sign that he was particularly able or well-informed, he had failed to detect the trend of English policy in the past two years, and his knowledge of conditions at the English Court had been notably inferior to that of the French ambassador; and now, since he was virtually confined to his house, his opportunities for getting information were very limited, even though the Spanish ambassador could help him. Yet he was able to send home details of English naval preparations (in a curiously simple substitution cipher based on A = 10, B = 11, C = 12, &c., which would not long mystify a schoolboy today). Not only that, but he was also able to report that there were English spies in all the Dutch naval ports, and that particular importance was attached by the English government to the advices received from the spy at Middleburg. He sent word that the English fleet had provisions for only a month and that there would not be sufficient money in the Exchequer to buy more (and we know from other sources that at this time the Foreign Committee was faced with such difficulties). He reported that some jealousy of France was developing at Court, and that advantage should be taken of this and of the absence of the Duke of Lauderdale to divide the Cabal and to persuade Charles to reverse his foreign policy.[1]

In its analytical method of presentation, its general attitude, and its allusions to the Duke of York and the possibility of dividing the Cabal, this last dispatch of 8/18 June 1672 is not unlike memoranda written by Du Moulin a few months later which we shall shortly consider. It is impossible directly to prove that it was he who was acting as Boreel's informant, but it is natural to suspect him: he was a keen and pro-Dutch observer of events, had connexions with the office of the Secretary of State, was directly accused by Burnet of joining with Howard to give the Dutch intelligence,[2] and was in fact forced to flee the country within two months on suspicion

---

[1] Dispatches of May–June 1672 in R.A. St.-Gen. 7332, especially those of 17/27 May, 28 May/7 June, and 8/18 June.   [2] Burnet, ii. 64.

of such activities. There can have been few people so well qualified to give the Dutch ambassador such accurate information, and it may well be that we have here Du Moulin's first entry into Dutch service.

It was followed by the first Dutch attempt to seek their salvation by separating the two kings who were at war with them. Separate embassies were sent to the camp of Louis XIV at Utrecht, and to Charles II at London, to inquire of each what his demands were. Dutch propagandists were later able to claim that Louis had shown some disposition to accept separate terms, but that his proposals were impossibly severe. The embassy to Charles II was equally disappointing, for after the Dutch deputies Halewijn and van Weede had landed at Gravesend, they were not allowed even to enter London, but were instead sent with Boreel to reside at Hampton Court where their activities could be watched and where they could be prevented from communicating with any discontented elements in London. At Hampton Court they remained in isolation until they were sent home at the beginning of August. They were interviewed there on 20 June by Arlington, Buckingham, Clifford, and Shaftesbury, but their arguments made no impression.[1] Charles kept always in close touch with the French ambassador, and sent first Lord Halifax, and later both Buckingham and Arlington on embassies to Louis XIV to concert joint peace terms or none.

The stay of the Dutch deputies at Hampton Court was therefore fruitless, but before it was over attempts to get in touch with them ruined both William Howard and Peter Du Moulin. Howard later told Burnet[2] that he had previously been over to Holland and had offered his services to De Witt, but 'found him a dry man', and had not reached terms. Burnet's continuation, to the effect that Howard waited on William 'as soon as the prince was raised' to the position of Stadholder, was inaccurate, since by that time Howard was in the Tower; and it seems more probable that Howard's intrigues took place entirely on his own initiative.

According to the account which he later gave to Clifford, on Sunday, 16 June, Howard received a visit from the

---

[1] See their dispatch of 20/30 June in R.A. St.-Gen. 6922.
[2] Burnet, ii. 64.

secretary of the Dutch deputies, an old friend of his named Kingscot, who urged him to do all he could to get his powerful relative, the Duke of Buckingham, to speak to the King in favour of an accommodation between England and Holland. Howard, nothing loth to act as an intermediary, reported this to Buckingham, and on Monday, while Kingscot waited patiently for several hours in a London coffee-house, was summoned to Windsor, where he had a long discussion with the Duke. The upshot of this was that Howard should draw up some proposed peace terms and give them to Kingscot as his own unofficial plan, while in the meantime Buckingham would do everything to get Charles to adopt them. On Tuesday Howard gave the proposals to Kingscot at the same coffee-house, insisting that they were quite unofficial, and Kingscot took them away to show his masters. Kingscot brought back their comments the same night, and again on Wednesday had a long discussion with Howard at the Red Lion in Brentford, after which an agreed amended copy of the terms was taken to Buckingham and a complete report given to him of all that had passed. That, Howard told Clifford, was all that he knew of any negotiations with the Dutch; and he implied that everything he had done had had Buckingham's approval. Indeed, he was still maintaining to a chance acquaintance in Flanders six months later that Buckingham had employed him for the purpose; and he may be right, in spite of Buckingham's disavowal and talk of documents being put under doors and found on desks. Certainly nothing in the Duke's character or career makes it unlikely.

What Howard did not confess in this detailed account to Clifford, however, was that at some point in this negotiation he had communicated it to the French ambassador in London, Colbert, with even a copy of the proposed peace terms. He was either in hopes of getting money from Colbert for this valuable information, or he wanted to sow distrust between France and England—or quite probably he had both objects in mind. His action proved, however, to be a bad miscalculation. Any financial profit which he made was more than offset when he was seized and sent to the Tower, where he stayed for the next five months, though no charge was ever preferred against him. Nor did he succeed in dividing the two allies, for Charles II reassured Colbert, telling him that he had not even read the peace proposals, that they had been disavowed both by Buckingham and by the Dutch deputies, and that he would on no account consent to a separate peace. At the same time Buckingham and Arlington went on their embassy to Louis XIV at Utrecht, the outcome of which was the signing of a new treaty binding each monarch not to make a separate peace.[1]

There is no evidence to connect Du Moulin with this intrigue of his friend, but in little more than a month the Foreign Committee of the Privy Council issued orders that he, too, should be taken and sent to the Tower for frequenting the company of the Dutch deputies.[2] By some means he had heard of the order before it could be executed, and decided to leave the country while the going was still good. His own version of the affair, as told to Halifax, was that the order for his arrest was simply the culmination of three years of persecution at Arlington's hands; that the long-sought opportunity to ruin him occurred when he attempted to pay two 'social calls' (*visites de civilité*) to the Dutch deputies at Hampton Court; and that, though innocent, he had fled from the country to escape the fate of one of Buckingham's relatives (Howard), who was kept in the Tower against all forms of justice; 'et j'ai toujours crû de la prison encore plus que de la pauvreté qu'elle n'a rien en soi de plus dur *quam quod homines ridiculos faciat.* De loin, on se justifie avec moins de peine; ou si l'on n'y réussit pas on s'en console plus aisément; et lorsque nos juges deviennent nos parties, le meilleur remède est de se tirer de dessous leur juridiction.' Similarly, in another letter to Shaftesbury, he maintained that his attempted visit to the Dutch deputies arose only from 'personal acquaintance and old friendship', from a desire to condole with them on the progress of the French armies, and from motives of civility, and he again complained of Arlington's 'implacable hatred'.[3]

---

[1] For this episode see Colbert to Louis XIV, 29 June/9 July (P.R.O. Transcripts); Colbert to Pomponne, 24 June/4 July and 4/14 July, with enclosures (Archives du Ministère des Affaires Étrangères); MSS. Carte 37, ff. 702 et seq.; Foxcroft, i. 80, n. 1.

[2] For. Ent. Bk. 177, 31 July 1672; *C.S.P.D. 1672*, p. 432.

[3] Drafts of both letters are in R.A. Fagel 253, and the original of the second letter is in the P.R.O., S.P. Chas. II, 319, f. 118.

It is not altogether impossible that these professions of innocence are true, but knowing his full career and his political views, and knowing that he could have been the man supplying Boreel with information, one may fairly be sceptical about these 'social calls'. Burnet's account was short and to the point; he 'gave the States very good intelligence [but] fearing that he was discovered, took the alarm in time, and got beyond sea'.[1]

So he left his broken career in England and passed over to try to build a new one in Holland by working against the English government. In Charles's view he was a traitor, and he would almost certainly have been punished as such if he had been caught; but if he was technically a traitor, his treason was not of the purely mercenary kind, but was that type which is based on political principle, and of which several twentieth-century examples are readily called to mind. In his case, the principle was one of hostility to France in the interests of Europe and of Protestantism. There is no reason to doubt the sincerity of the arguments repeatedly put forward in his letters and pamphlets, that it was essential in England's own interest to break off the French alliance and turn against Louis XIV; and if indeed he did write the great pamphlet *England's Appeal*, it was in no way inconsistent of him to take the *nom de plume* of 'A True Lover of his Country'.

In Holland he speedily entered the service of William of Orange, whose great aim in life was also to fight against Louis XIV. It is not certain how he came to William's notice. It may readily be inferred that he had friends in Holland dating back to his mission there in 1667 or before. It is also possible that Boreel may have recommended him. According to one later report he 'was altogether brought in by van Beuningen',[2] who might have met him when, as Dutch ambassador in Paris in 1668, he was co-operating with Du Moulin's master Trevor in support of the Triple Alliance against France. Van Beuningen was strongly impressed with the French danger and also a very devout Protestant, as Buckingham and Arlington had found, when on their em-

---

[1] Burnet, ii. 64.

[2] Williamson s Journal, 7/17 May 1674 (S.P. 105/222, based on notes in 105/231), being a report of a conversation with Monsieur de W[icquefort ?].

bassy they had had to listen to 'a multitude of arguments drawn from morality and conscience which took up a great deal of time'.[1] His fears of Louis XIV had led him to pass from support of De Witt to opposition, and finally to join William of Orange, and they obviously gave him an outlook similar to Du Moulin. After-events show them on good terms, and as his influence in the city of Amsterdam was very great, his patronage would be very useful. Burnet gives a picture of van Beuningen, in which he describes him as 'a man of great notions, but talked perpetually, so that it was not possible to convince him, in discourse at least; for he heard nobody speak but himself' (which cannot have been to the liking of the argumentative Burnet), but goes on to pay tribute to his honesty.[2]

A second important patron of Du Moulin's was Caspar Fagel, who after being greffier to the States-General, succeeded John De Witt in the office of Grand Pensionary, and became the right-hand man of the young and inexperienced William of Orange. He held his office long enough to see William established on the English throne, and his services to the Dutch state in the 1670's and 1680's were very valuable, so that, though he is not the best known of the Pensionaries of the seventeenth century, he is not the least great among them. Sir William Temple described him after the war was over as 'a person whose dispositions may, I am confident, be improved, to make him as partial to England, as those of his predecessors were esteemed to France, in case there were any competition of those two interests here. The point upon which I judge this to turn chiefly, is that of religion, in which I find him, by his discourses, very warm; and hear by others, that he hath it very much at heart.'[3]

It was probably through van Beuningen and Fagel that Du Moulin reached the presence of William of Orange. By this time William had been raised to the office of Stadholder by a great outburst of public feeling, in spite of the terms of the Perpetual Edict which had tried to ensure that the offices of Captain-General and Stadholder should never be combined, and about a week after Du Moulin's arrival, the

---

[1] Cit. Foxcroft, i. 86.   [2] Burnet, i. 588-9.
[3] Temple, iv. 37.

lynching of the two brothers De Witt by the mob at The Hague left him in unchallenged control of the national resistance. Thanks to the flooding of the country-side after the dikes had been opened, the French advance was held up, and William could begin to fight back with the assistance of the Emperor Leopold I and the Great Elector of Brandenburg from October 1672. At sea also the Dutch had at least held their own and indeed the worst of the danger was over. Yet William had as yet made no progress in his attempts to win his uncle Charles II from the French alliance. He saw Buckingham and Arlington on their way to Utrecht, but though he had some original success with the mercurial Buckingham, he failed in the end to shake their attachment to the French policy, and attempts to approach Charles personally were also a failure. In July van Reede had returned to Holland after an abortive mission to Whitehall on William's behalf, and a second attempt through Sir Gabriel Sylvius and William's physician, Dr. Rumpf, to induce Charles to agree to a separate peace even at the price of giving Sluys as a security and full satisfaction on the other points at stake, was equally unsuccessful at the end of the same month. Charles insisted that he would make peace only in conjunction with his ally Louis, and indeed he could not do otherwise.[1] William therefore needed some means of bringing extra pressure to bear on his uncle.

It was in this situation that Du Moulin was brought to him, offering to explain the motives behind English foreign policy and to suggest how it could be altered. Du Moulin's first task was to draw up an authoritative account of how, and by whom, the French alliance had been made. To understand why William and Fagel set so much store by his observations it is necessary to bear in mind that the dispatches of the Dutch ambassadors in London before 1672, whether public or secret, or private letters to De Witt, had on the

[1] For details of these negotiations, see Trevelyan, chap. xii; Foxcroft, chap. iv; Barbour, pp. 193 et seq.; de Wicquefort, iv. 440–55; Japikse, *Corres.*, II. i. 80, 86; Geyl, *Oranje en Stuart*, p. 480 et seq.; Japikse, *Prins Willem III*, i. 225 et seq.; Eliz. Korvezee in *Bijdragen voor Vaderlandsche Geschiedenis*, 6e reeks, vol. 7 (1928). Sir Gabriel Sylvius was a Dutchman who had passed from the service of William's mother, Mary Stuart, to that of the Duke of York, and his services as an intermediary were often used at this time.

whole been remarkably uninformative. It had taken them a long time to detect the change in English foreign policy between the Triple Alliance of 1668 and the attack on Holland in 1672, and they had not been able to explain it satisfactorily, nor had they been able to fathom the intrigues and differing outlooks of the King, his brother, and leading personalities at Court. In this respect, they compare decidedly unfavourably with the French ambassadors, though it is true that the latter had far better opportunities of getting to know what was going on because they were on more confidential terms with Charles and Arlington. One may therefore suppose that, unless William and Fagel had other sources of information, they needed someone who could throw light on conditions in England. Du Moulin was the very man for their purpose; he had been in a good position to use his great powers of observation and his acute political intelligence, and, moreover, he also possessed the ability to present the results of his analysis of the English political situation clearly and methodically.

This analysis is a remarkable performance.[1] It is not a complete penetration of all the secrets of English diplomacy —that could hardly be expected—but in several respects it comes nearer the truth than any other contemporary statement. It opens with the assertion that, surprising as the Anglo-French alliance might seem to those who knew little of the English Court, there were people who had observed the Court closely, who were not surprised, and had even predicted long ago what those who were most concerned did not believe until they were compelled to do so by experience. 'Je ne sais si j'oserais prétendre être de ce nombre, de crainte de paraître trop vain; mais puisque mon plus grand malheur a été d'avoir su trop de particularités de cette intrigue, je m'efforcerai de la démêler sans déguisement et sans fard ni sans affecter une modestie hors de saison lorsqu'il s'agit de dire la vérité.' After these preliminaries he went on to draw a contrast between the previous Anglo-Dutch war of 1664–7,

[1] The original drafts of this and the following memorial are to be found in R.A. Fagel 252, 1474, written and amended in Du Moulin's handwriting, and copies made later by William Howard are in the P.R.O., S.P. Car. II, 334, f. 44. The two memorials are undated, but from internal evidence must have been written in the autumn or early winter of 1672.

when anti-Dutch popular feeling had been skilfully worked up beforehand, and the present conflict, in which it was not the English *nation* that was waging war, though their prejudices were being utilized and their lives endangered. On this occasion Charles had been induced to make war not by public opinion but 'outre quelque inclination de lui-même', by the continued arguments and artifices of the Duke of York and some of the principal ministers. The King, so Du Moulin argued, had always been inclined to a French alliance as a result of his education in that country, and of his pro-French entourage, so that he had never preferred Holland 'à un climat qui était plus à son gré, et dont les mœurs étaient plus conformes à son génie'; and in addition he had been deeply wounded by the disgrace of the Medway episode in 1667. Nevertheless, he had not objected when Clarendon's successors had wanted to reverse Clarendon's French policy, and the result had been the Triple Alliance of 1668. At this period the Duke of York, who unfortunately for the United Provinces had always been prejudiced against them, for reasons well known to those who knew his character and inclinations, had had little influence on policy. But from 1669 onwards Charles had been subjected to pressure to return to the French alliance, and the war of 1672 was the result.

The decisive change, according to Du Moulin, had taken place about April 1669, precisely the time when he was falling out of favour in Paris. It was the result of the feeling of some of the King's ministers (and here it is to be supposed that he meant principally his enemy Arlington), who, finding that they had not made sufficient personal profit from saving the Spanish Netherlands from the French, determined to reverse their policy and seek terms with France. (It must be assumed that Du Moulin was led astray by personal rancour in ascribing the change to such purely mercenary motives.) For their purpose these ministers achieved a reconciliation with the Duke of York, and from about July or August 1669 they joined forces to work to bring Charles over to their point of view. The influence of Madame d'Orléans over her brother was used, in a stay of 'some weeks' at Dover, and it was there, so Du Moulin thought, that the first plan for the destruction of the United Provinces was made. Buckingham's two jour-

neys to France followed; Du Moulin accurately considered
that here Buckingham's vanity was being turned to account
by some of his colleagues. These colleagues (presumably
Arlington and Clifford) then continued their efforts to influence Charles against Holland, so that 'ses divertissements
mêmes étaient de continuelles batteries contre les Provinces-
Unies, diverses résolutions les plus violentes ayant été prises
dans ces moments-là'. Insulting medals, portraits, and pamphlets were found or forged; negotiations over Surinam were
hindered, to try to put the Dutch in the wrong, and the incident of the yacht *Merlin* manufactured for the same purpose;
the ministers' creatures, carefully planted in every European
Court, sent home misleadingly favourable reports of the
diplomatic situation; and the secret committee (*le conseil
secret*) was re-formed to exclude Rupert, Bridgeman, Robarts,
Ormond, Trevor, Holles, and other members who showed
some independence of view. Here Du Moulin went on to
make a distinction between members of the Cabal, which, so
far as one is aware, was made by no other contemporary
except those deliberately admitted into the secret: 'quoique
ce qu'ils ont nommé Caballe ne soit composé que de cinq
personnes, on a remarqué que deux d'entre eux avaient le
véritable secret, sans se découvrir au reste que lorsque les
choses étaient déjà résolues, ou à mesure qu'ils avaient besoin
de leur assistance'. He seems to have realized, what is well
known today, that Arlington and Clifford were in the inner
secret, and that the other three were only brought in afterwards as and when it was convenient.

Du Moulin goes on to say that the problem of how to get
money without calling Parliament was solved by proroguing
it, stopping the Exchequer, and drawing French subsidies:
and to make certain that Charles should make no attempt to
recall Parliament, the ministers persuaded him to issue the
Declaration of Indulgence at the same time as the French
alliance was made public, 'qui étaient les deux seuls points
sur quoi il restât quelque fermeté au Parlement, tout soumis
d'ailleurs à l'autorité royale'. In spite of all this, Charles still
remained doubtful, and some of his ministers might even
have been tempted to try to renew the Dutch alliance, if
arguments *à la française* (i.e. bribery) had not been used. But

Charles was induced to attack the Smyrna fleet to fill his coffers, and when this failed, he was persuaded to declare war, calling the Council together for the purpose in extraordinary haste, only an hour before a conference with the Dutch ambassadors at which it was known that the latter would concede the full right of the flag.

Following this narrative of the recent course of English foreign policy, Du Moulin proceeds to analyse the situation in England at the time of writing. For this purpose he begins by drawing a distinction between the English nation and the Court. So far as the nation is concerned, or rather its representatives in Parliament, submissive as they were generally to the wishes of the Court, the latter had not dared to call them together for two years, and if it were possible for the Dutch to treat with them in a body, there would soon be a firm and durable union between the two nations: all the more so if it were possible to have a general election and a new Parliament. Again, the Court itself could be divided into the war party and those excluded from office (and in default of a meeting of Parliament Du Moulin held that it was greatly to be desired that Charles should be induced to take the advice of *all* his Council), and even the war party might be subdivided into four sections: the Duke of York; the ministers devoted to him and in secret control (Arlington and Clifford); those ministers who had followed their lead; and the King himself. From James nothing was to be hoped, for he would hear anything in favour of the United Provinces only when constrained by sheer necessity. The same was true of his confidants except that their humbler birth made them act more cautiously. The other ministers might be easier to win over, but they would have to be given money to pay their debts, and a sufficient pretext for peace to enable them to persuade Parliament that they were 'dignes de lauriers au lieu d'une recherche criminelle'. They were less committed to the prevailing foreign policy and would risk less for it. As for Charles, he was too skilful in *l'art de régner* not to hide his desire for vengeance on Holland if he found it too difficult to satisfy it, and he must be aware that so far all the gains of the war had gone to France; like many others in all ranks of society he must be tired of a war in which he saw too late that there was everything to lose and nothing to gain. He was evidently held back from a change of policy only by the ties and obligations which he had taken upon himself, and by the difficulties of his present situation: he disliked the prospect of recalling Parliament after its long intermission, having to face the unpopularity of the French alliance, the Stop of the Exchequer, the Declaration of Indulgence, the giving of posts to Papists, the standing army, and the new debts which would have to be paid off, so that however tired he was of the war he would only make peace (if he was not forced to do so) on terms sufficiently advantageous to disarm opposition.

At this point Du Moulin broke off his report, saying that the discussion of the means by which a change in English policy could be brought about needed a separate discourse, to be submitted if the first one was found acceptable. This summary can scarcely do justice to a report which deserves quotation in full to show the lucidity of its analysis and the acuteness of its observations. Obviously the author is wrong on several important points. The account of the formation of the alliance with Louis XIV can be corrected in the light of our knowledge from other sources not open to him of what happened before and at the Treaty of Dover. Far too much importance is given to James, and to the author's personal enemy, Arlington, who was Charles's agent rather than his evil genius, and was later the first of his ministers to have misgivings about the French alliance. Du Moulin greatly underestimated Charles's personal control over foreign policy and assumed too readily that he could be easily induced by the suitable application of pressure to follow policies contrary to his own true interests. This was an error common to many of Charles's contemporaries, friends and enemies, the French ambassadors as well as his own ministers, his brother James as well as members of the Country Party; though perhaps some modern historians err in the opposite direction and credit him with a consistency and firmness of purpose which he did not possess. It is, however, noticeable that the concluding section of Du Moulin's report attributes to Charles more shrewdness than the narrative part of it, and it may be that the author was afraid of offending Charles's nephew William by too great outspokenness; or, quite probably, he considered that William might have some compunction about engaging in underhand intrigues against his uncle the King, but would have no scruples about working against wicked ministers in the King's own true interests. This would be consistent with later writings and with Dutch propaganda throughout.

In any case, for our present purpose, the accuracy of Du Moulin's analysis is not so important as the fact that, whether it was right or wrong, it found favour with William and Fagel, and on it Dutch policy with regard to England was based. We know from William Howard's later letter to Arlington[1] that William and Fagel thought highly of it, and we know also that, presumably with their approval, Du Moulin did follow it up with a second memorial, devoted to suggesting means by which a change in English foreign policy might be brought about.

For this purpose Du Moulin divided England into four sections: the Cabal protected and supported by the Duke of York; the person of the King; the Parliament; and, lastly, the bulk of the nation. With this last section Du Moulin does not deal, on grounds of lack of space, and because an appeal to it would only be necessary after all other means had been tried.

With regard to the Cabal, there was little to be hoped from them as long as they had any hope left of defeating the United Provinces; but as no opportunity was to be neglected, and as the growing difficulties of the war might induce them to withdraw from their policy before it was too late, something might be done to convince them of the dangers of their present course and to provide them with a convenient way out without dishonour. The argument that the members of the Cabal would be in grave danger of attack in the House of Commons should not be openly used in negotiation with them, but attempts should be made to work underhand to foster and increase the general discontent and by making it more vocal to intimidate them into desiring peace. At the same time the Cabal must be convinced that, as France and England had been unable to achieve a decisive success in the exceptionally favourable circumstances of 1672,

[1] See p. 81 below.

it was unlikely that they could hope for speedy success in 1673, and they might even be defeated. In this connexion Du Moulin made the acute observation from past experience of naval wars between England and Holland, that the Dutch fleet could not be compelled to fight, and even if a battle did take place, so long as the two fleets were approximately equal a decisive sea victory was most unlikely. To these indications of the risk to the Cabal of continuing the war without much prospect of success, must be added the provision of peace terms which were sufficiently honourable without making any serious concessions. The English Court must be reminded that their grievances were the work of John De Witt with his persistent diplomatic evasions and his hatred of the Stuart family; now that the De Witts were dead and their party without influence, a firm and durable understanding could be reached between Charles and his nephew William, in whose interests he had professed to be fighting against the Dutch Republicans. The grievances alleged by England could be met by blaming them on De Witt's rule, and by satisfaction on the question of the flag and the minor matter of Surinam. In Du Moulin's original draft there then appears a suggestion of the advantages to be gained from proposing a marriage between William and the Duke of York's eldest daughter Mary (then aged 10), which the King could hardly fail to approve and which would also find general favour in Parliament: even if the proposal were not successful, it could be used to divide the Cabal, and show some of them how generous William could be. This suggestion, however, was omitted from the fair copy of Du Moulin's memorial. It was a fairly obvious one, to be considered many times before the marriage took place in 1677, but Du Moulin may have felt that he was here encroaching on personal matters.

If it appeared that the ministers of the Cabal were not likely to be shaken, recourse must be had to the King, who should be approached privately, 'où d'ordinaire il parle des affaires avec plus de liberté comme il en juge avec moins de prévention'. He must be persuaded of the danger of continuing the war, which, even if it resulted in a Dutch defeat, could only bring advantages to France. If necessary, and after trying 'toutes les voies de douceur', an attempt must be made to denounce the ministers to the King for their conduct. Even if Charles did not believe everything, sufficient suspicion would remain to weaken the government.

If in spite of repeated efforts the King and his ministers refused to abandon the French alliance, then the only remedy left would be to turn to Parliament to prevent them from giving Charles money to continue the war. Precedents must be sought for foreign ambassadors dealing with Parliament, and at the same time suitably influential members of both Houses should be sounded for their support. As many intelligent and right-minded people as possible should be engaged to inform M.P.s, by word of mouth and in writing, of the issues at stake, and lastly the States-General should publish a manifesto which should be a reply to Charles's declaration of war and yet full of deference and respect for Charles personally.

In this memorial there are foreshadowed all the methods to be employed by Dutch policy in the eighteen months between Du Moulin's arrival in Holland and the Treaty of Westminster—attempts to persuade, divide, and intimidate the Cabal; attempts to persuade Charles and lead him to distrust his ministers, and, finally and most important, attempts by intrigue and propaganda to cause trouble for Charles and danger for his ministers by giving Parliament a sense of the dangers of the French alliance and by joining hands with the Country Party in opposition. The general hope that difficulties with his Parliament would prevent Charles from continuing the war was obviously one which the Dutch might reasonably have held in any case without any detailed knowledge of or interference in English politics, but this memorial made it something more than merely a pious hope: it paved the way for a systematic attempt to increase Charles's constitutional difficulties when the other methods had been tried and failed.

It seems likely that William would probably have preferred to achieve his aim of securing peace with England in order to concentrate on France, by reaching a personal arrangement with his uncle Charles II. At no time in his career in Holland or in England did he desire to encourage opposition parties unless that were the only possible means of securing his interests and furthering his great aim of checking Louis XIV. Intrigue with Charles's discontented subjects and the fostering of Charles's constitutional difficulties was a dangerous game to play. Apart from anything else, if Charles were completely alienated there would be no hope of eventually bringing England into the coalition against France; and, looking farther ahead still, William was well aware that he stood near to the English succession and had no wish permanently to weaken the royal prerogative. (We shall find that, after the second marriage of James of York in 1673, Dutch agents in England were almost immediately discussing the chances of James having a healthy son.) Nor was he a conspirator by temperament, though he was prepared to stoop to it if there was no alternative.

William therefore made a series of attempts in 1672 to reach terms with Charles II. The missions of van Reede in July, and Rumpf later on have already been noted, and van Reede paid a second visit to England in September. It is clear that William was even prepared to contemplate the loss of Sluys to secure peace, though it is doubtful whether he would have agreed to this in permanence, or could have secured the approval of the States-General when it came to the point. Nor was Charles reluctant to make peace; his warlike enthusiasm soon evaporated, and shortage of money, if nothing else, made him anxious for an early and satisfactory ending to the war. Charles indeed was prepared to make the most of his relationship with William, and tried persistently to pose as William's patron, keen on securing the interests of his nephew. There is an illuminating account of a discussion in the Committee of Foreign Affairs after the death of De Witt, on whether to write to William 'to mind him that this accident may make a fair way for a peace', as a result of which Charles resolved to write a personal letter to his nephew.[1]

There was never, however, the slightest chance that such attempts as this would be successful. William wanted a separate peace to enable him to concentrate on France, while Charles neither would nor could agree to a separate peace without the French ally to whom he was tied; and the result was deadlock. Charles has a reputation among historians for

[1] For. Ent. Bk. 177, 18 and 20 Aug. 1672; Japikse, Corres., II. i. 96.

his shrewdness, but he made one of his worst miscalculations in his appraisal of William in 1672. For all his youth and inexperience, William was the last person to accept the position of Charles's protégé; nor was he the sort of person easily deterred by cheap threats. Reede's last interview with Charles in London in September was a stormy one in which Charles accused William of plotting to stir up trouble for him with English malcontents, and even went so far as to threaten that if he so desired it would cost him little to procure for William the same grim fate as the De Witts had suffered at the hands of the mob of The Hague. Eighteen months later Williamson found it worth while to note down in his journal a reference to 'Reede's unlucky report to the Prince a year ago of the King's saying, He could with a little cost put the Prince where De Witt was, &c.'[1] This episode, which shows Charles in rather a poor light, had the opposite effect to the one Charles intended. William wrote dignified letters to Charles and Arlington, denying that he had been plotting against the King's interests ('comme si je voulais tramer quelque chose contre les intérêts du Roi'), but saying that he was not afraid of threats. 'Je ne suis point craintif de mon naturel.'[2]

Any compunction which William might still have had in intriguing against his uncle was probably dispelled by this threat; but it would not be correct to infer from his carefully phrased reply that he had not previously been employing agents in England. We do not certainly know whether he had yet read or approved Du Moulin's two memorials, which are undated, but it is clear that Dutch agents were active in England by September: whether or not their activities were 'against the true interests of the King' gave scope for equivocation. Details of their doings are unfortunately meagre, but Johan van Wachtendonck, Commissioner for the Dutch prisoners of war, was committed to the Tower on suspicion of activities against the King, and in spite of his protestations of innocence he remained imprisoned until after the end of the war.[3] More important, we have an uncorroborated hint

---

1 7/17 May 1674, in S.P. 105/222 (based on notes in S.P. 105/231). *Note*: It appears from Temple, iv. 95, and William's letter to Arlington (see following note) that Arlington made a similar remark.

2 Japikse, *Corres.*, II. i. 114–16.

3 Cf. his report dated 3/13 Sept. 1672, in R.A. St.-Gen. 6922.

that at this time an attempt was made to approach Shaftesbury and Lauderdale, and so divide the Cabal in its attitude to the war. The writer of a letter dated 10 October/31 September [*sic*], reported to Du Moulin that 'Your friends and their inclinations are as before, no good can be done neither on the little or great man. I am certain all [the Cabal?] are united in this work, though otherwise they have their envyings.'[1] This cryptic statement seems to imply an attempt to sound Shaftesbury and Lauderdale, two friends (soon, however, to become bitter enemies), whose shortness and tallness of stature respectively were a matter of comment: a Scotsman some years previously had referred to them as the 'lickell man' and the 'mickell man' respectively.

There is no confirmation of this available from any other source, and no indication that any such approach was authorized by William. Yet such an attempt would obviously have been fully in line with the policy laid down in Du Moulin's memorial of dividing the Cabal or of sowing suspicion in the King's mind or both. It would fully explain Charles's indignant outburst to van Reede. And the single hint which we do possess is contained in one of the first few letters from England which are preserved in Du Moulin's papers.[1] Was it the first-fruits of the organization which Du Moulin began to build about this time?

[1] R.A. Fagel 244.

IV

THE FIFTH COLUMN

BEFORE the strict narrative of events is continued from the autumn of 1672, it is convenient to describe the 'fifth column' which then began to operate, and to indicate generally the ways in which it functioned, and the work which it performed during the next eighteen months. It is a strange story of spies and secret agents, smugglers, and conspirators, which at times reads more like historical fiction than sober fact; but the evidence for it is ample, even though there are some tantalizing gaps in it.

The headquarters of the organization, from which its activities were controlled, obviously had to be in The Hague. There the general lines of the policy to be adopted to turn England against France were laid down by William and his Pensionary Fagel. They also enjoyed the assistance of the Imperial ambassador, Lisola, one of the greatest diplomats of the age even if his greatness is to some extent exaggerated by his German biographer.[1] By his diplomatic intrigues and his skill as a pamphleteer he had already proved a thorn in the side of Louis XIV, who regarded his attempts to build up an anti-French coalition as so dangerous that he was even prepared to try to capture him in spite of his diplomatic immunity. As he had been ambassador in London, he had some first-hand knowledge of English conditions, and was no doubt able to appreciate Du Moulin's analysis of them.

Du Moulin's own precise position in William's entourage is not certain, until in the course of the summer of 1673 we find him definitely employed as a confidential secretary to deal with foreign correspondence; but long before that he enjoyed William's full confidence, and was authorized to deal with all 'intelligence' coming from England and to proffer suggestions on policy. Master and agent had clearly much in common in their outlook on international affairs, and it seems that during their collaboration William may even have acquired some liking for the Huguenot refugee,

[1] Pribram, *Lisola* (Leipzig, 1894).

since he wrote that 'poor Du Moulin is dead' when the news reached him in 1676, and there were not many people of whom he would have written in that way. Certainly Charles and his ministers came to regard Du Moulin as a sort of evil genius of William's, who led him astray from his proper duty to his uncle and induced him to take part in disloyal intrigues; and how obnoxious Du Moulin was to them on that account is shown by the attempts made to ruin him after the war. It is relevant, however, to remember that when these attempts were being made, he wrote that the English ministers 'me font trop d'honneur de me donner auprès de Son Altesse [William] une place que je ne mérite point et que je n'ai jamais possédée. Toute mon ambition s'étend à bien exécuter ses ordres, et il n'est pas besoin que je vous dise que Son Altesse est trop éclairée d'avoir besoin de mes avis dans les résolutions qu'elle a à prendre.'[1] If this statement of the relationship between the two men is accepted (and there is no reason to doubt it, particularly when our knowledge of William's character in later life is taken into consideration), then it is probable that, though Du Moulin may have had considerable freedom in detail and was able to make very influential suggestions based on his personal knowledge of English conditions, William always retained full responsibility for the broad lines of policy, and his authorization of what his agents did was no mere formality.

Du Moulin's first task was to write to as many of his old friends in London as possible, and to persuade them to enter into a regular correspondence with him, providing him with 'intelligence' of what was going on in England. This was done in the autumn of 1672 and the following winter. Naturally some of them were reluctant to engage in anything which might get them into trouble with the English government: whatever their sympathies might be, they were conscious of the hazards of entering into a correspondence which might be regarded as treasonable. This attitude is forcibly expressed in a letter signed by the initial 'N', and addressed to Monsr. du Moulin, without date:[2]

I answered yours by the bearer, as soon as I received it according

[1] Du Moulin to van Beuningen, 13/23 Aug. 1674, in R.A. Fagel 274.
[2] Like the rest of this correspondence this letter is in R.A. Fagel 244.

to your direction, and very sorry to hear from Mr. Child[1] that he is informed that you are very busy against our rulers, and full of passions, and it is generally discoursed by all that know you and others, as also that there was a design to address from Holland to the Parliament, which they could not receive, it being His Majesty's undoubted prerogative to make peace and war, receive or send ambassadors. I beseech you to meddle not, which would hinder you from a capacity of ever dwelling in England, and they say you write hither with much passion. I am glad I know none of them to whom you write, but do beseech you to consider that none can receive such letters and you may bring your friends into trouble, nor is it to any advantage. Pray never descant upon the persons or undertakings of our rulers: nor query of our affairs. I care not to hear often, but should be glad to understand sometimes of your health, and as to news, only matter of fact without reflections. Pardon my freedom, I know what and why I write, and shall ever remain, &c.

Not all the replies were so discouraging, however. There must have been many writers whose letters and names have not been preserved, but we know with certainty who were the two principal members of the London end of Du Moulin's organization. They passed under the false names of 'Mr. Freeman' and 'Mr. Smith'. Mr. Freeman, according to one English counter-espionage agent, was in character 'a man of great parts and of few words', and in physique 'a tall, lean man'.[2] The same man noted that Smith, 'and sometimes his company call him Sir Nicholas, appears to have been born about Chippenham in Wiltshire. Is a devilish fellow, set thick, about 45 years old',[3] or, as another account has it, 'a pretty fat plump man'.

The real name of one of them was William Medley, a member of the sect of Fifth Monarchists whose extreme political outlook had caused concern both to Cromwell and to Charles II. He had been one of the principal twenty-one Fifth Monarchists involved in a plan for an insurrection against Cromwell in 1657, and had signed himself 'W. Medley, scribe', to the printed manifesto of the rioters, *A Standard Set Up*. As a result he was seized by the Protector's

[1] Probably to be identified with the famous East India merchant, later Sir Josiah Child, who would have known Du Moulin on the Council of Trade.

[2] Puckle to Arlington, 25 Nov. 1673, in S.P. 84/195, f. 104.

[3] Williamson's Journal, 6/16 May 1674, in S.P. 105/222.

government and spent nearly two years in the Tower. Perhaps because this experience disillusioned him about the methods by which the millennium was to be achieved, he does not seem to have taken part in the futile escapade known as Venner's rising in 1661 even though he was Venner's son-in-law; at all events, after that handful of Fifth Monarchists had terrorized London, he was not one of the prisoners taken when the rising was put down, and in spite of his relationship to Venner he escaped the government's attention, and was still living in London at the end of that year. In November 1661 an informant of the Secretary of State wrote:

There is Mr. Medley in Seething [?] lane, that married Venner's daughter, who is as right as his father [in law] for rebellion. He is the scribe and accomptant for that faction, and he hath not only a list of their party, but he had, and I conceive hath now, the keeping of all the letters and papers of correspondence between that party in every country, as also what stock of money they have; and this I was certainly informed of by my old friend Mr. Pugh, but lately before he went to Holland; and if he were suddenly and secretly surprised, I am confident some papers would be found to your content. . . .[1]

There is no record that this information was ever acted upon, and indeed in the following years we know little about the remnants of this sect in days when the millennium seemed farther away than ever. Some of them found it expedient to take refuge in the comparative freedom of Holland, whence from time to time Charles's government received alarmist reports that such Fifth Monarchists as Dr. Richardson of Leyden were engaged in plots; but Medley himself disappears entirely from view until we meet him again in 1672, hostile to the Restoration government and ready to co-operate with Du Moulin in conspiring against it in a more methodical way. He was identified by one of his colleagues, William Carr, who turned informer, with 'Mr. Freeman' (after another informant had argued that this Freeman was the notorious Republican Ludlow, returning from his exile in Switzerland to plot against the government), and had a relative with a commission in the English forces in the pay of

[1] Quoted in an article on 'Fifth Monarchy Insurrections', by Champlin Burrage, in *E.H.R.*, vol. xxv, 1910, from which these facts about Medley are taken.

the States-General, who is always referred to in the correspondence as 'the Captain'.

Medley worked in conjunction with another man whose true name was Trenchard, and who was said by Carr to be 'brother to him that was of the House of Commons lately', namely, the member for Wareham in Dorset who had recently died. The Trenchard family, which came from the West Country and particularly from Wiltshire and Dorset, had supplied several zealous Puritans in the time of the Civil War; and a namesake who was the nephew of our Trenchard, was later to become Whig M.P. for Taunton, to be high in the counsels of the Whig Party in the Exclusion Bill crisis, and eventually, as Sir John Trenchard, to rise to be Secretary of State under William III. The general political outlook of these Trenchards is obvious enough, and it is also clear that the brother of an M.P. would have special opportunities and might be able to make use of his acquaintance with other members to further Du Moulin's schemes.

Carr identified 'Freeman' as Medley, and 'Smith' as Trenchard, and he was well placed to know: but there is a possibility that he was mistaken. On examining that part of Du Moulin's correspondence which survives, we find no letters signed by 'Freeman', several signed 'Nic. Smyth', but more (the most valuable letters of all) signed 'J. T.', 'J. Turner', 'J. Thompson', 'J. Tanner', and other variants of the same initials, which it would be more natural for Trenchard to adopt than Medley. One is inclined to wonder whether Carr may have been wrong in identifying 'Smith' and Trenchard: perhaps 'Freeman' and 'J. T.' were Trenchard, and 'Nic. Smyth' was Medley or a third person: all that can be said definitely is that Carr's identification was accepted, and acted upon, by the English authorities.

This William Carr is one of the least reputable of the intriguers, since there is no sign that he cared anything for either politics or religion, and every indication that he was prepared to sell his services to the highest bidder—or to more than one bidder. After being in Lord Gerrard's household, and spending some time as Clerk to the King's Horse Guard, of which that peer was Colonel, he went (or had to flee) abroad, and wrote from Rotterdam in November 1672 to offer to correspond with the Secretary of State's office. He cited as qualifications his travels in Dalmatia, Hungary, and elsewhere, and 'his study in chemistry'—a somewhat surprising asset to mention, probably dragged in to prove that he was a man of some education—and suggested that he should write weekly accounts from Holland of what was happening there, being particularly acquainted with Fagel and De Ruyter.[1] During the year 1673 he is to be found, on the one hand, sending to Lord Arlington copies of Dutch propaganda pamphlets and trying also to approach the English ambassadors at the Cologne peace congress, and, on the other hand, in company with Du Moulin at The Hague and earning a living by joining with Howard to sell to English merchants passes giving them immunity from Dutch privateers. It does not appear that Carr was ever trusted very far by anyone who came into contact with him, and his importance lies not in any work which he was allowed to perform, but in the fact that in May 1674 he had an interview at Rotterdam with Sir Joseph Williamson, on the latter's return from his fruitless embassy to the Cologne peace conference. In this interview he gave Williamson valuable information about Du Moulin, Howard, Freeman, Smith, and their group, and the record in Williamson's Journal fills some important gaps in the evidence, although he is not implicitly to be relied on.[2]

Among the information then given by Carr, Williamson records a statement that:

There were certain young gentlemen relations to Parliament men, that had managed all this matter here [in Holland], during the last session of Parliament [the session of Jan.-Feb. 1674]. They have come over twice or thrice. Once came over a Parliament man under the name of Mr. George by du Moulin's order, was but one night at The Hague, and having spoken with the Prince returned. Carr saw him, was a thick short man, as Carr judged much like Marvell, but he could not say it was he, though he knows, as he says, Marvell very well.

This reference to the famous poet and M.P. for Hull, Andrew Marvell, is curious. Of course, Carr's statement is

[1] Silas Taylor to Williamson, 28 Nov. 1672, in *C.S.P.D. 1672-3*, p. 215.

[2] See Williamson's Journal for 6/16 May 1674 in S.P. 105/222, summarizing information given by Carr and by the printer Crouch, who had also turned informer.

so vague (perhaps deliberately so) that, taken by itself, it is quite untrustworthy evidence of the true identity of the mysterious 'Mr. George' whom he saw for so short a time. There are, however, one or two other indications that Marvell may have been involved in Du Moulin's organization in 1674. In a letter among Du Moulin's papers, dated 22 June/ 2 July 1674, code names are allocated to the most important politicians of the day and to Dutch agents, for use in correspondence between London and Holland. In the second column of the list there appears a group of four names, those of A. Marvell (to be called 'Mr. Thomas'), Williams, Ayloff, and Fanshaw.[1] The last three of these men were definitely members of Du Moulin's group, and it is natural to suspect that the same was true of Marvell, particularly as he is the only member of the House of Commons to whom a code name is given. Again, in the next letter, written from London by 'J. Thompson' to 'Mr. Miller' (obviously Du Moulin), dated 30 June/10 July 1674, the writer says: 'Mr. Thomas [Marvell] is in the country, and will not return for some time. Mr. Godfrey [Ayloff] has written to all his friends here of our difference, as if all the world were to be concerned in his impertinencies. The Dr. [identity unknown] was told of it some time since, but also by the relater, that he believed it was Mr. Thomas's [Marvell's] fault. . . .'

It is difficult to understand why Du Moulin's correspondent should preoccupy himself with Marvell and his movements, under a code name, and why Marvell should be concerned in disagreements among the conspirators, except on the supposition that he was one of them. Such a supposition would be in no way inconsistent with Marvell's record from 1674 to 1678 as a notable member of Shaftesbury's Country Party and author of the *Growth of Popery*: it may well be that Marvell's hostility to France dated back to 1673 or earlier and that he helped the Dutch to break the Anglo-French alliance in that and the following year, particularly as his biographers can supply few details of his activities at that time. He would be a valuable acquisition to Du Moulin's group, both on account of his position in the Commons and

[1] R.A. Fagel 244. See p. 63 below.

his skill as a political pamphleteer; but there is no evidence to connect him with any particular pamphlet which the group distributed.

Others who joined the group between 1672 and 1674 may be more briefly mentioned. Williams, to whom reference has been made, offered his services in December 1673 in a letter whose style is so windy and verbose as to suggest that he was probably a very bad conspirator: yet he seems to have been genuinely interested in the cause, and no mere adventurer. John Ayloff, a lawyer, was the person responsible for causing a considerable stir in October 1673 when he put a French sabot under the chair of the Speaker of the House of Commons to indicate the danger of England falling under the domination of French despotism, Popery, and the 'wooden shoes' and poverty that went with it. He was later concerned in the Rye House Plot to assassinate Charles II in 1683, and was finally executed for his part in Monmouth's rebellion two years afterwards.[1] Fanshaw was 'a young fairfaced man, is with them at present by another name. He is about 23 or 24 years old with a great periwig'; information given to Williamson by the printer R. Crouch, or Cross, when he turned King's evidence at the same time as Carr. It is to be presumed that Crouch was one of the men responsible for reprinting in London many of the Dutch propaganda pamphlets and anti-Popery writings: among various pamphlets printed by 'R. C.' is one entitled *The Burning of the Whore of Babylon*, appropriately issued on 5 November 1673, and in Du Moulin's papers there is one letter signed by the same initials. Among those whom Crouch betrayed was one Goodenough of the Temple, at whose chambers and house 'at the corner of Shoe Lane over against Baxter's meeting-house' his colleagues were said to lodge when in London. Scotland was represented among the conspirators by William Carstares, then serving the apprenticeship for a long career of restless activity and intrigue.[2]

Like all such groups of men, they included both enthusiasts and adventurers seeking their own profit from the

---

[1] See *Hatton Correspondence* (Camden Society), i. 118.
[2] Cf. R. H. Story, *William Carstares* (1874), and J. McCormick, *State Papers and Letters Addressed to Wm. Carstares* (Edinburgh 1774).

under-ground work in which they engaged; they co-operated to run great risks to achieve their objective, and then when that objective had been achieved quarrelled among themselves and even betrayed one another; and they claimed to be patriots as they indulged in their treason. Any general opinion about them is likely to be influenced by approval or disapproval of their aim of co-operating with England's enemies to break the Anglo-French alliance: but any observer can admire their daring and their success in a difficult task against all the resources at the disposal of Charles II and his government.

Du Moulin's first purpose was simply to obtain information of what was going on in political circles in London. The letters which survive in the Rijksarchief at The Hague (Fagel 244) contain occasional references to naval and military preparations, but they were in the main concerned, not with ordinary spying, but with *political* intelligence work. They extend from September 1672 to September 1674, and on reading them it is impossible not to feel regret that the full correspondence has not survived: it would provide a mine of information for the historian of these two critical years. As it is, he must be grateful that those which do still exist treat fully of the months January and February 1674, when the Dutch were finally successful in forcing Charles II to make the Treaty of Westminster.

Twenty-three out of approximately fifty letters relate to these two months. The best of them are without doubt those written by 'J. T.', 'J. Thompson', 'J. Turner', 'J. Tanner', and other signatures which hide the identity of the same writer. They are the work of a keen intellect, admirably phrased in the best trenchant style of the period, at once instructive, interesting, and entertaining, and on the whole giving a favourable impression of the writer's personality. The quality of the views expressed may be judged from what follows in later chapters: but the views are also diversified by anecdotes which are amusing even when their authenticity is suspect. Some of these stories are familiar: one has heard elsewhere how 'my Lord Rochester fled from Court some time since for delivering (by mistake) into the King's hands a terrible lampoon of his own making against the King, instead of another the King asked him for': but there were others, alike only in their disrespect to Charles. When Williamson had his interview with Carr in May 1674 he solemnly recorded that 'these Caballists have by late letters advice of the King's being taken by the constables in Mother Moseley's common house, That the constable was malicious to discover it was the King. That His Majesty had there the Earl of Rochester, etc., a set of such young noblemen, some of whom told him at table, that though they had been bred very loosely, yet they could not but observe to His Majesty, that they had never till then heard such talk as he used at table.' Williamson's reflections on hearing this rumour about his master are, unfortunately, not recorded.

It was not particularly difficult to smuggle letters from London to Holland, in spite of the war which was going on. The usual packet-boats continued to operate between Harwich and the Brill (except when a sea battle was thought to be imminent), since it suited the convenience of the spies of both governments alike to continue the service; and so, surprising as it may sound to modern ears, it was even possible to send letters by ordinary post in the normal way. An alternative route which could be used was through Flanders, for the Spanish Netherlands were neutral, and incidentally full of secret agents of both countries on that account. Of course, there was always the danger that letters might be intercepted, opened, and read before they reached their destination. One English agent in Flanders guarded against this by writing most of his reports in invisible ink, which became legible when the letter was held before a fire: the letters in which this device, reminiscent of the *Boys' Own Paper*, was actually used can be inspected in the State Papers (Flanders) in the Public Record Office. Cipher could also be used, but Du Moulin's agents generally employed simpler, and yet subtler methods. Their letters were written in suitably veiled language and concocted to look like ordinary letters written from one merchant in England to another in Holland, to 'Mr. Smith, coffeeman at his house in Rotterdam', or some similar accommodation address. One or two examples of the language used may be given, with the secret meaning interpolated in square brackets.

Good cousin, I am of opinion that your business here is in a good and hopeful condition. My cousin [Charles II] is resolved to stick close to my brother-in-law [James] and to Mistress Lloyd [Louis XIV], so that I doubt not but the linen will be freed from the attachments laid upon it [? the pamphlets which we brought over will be released]. We expect a good parcel of tobacco [more pamphlets] but no other commodities. My old neighbour [Parliament] is gone out of town [adjourned] till Monday next, but he has already given order for his picture to be drawn for you [reports of its proceedings will be sent], but we cannot persuade him to answer my cousin's letter [to answer the request in the King's Speech for money] till those differences between them be accommodated. Mr. Thompson [?] is preparing for his journey but will not be ready in a long time. Mr. Tompkins [? Buckingham] has exhibited a bill against Mr. Steel [? Arlington] who besides is like to lose all his preferments. Those goods [pamphlets] which you consigned to Mr. Jones are not come to hands, so that I fear some miscarriage, but the linen [pamphlets] by Mr. Smith is safe arrived, and is like to come to a great market, the merchants striving for it [and they are likely to be in great demand]. . . .

Or:

My cousin [Charles II] is apoplectical and often ill, my brother-in-law [James] is diseased as I writ you in our last, therefore I see not but that the estate [the Crown of England] is like to fall to Mrs. Ford [William of Orange][1] and I am rather glad of it because she is a very good woman, and most here speak well of her. My cousin [Charles II] is grown so doltish and has been so often foiled in Chancery [Parliament], that I believe for a little matter he might almost be persuaded to surrender. He is now become rather an object of contempt and pity than of fear. . . .

In June 1674 this language was partly codified in the following way:[2]

King	= Mr. Young.	Parliament	= the traders.
D. York	= Mr. Cox.	Peers	= the merchants.
Duchess York	= Mrs. Cox.	Commons	= Ironmongers.
Monmouth	= My nephew.	Court Party	= Mr. Simpson.
Arlington	= Mr. Smith.	Country Party	= Mr. Panton.
Lauderdale	= Mr. Greene.	New Parliament	= Mr. Newton.
Keeper [Finch]	= Mr. Simpkins.	City of London	= the stonecutters.
Treasurer [Danby]	= Mr. Norton.	Fanatics	= the dyers.
Ashley [*sic*].	= Mr. Benson.	Papists	= the stone-chandlers.

---

[1] This identification is clear from other references.

[2] These quotations are taken from letters dated 9 Jan., 29 Jan., and 2 July (N.S.) 1674, in R.A. Fagel 244.

Ireland	= Mr. Winter	A. Marvell	= Mr. Thomas.
Scotland	= Mr. Jenkins.	Williams	= Mr. Worthington.
Scotch Parliament	= Mr. Thornton.	Ayloff	= Mr. Godfrey.
		Fanshaw	= Mr. Wildgoose.
Hamilton and party	= Mr. Soames.	Dutch ambassadors	= Our partners.
French	= drapers.	Sir William Temple	= Mr. Foxcroft.
Prince of Orange	= my godson.		
States[-General]	= Mr. Greene [sic].	The East India Company	= the grocers.

In this way the writers in London were able to hope that, even if a letter was intercepted, it might escape detection by the English government: and yet the researcher in the twentieth century, with a series of the letters in front of him, can usually piece together the hidden meaning with fair certainty. Sometimes, however, the writers felt that their reports were too important to rely on the ordinary post, and that it was safer to use messengers. These messengers might travel by packet-boat from Harwich to the Brill, or from the Thames to Nieuport, or they might prefer to use unofficial transport of their own: there were many skippers of fishing-boats, yachts, and other small vessels who were prepared to risk the crossing for a suitable consideration, and especially one known to us only as 'Captain George'. This was a safer means of transporting packages of pamphlets than the packet-boat.

A third method of communication between the two countries which was definitely used in the winter of 1673–4 was that of the Spanish 'diplomatic bag'. Spanish diplomats had by then abandoned the traditional hostility of their country to the Dutch provinces which had broken from it, to co-operate with William of Orange against the French danger. Monterey, the Spanish governor at Brussels, Don Emanuel de Lira, the Spanish ambassador at The Hague, and Don Bernardo de Salinas, another Spanish diplomat, were frequently in consultation with William and co-operated in his policy towards England. So, too, did the Spanish ambassador in London, the Marquis del Fresno, though as a member of 'the old school' he sometimes had misgivings about the unorthodox methods being used; and the Spanish consul in London, Fonseca, was so active in his relations with the opposition to Charles II that the King seized the first suitable opportunity, in 1676, of ordering him to leave the country.

Du Moulin seems to have used the Spanish 'diplomatic bag' to transmit instructions to his London agents, who had only to call at the embassy and collect them.[1]

By these means, therefore, Du Moulin received reports, forwarded pamphlet propaganda, and sent instructions to his agents in London. These functions were performed, on the whole, with remarkably little interference from English counter-espionage, but this was not because Charles was not aware of the danger. He knew from the beginning of the war that the weak point in his position was the possibility of a combination between the Dutch and sections of his subjects. Accordingly, he did his best in 1672 to foster national hatred of the Dutch by propaganda of every kind, including, for instance, a revival of Dryden's *Massacre of Amboina*; and while Boreel had been in London, and later when the Dutch deputies had been at Hampton Court, precautions had been taken to prevent them from communicating with English malcontents. Naturally the government became increasingly sensitive to the danger of the Dutch maintaining 'correspondences' in England when a session of Parliament was in prospect, and long before the end of the war it had a good idea of the intrigues which were being carried on, but was unable to find and seize the persons responsible.

At the beginning of the war espionage was primarily under the supervision of Arlington's Under-Secretary, Sir Joseph Williamson, who, having progressed from his father's Cumberland vicarage via Queen's College, Oxford, into politics, was not a front-rank statesman, but showed great industry in the methodical collection of information of every kind, both domestic and international. His correspondents included some in Holland and Flanders who supplied him with news of the war and such scraps of other information as came to their notice, but they were rarely able to penetrate the secrets of Dutch policy or to give advance details of the activities of Du Moulin and his fellow exiles. They were either men of limited ability, such as 'the Machiavellian Puckle', who apparently was not 'Machiavellian' enough, or capable men like Richard Bulstrode and de Vic who wrote far from the scene at Brussels, or untrustworthy men like Howard, who,

[1] See especially the letter of 'J. T.', 6/16 Mar. 1674, in R.A. Fagel 244.

as we shall see, was employed on an important mission in 1672. In general they were not the equals of Du Moulin and his colleagues.

Nor was the government more successful in its attempts to ferret out the Dutch agents in London. Here Williamson made use of the famous Colonel Blood, who had distinguished himself by his attempt on the life of the Duke of Ormond, and still more by the well-known attempt to steal the Crown jewels from the Tower of London—an attempt in which he was only foiled by an unlucky accident. He and his accomplices had laid out the keeper, put the crown under the cloak of one of them, pushed the orb down the breeches of another, and were at work filing the sceptre into two when they were disturbed by the arrival of the keeper's son, who chose that precise moment to return from abroad.[1] It used to be thought that Charles II pardoned Blood out of sheer admiration for his nerve, but there were certainly other reasons as well: for Blood could and did supply valuable information to the government about the activities of the political and religious 'underground' of the time, through his friends among them. He had been useful in this way in the autumn of 1671, reporting on the factions among the Puritan sects when the introduction of a Declaration of Indulgence was being considered, and after that Declaration had been issued he was instrumental in procuring some of the licences for Puritan ministers. On the strength of these activities he has even been described as 'possessed of aims and ideals which were largely lofty and unselfish, and [this] leads the candid student to regard him as a Reformer spoiled in the making, a knight-errant of civil and religious liberty, by ruthless oppression turned into an Ishmael, until an erratic outburst of Royal favour restored him to his more natural role of a protector of the weak and a champion of the oppressed'.[2]

However this may be, in the war against the Dutch, Blood

---

[1] For Blood's career before 1672, see W. C. Abbott, *Colonel Thomas Blood, Crown-stealer*, reprinted in *Conflicts with Oblivion* (New Haven, 1924), and also M. Petherick, *Restoration Rogues* (1950).

[2] G. L. Turner, *Original Records of Early Nonconformity* (1911–14), iii. 160, cf. 218 et seq. It is argued that Blood did not really try to kill Ormond, and that if he tried to implicate Littleton and the other Navy Treasurer, then they must indeed have been involved.

was used against those more extreme Puritans who might be suspected of relations with Holland; he collaborated in the vain attempt to seize and confiscate Dutch propaganda pamphlets, and he was responsible, on some occasions at least, for passing on instructions to spies such as Puckle on their way into Holland.

All the efforts of Blood and the government were, however, unavailing; Dutch pamphlets came into the country unchecked, and Du Moulin's agents continued their work unmolested. It is fair, however, to remember that Du Moulin would have had a formidable adversary to contend with if Sir Joseph Williamson had not left England in May 1673 as English ambassador to the peace congress at Cologne, where he remained for nearly twelve months. In his absence the counter-espionage of the English government was decidedly inferior, but after his return in the spring of 1674 he soon broke up the remainder of Du Moulin's organization: so that from the Dutch point of view his appointment to the unavailing Cologne embassy was perhaps a fortunate accident.

V

ZAS AND ARTON—THE FIRST
FAILURES (SEPT. 1672–FEB. 1673)

B Y the autumn of 1672 it was clear that the Dutch were
not going to be completely overwhelmed by the French
armies. Behind the floods made when the dikes had been
opened in June, they held on in safety, united under William's
leadership. A last attempt made by the French general
Luxembourg in December, to take advantage of a heavy frost
to cross the frozen waters, was foiled by the thaw. To that
extent there seemed to be grounds for optimism. Yet the
Dutch did not meet with success in their attempts to fight
back, expel the French, and restrict the aggressive tendencies
of Louis XIV. William began a long career of military
failures with repulses at Naarden and Woerden, and an
attempt to strike at the French communications and surprise
Charleroi had no better fortune. The French remained in
occupation of Utrecht. Equally the hopes placed in allies
against the French failed to materialize after promising much.
The Great Elector of Brandenburg and the Emperor Leopold
were sufficiently convinced of the danger to take part in a
campaign on the Rhine in the autumn and winter of 1672–3,
but the joint Brandenburg and Imperialist troops had so little
success against the genius of Turenne that the Great Elector
withdrew from the war in April 1673. The Emperor by
himself could do little at a time when Hapsburg resources
were unusually low; and though the governor of the Spanish
Netherlands, Monterey, had given William some help in his
expedition to Charleroi, Spain did not declare war. The task
of building up an anti-French coalition had, in fact, to be
taken up again in the summer of 1673.

The sea war with England followed a similar course.
During the campaign of 1672 the Dutch navy had avoided
decisive defeat, and indeed had held its own remarkably well,
foiling all Charles's hopes of effecting a landing on the coast
of Zeeland to take his share of the partition of the United
Provinces. So the Dutch survived, but here again all their

hopes of inducing England to make peace before operations were resumed in the following spring were disappointed, and their efforts had to be renewed in the autumn of 1673. This chapter is devoted to an account of their preliminary failures in the winter of 1672–3.

Reference has already been made in Chapter III to the failure of several attempts to negotiate with Charles II between June and September 1672, and to a possible endeavour to divide the Cabal by approaching Shaftesbury and Lauderdale. The letter which seems to hint at this[1] is the earliest which survives in Du Moulin's papers, and in other respects, too, it cannot have been very encouraging, for it played down rumours of discontent in England. Just as the Cabal were united in their attitude to the war, 'though otherwise they have their envyings', so the people had no complaint about the war, whatever their opinions about other aspects of royal policy:

And the people have not those clamours about the war as beyond sea is thought. The fanatics, your best friends, rest quiet from the sweetness of their enjoyed toleration, and do not so much as mutter publicly. The episcopal dissatisfied only on a church account, think only on the confirmation of coercion in religion, and men may give money for it in Parliament when it comes: as for Papists (none of your best friends) they create no discontents, partly in that fanatics enjoy their liberty too, and partly in that they do continue close in their profession and act wondrous wisely, and the great men amongst them do dissemble their religion . . . the Duke [of York] says he will receive the sacrament at Xmas. . . . And lastly as to the merchants, their losses have been great, especially about the Straits, and *majore tumultu planguntur nummi quam funera*—yet that very love of money makes them cautious of uttering discontents; besides they feed on the promise of powerful convoys which are providing. But (if all this will not satisfy) to strike the nail on the head, the Parliament has been prorogued this fortnight to 4th February and when they will sit, *alias dicat*; most men think not at all during this war. Next as to your hope from the prince [William], *Carthago delenda est* [even] though he be their Hannibal. . . .[2]

This last curious anticipation of Shaftesbury's famous

phrase in his speech at the opening of Parliament on 4 February 1673 was intended to dispel any lingering hopes that William, as Charles's nephew, might be able to secure better terms for the Dutch than the Republican De Witt: in this third Anglo-Dutch war the power of England's greatest rivals at sea was to be as effectively destroyed as that of ancient Rome's Carthaginian enemies, whoever was the Dutch leader. With this governmental policy there was as yet no popular discontent: there was no realization, either on the part of those Nonconformists who benefited from the Declaration of Indulgence, or from those Anglicans who opposed it and wanted to restore 'coercion in religion', or even from those who feared it as the first step towards Popery, that Charles's religious policy at home was bound up with the French alliance in foreign affairs. And in any case, such dissatisfaction as there was had no means of expression, since Parliament had been prorogued until February. 'Pardon this unwelcome discourse from him, who loves not to lie under mistakes, nor would not his friend in any.'

The position, however, was not quite as gloomy as Du Moulin's correspondent considered it to be. The very fact that a meeting of Parliament (which had not sat since the spring of 1671) had been postponed still further from October 1672 to February 1673, indicated a weakness in the position of Charles and his ministers; and if a second naval campaign was to be fought in 1673, an appeal to Parliament for a subsidy sooner or later was indispensable. The longer this session was delayed, the keener the criticism of the Declaration of Indulgence would be, and in addition the government was not fully confident that the Commons, having last voted money for the Triple Alliance with Holland against France, would readily vote money for the French alliance against Holland. When the Committee of Foreign Affairs had met as far back as 18 August, one of the reasons why Arlington had then urged the advisability of negotiations was that it would have a good effect on Parliament, and Williamson noted 'N.B. Seemed concluded on all hands no Treaty of Peace could be depending while the Parliament sits, for the infinite danger there may be in having all the circumstances of it misrepresented by secret whispers to leading men in the House, by which the King's business in the House would be obstructed and his reputation abroad lost, and so he fall lower in the terms of the Peace.' On 15 and 16 September the decision to prorogue Parliament was finally taken, to prevent the Dutch from making use of 'bad humours' in the House of Commons which might prejudice peace talks.[1] The ministers clearly knew their danger.

This hope of negotiations, as was seen in Chapter III, finally faded in September and October 1672, and Charles was faced with the unpalatable prospect of an appeal to the House of Commons for money to enable him to continue the war. On 24 November, over two months before Parliament was due to meet, they began to discuss who should be the new Speaker.[1] A week previously Charles had sought to increase the unity of his ministers by appointing Shaftesbury Lord Chancellor, not because he ever trusted that elusive earl very far, but because he thought that the best way of controlling his dangerous abilities. Also in the month of November the government reached an agreement with William Howard, who had been in the Tower since his unlucky escapade in the summer.[2] In return for his freedom Howard agreed to cross secretly to Holland and to try to discover the hopes and the plans of the Dutch. He received his instructions on 29 November,[3] and early in December he crossed into Flanders, travelling under the false name of 'George Carter'. From Nieuport, where he landed, he proceeded to Antwerp, and there he waited. Before venturing into Holland, 'George Carter' wrote to a correspondent in The Hague, who was in all probability his old friend Du Moulin, to find out whether it would be safe to proceed. He did not receive any immediate reply, but he resolved to take whatever risk would be involved in venturing into Dutch territory without one. In view of his friendship with Du Moulin the risk was probably small, but before leaving Antwerp he reported his plans to the English government, solemnly asserting that 'the service of my King and country ought to preponderate all considerations of my own danger and safety'. If his life-long record of conspiracy is considered, it is impossible not to wonder whether his tongue was in his cheek when he wrote this; and he may already have been wondering how far he should carry out his instructions of discovering Dutch plans, and how far it might be better to throw in his lot with Du Moulin.[1]

The latter, and his Dutch employers, had several schemes on foot in this same month of December. Early in the month another of the series of unofficial Dutch envoys landed in England, an advocate named Gerbrand Zas. He came without official credentials of any kind, ostensibly on his way to Sir Gabriel Sylvius, the Dutchman in the Stuart service, and carrying letters from the Grand Pensionary Fagel which might supply a basis for negotiation. Henry Coventry, who was now Arlington's colleague as Secretary of State, immediately suggested that 'This is only to give intelligence, and make ill impressions on the people', and Clifford also argued that 'It's meant only to prepossess the Parliament, to raise jealousy with France, etc.' Accordingly Charles decided that Zas should be sent back promptly to Holland, and a letter written to the effect 'that the King has been so often and so long abused by these amusements, that he looks upon them as artifices only', and Zas was warned not to return without an official passport.[2]

We do not know precisely what William hoped to achieve by this mission, but it is probable that he had now given up all hope of inducing Charles to change his policy by persuasion, and was now relying more on the possibility that Charles might be forced out of the war by Parliamentary pressure. On 19/29 December an English correspondent named Nipho recounted an interesting conversation with William on English politics in which this hope was expressed.[3] William did not, however, intend to wait passively in the meantime: he and Du Moulin were engaged in certain plots and preparations which were intended to take effect before Parliament met.

The folder in Du Moulin's papers which contains letters received from England gives little help at this time. There are only three letters, all written from 'J. T.' to 'Mr. William

[1] Letters of 15/25 and 21/31 Dec. 1672, S.P. 77/41, ff. 199 and 215.
[2] For. Ent. Bk. 177, 11 Dec. 1672.
[3] S.P. 77/41, f. 210.

Arton, public notary at his house in the West end in the Hague', giving no information of great importance, and all inquiring why Arton did not reply:[1] the reason for Arton's slackness will shortly appear. For the moment some of Du Moulin's more highly placed connexions might be of more assistance than 'J. T.' Among the prominent English politicians with whom he could claim an acquaintance was Lord Halifax, then at the beginning of a long career in which he was consistently hostile to Louis XIV and therefore a natural ally of William's. Halifax's views on foreign policy may have been well known to Du Moulin as a result of their common connexion with the Council of Trade, and Halifax's conduct on his journey through Holland to the camp of Louis XIV in the summer of 1672 had also given grounds for the Dutch to suspect his dissatisfaction with the official English policy of alliance with France.[2] To Halifax therefore, Du Moulin, acting on William's instructions, drafted a letter to endeavour to enlist his support, and with a second purpose embodied in the postscript.[3] The letter begins with the justification of Du Moulin's flight to Holland to which previous reference has been made, and then goes on to say that in view of past conversations it would be idle to deny his (Du Moulin's) opinions about the war: 'et si c'est un crime de souhaiter que la Triple Alliance eût subsisté pour le bien de toute l'Europe; et s'il n'est pas permis de craindre que la France devienne trop puissante et qu'il soit du devoir d'un bon sujet de renoncer presque au sens commun en faveur du Roi très Chrétien; j'avoue que je ne suis pas innocent...'. Knowing Halifax's views, in fact, he prided himself on his anti-French opinions instead of apologizing for them; he argued that the war could no longer be of any advantage to England, even if England were successful, since any conquest made would be dependent on the goodwill of Louis XIV; that in any case Holland was now stronger and more united than when Halifax had been there on his embassy, and had powerful allies; that Holland could now be conquered only at the

---

[1] Letters dated 17 and 31 Dec. 1672 and 17 Jan. 1673 (R.A. Fagel 244).

[2] Cf. Foxcroft, chap. iv.

[3] Draft of the letter is in R.A. Fagel 253. It is undated, but from internal evidence seems to have been written between Nov. 1672 and Jan. 1673.

price of universal monarchy for Louis XIV; in short, that England had everything to lose and nothing to gain from continuing the war. 'Et d'ailleurs, comme j'ai l'honneur de connaître parfaitement vos sentiments sur ce sujet-là, je n'ai pas besoin non plus de m'efforcer davantage de vous convaincre d'une vérité dont vous êtes déjà persuadé.' Reminding Halifax of their last conversation in England, when Halifax had said that England had let loose on Europe a raging lion in Louis XIV, and had deplored the poor prospects of internal tranquillity as well, he went on to suggest that this tranquillity could only be restored if Charles joined in alliance to force France back to the boundaries of the Treaty of Vervins of 1598. (This would have meant not only the reconquest of the French gains in Flanders at Aix-la-Chapelle in 1668, but also of Artois and Roussillon, ceded at the Peace of the Pyrenees in 1659, and most of Alsace, ceded at the Treaty of Westphalia in 1648. Such far-reaching aims would only have been confided in someone whose attitude was already assured.) Du Moulin concluded with some philosophic observations on his own enforced exile from England: 'Si les choses générales se rétablissent, la disgrâce des particuliers ne continuera pas; et si l'orbe britannique continue à tourner sur les memes pôles, il faudra se souvenir que nous sommes tous citoyens du monde, et encore que l'air de La Haye ne soit pas aussi pur que celui de Montpellier, on ne laisse pas d'y vivre aussi agréablement.' (Montpellier was the place where Clarendon was living in exile.) Du Moulin's conception of himself as a 'citizen of the world' is not the least interesting part of a letter which reveals much of his outlook.

There then follows a significant postscript, which may have been the most important part of the letter for William. Du Moulin informed Halifax that he had just learned that France had recently offered secret peace terms to Holland, and would be quite ready to desert her English ally if the terms were accepted. If Halifax would pass this information on to the King, William would be able to give further information about this offer—but Du Moulin's name must not be mentioned as the source of information, for it would not then be believed.

The endorsement of the draft of this letter, and an

accompanying note which Du Moulin sent with the draft to William, make it clear that both letter and postscript were drawn up on agreed lines and then submitted for William's approval. In his letter to William, Du Moulin hoped that this attempt to influence English policy by insinuating distrust of France would be successful, but considered it unlikely in view of the care which the government had taken to pay off the fleet at the beginning of winter, and in view of the precedence which the English ambassador to Louis XIV had recently yielded to the French Princes of the blood for the first time—a punctilio to which great importance was attached, as Du Moulin knew from his personal experience in 1669. Reminding William of his own previous analysis of the English Court, he saw no reason to alter his views, but hoped he would be mistaken; and, observing that the success of this intrigue depended on the way in which first Halifax and then Charles reacted to his letter, he went on to point out that a means of bringing real pressure to bear on England would be a close alliance with Spain. Such an alliance was practicable, he argued, because Spain more than any other Power had an interest in opposing France in the Low Countries and England in the New World; and irrespective of its military value, such an alliance would be most unpalatable to English merchants, for Du Moulin well knew the importance of trade with Spain to the City of London. In this observation Du Moulin showed some prescience, for in the autumn of 1673 fear of a war with Spain did prove to be an important factor in the growth of hostility in London to the French alliance.

There is no record of the reception which this letter received in England, but clearly it had no effect on English policy. Halifax was not yet the influential person that he later became in his 'trimming' days, and as Du Moulin had feared, the connexion between Charles and Louis was too close to be broken by insinuations that France was meditating a separate peace. From his letter to William it may be safely inferred that he had always believed more drastic measures to be necessary for their purpose. More characteristic of his policy was a second letter written in the month of December to a more important English personage, no less than the new Lord Chancellor, the Earl of Shaftesbury, who had been described by 'J. T.' as 'very active in his office, and has gained great reputation in the administration of the Court, so that he bears his authority high'.[1] Like the letter written to Halifax, that for Shaftesbury was skilfully framed to suit the person whom Du Moulin was trying to win over.[2] It opened as a message of congratulation on the Earl's new appointment, trying to play upon his vanity by means of skilful flattery. This was followed by a justification of Du Moulin's flight from England, which he ascribed to Arlington's hostility and a misinterpretation of his attempt to visit the Dutch deputies at Hampton Court. A desire to condole with them on the disasters befalling their country, 'with my personal acquaintance and long friendship with the Dutch deputies, prompted me to give them a visit at Hampton Court, and having attempted it twice in vain, my intended condoling was looked upon as a great crime, and I was forced to fly to avoid an undeserved confinement. . . . I do not well see how a visit of civility could be of so heinous a nature. . . .' He defended his flight into the country of the enemy by saying that only there had he friends.

My comfort is that since I had the honour to be one of His Majesty's subjects, my conscience beareth me witness I ever had a true English heart. . . . But to give your Lordship a new and a more essential proof of it, I am to tell you that if I might with safety see your Lordship in private, I have those things to propose to you which would fully satisfy you how far I am an Englishman: and I send this express to your Lordship (who is an Englishman's son and a very honest man) to know how far and upon what grounds I may venture to go privately over.

For his journey to submit these proposals 'which cannot be trusted to paper', he needed a safe conduct, either a private pass from the King to which only Shaftesbury and Lauderdale were privy, or preferably one from Shaftesbury alone, so that he could at first be the sole judge of the proposals. It will be noticed that the appeal here was as frankly national as that to Halifax had been European. We do not know what precisely the proposals would have been had Du

[1] Letter of 17 Dec. 1672 in R.A. Fagel 244.
[2] Letter of 30 Dec. 1672, now in S.P. Car. II, 319, f. 118; draft in R.A. Fagel 253.

Moulin been able to make his journey, but it can hardly be doubted that they would not have been important in themselves but only as a means to divide Shaftesbury and Lauderdale from the rest of the Cabal. Du Moulin was basing his plan on his theory that some of the King's ministers were much more devoted to the French alliance than others.

This letter, dated 30 December 1672, was to be carried by that same William Arton, 'public notary, at his house in the West end of The Hague' to whom 'J. T.' had written three times in vain: the reason why there had been no reply was quite simply that Arton might be able to deliver it in person. With Arton there travelled the advocate Gerbrand Zas whose first trip to England has already been noted. He had been warned not to return without a passport, but nevertheless he agreed to take the risk. His instructions, drawn up, according to a marginal note by the Pensionary Fagel, in William's bedroom, reminded him that for reasons already agreed upon, he was to travel again without public credentials, and did not specify the purpose of the negotiations. There is also in existence a draft of a document authorizing Zas to go to England to negotiate a truce in the war at sea between the two countries for one year from 1 April 1673, and to spend a million guilders for the purpose.[1] It is natural to wonder whether this remarkably large sum of money was to be used for bribery, and if so, whether it was intended for ministers and courtiers, or for members of the House of Commons which was to meet on 4 February. There are, however, no indications of the means by which Zas hoped to achieve the highly desirable end of freeing the Dutch from the war at sea in order to concentrate on the land-war against the French; nor is it possible to tell whether he had other secret purposes.

His conduct in England gives us no help to elucidate these points, for he was immediately intercepted. He and Arton left The Hague together at the beginning of January 1673 and, crossing by the ordinary packet-boat, landed at Harwich. There, however, they were promptly arrested by the Mayor of Harwich, Robert Seaman, and detained until orders were received from London; for only three days pre-

[1] R.A. Fagel 28: printed by Japikse, *Corres.*, II. i. 321, n. 1.

viously a warrant had been issued for the arrest of all passengers coming from Holland or Flanders on pretence of public business or other negotiations.[1] While they were waiting at Harwich, Zas was apparently little daunted, for he still 'looked upon himself as the chief engine on which the probability of a peace between England and Holland was to move'.[2] Arton also produced the letter to the Lord Chancellor Shaftesbury which he was carrying, apparently thinking that the possession of a letter to so exalted a personage must immediately lead to his liberation.

The government's warrant was probably not the result of any foreknowledge of the Dutchmen's mission, so much as the outcome of their general fear of the arrival of Dutch agents to stir up trouble in Parliament. It was natural that, rightly or wrongly, they should jump to the conclusion that that was the real reason why Zas and Arton had come over, and they were probably confirmed in that opinion by a letter which came over on the same packet-boat from their spy at the Brill, Mr. Dale. This gave an unflattering picture of Arton:

He knows much the secrets of this state, rails much against the King, 1. saying he need not make use of Parliament to raise money so long as he can break the bankers who will break thousands. 2. that he hath falsely broken his oath and truth of that peace made last at Breda, and consequently not [obliterated] to be treated withal. 3. that he would never leave off his knavery till the commonalty had served him as some served his father. All which he hoped the next Parliament would take some effect and that he should be [?] advised of the Dutch in England to side with any party that should arise against His Majesty. . . .[3]

The person responsible for such rash remarks as these was not likely to get a good hearing in London, and those who believe in clairvoyance will not be surprised to learn that the wife of 'J. T.' (who was anxiously awaiting the arrival of his 'honest fellow-traveller' [sic]) 'was much afflicted in a dream the other night . . . for him and saw his wife and children taking on'.[4]

[1] C.S.P.D. 1672–3, pp. 417, 428.
[2] Silas Taylor to Williamson, 1 Feb. 1673, ibid., p. 505.
[3] Letter of 6/16 Jan. 1673, S.P. 84/193, f. 63.
[4] Letter of 17 Jan. 1673, R.A. Fagel 244.

It was ordered that Zas and Arton should be taken to London for an examination by the King's ministers, at which Charles intended to be present in person, such was the importance that he attached to them. The examination was due to take place on 25 January, but on the previous day an even more disastrous blow than Dale's letter placed them in still greater jeopardy. For a long and detailed report from William Howard was read that day in the Committee of Foreign Affairs.

We last left Howard at Antwerp, under the false name of 'George Carter', about to venture into Dutch territory on 21 December. After that date he wrote nothing to his employers for a month, but his 'great narrative' of 17/27 January more than made up for his previous silence, both in length and importance.[1]

Howard begins by recapitulating the instructions which he had received from Arlington, namely, to inquire '1. What disposition this State seems to have to peace. And 2ly. Upon what confidences they principally support themselves in the furthest prosecution of the war.' There follows a description of his arrival at The Hague, which he states inaccurately to have been on a Saturday, 28 December N.S. but was probably on 28 December O.S. On the same day as he arrived in The Hague he met 'my friend'; from the phrasing it seems that he had previously mentioned to Arlington that he had a friend in Dutch service from whom he could get information, but, curiously, he does not name him. From the sequel it is clear to us, but perhaps not to Arlington, that his friend was in fact Du Moulin. Du Moulin welcomed his unexpected visitor, 'and to convince me, how welcome I was, he had me to his table, and showed me a letter, which he was then writing to me, by the direction (as he said) of Monsr. Pensionarius Fagel, who had ordered him to send it to me by an express, together with another letter to a person of great eminency, of whom more hereafter [Shaftesbury]'. Du Moulin then inquired of him the state of English opinion with regard to the war and the approaching Parliament, so as to be able to pass on this information to Fagel; and in order to ingratiate himself, Howard did this, and in his report, appa-

[1] S.P. 84/193, ff. 69-72.

rently rather unnecessarily, gives a long account of what
he said.

He told Du Moulin (so he wrote) that he had

made it much my business to feel the inclinations of such Members of
Parliament, as were generally reputed to be the most leading men, and
that as many as I had discoursed [with] did all concenter in this one
sense; that the excessive greatness of the French monarch had long
been the fear of all Europe, and ought to be no less the jealousy of
England . . . that for the prevention of this, they were resolved to use
their utmost endeavours to awaken the Parliament and the whole
nation to a timely sense of their danger, and to stir them up to make
it their humble advice to the King, that he would put an early stop
to the French victories, by withdrawing himself from an alliance,
which was likely to prove so destructive to him, and to his subjects.
But withal, I told him that the greatest discouragement they met with
in this undertaking, was the inflexible and stiff deportment of the
States, who . . . sought rather to dare and menace the King out of his
present league with France   . than to win and tempt him to their
friendship by any reasonable condescensions to his demands.

In short, Howard argued that if Holland's friends in Parliament were to achieve anything when it met on 4 February
they must be assisted by Dutch concessions in their peace
proposals. This was an odd way of insinuating himself into
the confidence of the Dutch; if Howard's story is indeed
correct, he could hardly have adopted a method more calculated to confirm Du Moulin's analysis of the situation.

Howard went on to report that these views of his were
answered next day, to the effect that the Dutch were willing
to make concessions on the questions of the flag, the fishery
disputes, Surinam, and a war indemnity, but that they were
determined not to agree to any cessions of towns either
permanently or 'by way of caution' until money payments
were made. This question of the towns was that by which
Charles and his ministers set most store,[1] and Howard developed his own views and the Dutch replies at some length.
He then went on to make 'some inquiries concerning preparations for war; in which there needed not much art to gain all
the information I desired, my part herein being little more
than to give occasion to the discourses of my friend, who of

[1] See For. Ent. Bk. 177, *passim* during the winter of 1672–3.

his own accord was forward enough to set before me a scheme of all the encouragements they had to prosecute the war'. No details of military or naval dispositions are given: but a description is given of Du Moulin's view of Holland's greatly increased internal strength under William; of Holland's hopes of assistance from the Emperor, Spain, Brandenburg, and other allies; while, on the other hand, Louis was supposed to be exhausted by his efforts, and Charles could expect difficulties from his Parliament who would inquire into the French alliance and its authors.

To kindle this fire, all hands are at work to provide combustible matter, and no endeavours will be omitted to blow it up into a flame. That in order to this Monsr. Fagel was preparing an elaborate Manifest and Remonstrance which should be ready to come forth at the first session of the Parliament. To keep time with this there is another Tractate (under the pen, and almost finished) by an anonymous author, intended to be addressed to the Parliament, entitled England's Appeal from the Private Cabal at Whitehall to the Supreme Council of the Kingdom, the Lords and Commons assembled in Parliament. The general scope of which is 1. to show them the designs of all the Kings of France for a long time to make themselves universal monarchs, together with the ways and means by which the Princes of Europe jealous of their aspiring purposes have hitherto prevented them, etc. 2. To detect the frauds and violations of faith practised by the Court of France in all treaties, alliances, oaths, and promises. 3. To set forth the apparent hazard of ruin to England by the continuance of this alliance. 4. To discover all the arcanas of our late counsels in contriving this alliance. And lastly, to make known the pernicious ends and aims of the contrivers of this war and league, viz. for the destruction of the Protestant religion, and the subversion of the fundamental laws of the kingdom. To make way for all this, suitable preparations have been made upon several members of both Houses, a good understanding settled with some Lords of the Council, viz. the Lord Halifax and the Lord Holles. And to divide the Cabal itself, a letter (which is the same I hinted at in the beginning) was sent from hence by an express who took shipping (upon Sunday last) to the (now) Lord Chancellor, to be communicated to the Duke of Lauderdale; by which 'tis hoped (upon what grounds I know not) that they will be taken up from the further prosecution of those dangerous counsels, and will lend a helping hand to incline the King to hearken to the safer advice of his Parliament, and to disentangle him out of that pernicious league, into which the artifices of evil ministers (this is the style we speak in) have ensnared him.

To support this account of Dutch policy, Howard enclosed copies of '2 politic discourses written in French, not a little valued by Mons. Fagel'—these were Du Moulin's reports on English politics, previously summarized.[1] To these Howard says he had intended to add 'a copy of the Remonstrance, before it is translated, and fitted for the press, but Mons. Fagel's indisposition of health has given 2 or 3 days' delay to the despatch of it'. He summed up Dutch aims as being to convince Parliament of the dangers of the French alliance, to urge them not to give supplies for a war in French interests, and to attack its authors, especially Arlington and Clifford; and he expresses the view that the best way to foil the Dutch would be to postpone the meeting of Parliament until the King's position was strengthened either by an advantageous peace or a triumphant victory. He concludes his long report by describing meetings on the previous day (16 January) first with Fagel and then with William, 'who gave me a good opportunity of privacy with him in his bedchamber, where he was pleased to allow me the freedom of above an hour's discourse with him'. At this meeting Howard suggested that William should write to Charles, 'assuring him of the willingness of the States (as far as possibly they could) to comply with all His Majesty's demands, and desiring him that for the more speedy settling a good understanding, he [Charles] would be pleased to send some person to them with a project of proposals. . . .' William at first would agree to such a proposal only 'upon this condition, that his letter should contain in it an exception to the King of France, of whom he did profess so great an abhorrence, that he said he would never give anything to buy a peace with him, to whom he was resolved to be an enemy so long as he lived'; but Howard had hopes of getting William to waive this, and possibly had visions of himself as the negotiator in question. There are also brief references to Dutch naval and military preparations, including a statement (incorrect, as it turned out) that 'the general sense of the grandees is, to set out no men of war, but to guard all their sea coasts strongly, and to make war at sea only with capers'; and Howard asked finally to be informed by the return of his messenger, or through Colonel

[1] See pp. 41–48 above.

Blood, whether he was to stay in Holland or to return home.

On the surface it certainly seems that Howard had carried out his instructions and devoted his energies successfully in Charles II's interests to discovering Dutch policies. Yet Howard's later record of co-operation with Du Moulin in the Dutch interest, and of double-dealing in many respects, makes one consider one or two portions of his story with some suspicion. Why did Howard not mention the name of his influential friend from whom he derived so much of his information, and who was clearly so important in the Dutch counsel? Why did he make no report to Arlington between his arrival at The Hague at the end of December and this letter written on 17 January? Howard makes the excuse that he had no material for a weekly letter; yet nearly one third of his report is devoted to a description of two important interviews with Du Moulin which took place *on the day of his arrival and the day following*, and could well have been reported to his employer in less than three weeks. Again, how much of this report of 17 January was a revelation of matters which the Dutch (or at least Du Moulin) wanted to keep secret? The Dutch case about the dangers to England and Europe of the French alliance was given in full, together with concessions which the Dutch were ready to make on all points except that of the cautionary towns. If the Dutch policy is regarded as being a combination of inducements of this sort with threats to make trouble for Charles by creating divisions in his ministry and in his Parliament, then, it could be argued, this letter was admirably directed to that object. It may be objected to this, that Howard's revelation of Du Moulin's letter to Shaftesbury ruined any Dutch hopes from that device; but even here, that depends on how much they hoped to achieve directly in that way. If the object of that letter was simply to create discord among the ministers by arousing suspicion that Shaftesbury and Lauderdale were secretly intriguing against the French alliance, then nothing could have achieved that object more readily than to write the letter and then reveal its existence to Arlington afterwards—Arlington, who, with Clifford, was most committed of the Cabal to France, and might fear most from a parliamentary attack upon him. It is noteworthy that Howard did not write about Arton's mission to Shaftesbury until five days after Arton had sailed, thus giving him a good start; and in spite of his intimacy with Du Moulin, he makes no mention of the envoy Zas, who travelled with Arton, and of whose existence he was just as likely to know. Perhaps Zas's mission, unlike Arton's, was really intended to be a secret one, and was only forestalled by the unexpected arrest of both Zas and Arton immediately on their landing at Harwich. These suspicions of Howard's actions at this time cannot be proved—all that can certainly be said is that he was deceiving either England or Holland, or possibly both—but it remains at least possible that Howard was co-operating with his friend Du Moulin, as he may have done six months earlier and certainly did six months later.

The most direct effect of this 'great narrative', as Williamson called it, was that it greatly worsened the chances of Zas and Arton after it had been read to the Committee of Foreign Affairs on 24 January. The Committee resolved, after hearing it, 'to cut him [Howard] short, by no means to have him meddle with any negotiation or treaty, no such underhand dealings by any hand to be encouraged, only the mediators.[1] Yet by all means to let him stay there as a spy, etc., and only to apply himself to know their preparations . . . and especially what correspondences here in England and in the Parliament.'[2] Having restricted Howard in that way, they proceeded to examine Zas at their meeting on the following day, 25 January. He appeared before Shaftesbury, Clifford, Lauderdale, Buckingham, Arlington, and Henry Coventry;[3] Charles was not present in person, in spite of his previous declaration that he would examine the prisoners himself. Zas was closely questioned, and the worst possible interpretation placed on every circumstance. He was compelled to agree that he had been warned not to return after his previous visit; and all he could exhibit in the way of

[1] Sweden had been accepted as official mediator between the combatants, and was now trying to arrange a peace congress which eventually met at Cologne in June 1673. See p. 112 below.

[2] This and following accounts of the Committee's meetings are taken from F or. Ent. Bk. 177 under the dates given.

[3] Henry Coventry had succeeded Trevor as the second Secretary of State.

credentials was a letter from Fagel giving him 'power and authority in the Prince's name to do all things, and that they should be as valid and firm as if he had a character [public credentials]'. As Lauderdale pointed out, 'This is of credence to nobody knows who', and though Zas maintained that it was for the benefit of Charles and his ministers, Shaftesbury argued that 'this credence serves any of the King's subjects [just] as well as the King'. This possibility, that Zas's real purpose was not to negotiate with the King or his ministers but with discontented members of the Commons, was in everyone's mind. Zas was allowed to repeat his peace proposals of his previous mission, but as he repeated the steadfast refusal of the Dutch to cede any 'cautionary towns', this did not help him. Finally, Buckingham declared that on the evidence of his own story, he must be a spy, and Shaftesbury agreeing, said openly what all must have been thinking, 'Is not this a time (to speak plainly) of disturbing the King's service? The Parliament approaches.' The lords then agreed that Zas must be a spy come to influence the Parliament, and sent him to the Tower.

The question what was to be done with him was taken up at another meeting on the following day (26th), in which the results of this examination were reported to the King and his brother, the Duke of York. The resulting discussion gives an interesting picture of the characters of Charles's leading ministers, none of whom cared to seem backward in dealing with the Dutchmen. After the Attorney-General had proposed 'martial law' (that is, that Zas should be tried as a spy by court martial), Lauderdale broke in with the brutal advice, 'First rack him and then hang him', which was no doubt what he would have wanted to do in his native Scotland. Clifford was in favour of hanging only, a rather more humane treatment, though it would have been cold comfort to Zas; but as Henry Coventry pointed out, 'His confessions were of much more consequence than his death', and accordingly he wanted 'to rack him as much as he can by law be racked [a qualification introduced, perhaps, because Coventry might have to defend it in the Commons]. . . . Ergo keep him under racks and torments and yet with hopes upon confession.' Buckingham agreed that it was better to get to the bottom of

Zas's design than to take away his life, but it was left to
Shaftesbury, with characteristic clarity of thought and ruth-
lessness, to point out the obvious solution, 'Go as far to
torment him as you can. Show him the rack, tell him of it,
but not execute it.' Accordingly it was resolved to set up a
court martial to try Zas, and that in the meantime on the
following morning Lauderdale and Henry Coventry should
show both Zas and Arton the rack in the Tower.

The results of this threat and later examinations were,
however, disappointing. Arton steadily maintained that his
only purpose was to deliver a letter to Shaftesbury 'from one
Du Moulin; which at first he saith he refused but Du Moulin
told him it was nothing but a congratulation, to desire a
pass for him to come into England'. Zas also tried to explain
away his lack of credentials by the tame, but not easily dis-
proved excuse that it was 'to spare expense and make the
greater haste', and various letters on his person were intended
only to settle a son-in-law of his in England, and to try to
secure the liberation of one Payne from the Tower.[1] This
was a poor result from the terrible threat of the rack. It is true
that the Duke of York's chaplain wrote about a meeting of
the Privy Council at which this examination was discussed,
''tis said they have owned that they were particularly directed
to have treated with my Lord Holles and my Lord Halifax.
Both these Lords were then at Council but not at all blanked
with the report, because no way conscious to their intentions. . . .'[2] There is, however, no confirmation of this rumour
elsewhere, and it seems more likely to have been derived
from something of Howard's letter which had leaked out.
On 1 February, when the Committee of Foreign Affairs was
discussing the terms of the commission to be set up to court-
martial Zas and Arton, it was agreed that torture should
actually be applied to get at the truth, 'yet not so as to lame or
disable him'. The commissioners, however, were no more
successful in eliciting information from the prisoners, although
they examined them repeatedly during March.[3] Arton ampli-
fied his story to say that he came over on private business for

---

[1] S.P. Car. II, 332, f. 217.
[2] B. Woodroffe to Earl of Huntingdon, 30 Jan. 1673, H.M.C. *Hastings*, ii. 161–2
(cf. also letter of 28 Jan.).   [3] *C.S.P.D. 1673*, pp. 53–54, 95.

two ladies, Lady du Tour and the eldest Lady Williams, as well as to deliver Du Moulin's letter to Shaftesbury; Zas let slip something about the large sum of money at his disposal; but in spite of all threats, neither would give names of Englishmen he hoped to meet or any indication how the money was to be spent. In April a second commission was ordered,[1] but this was no more successful than the first had been. Zas and Arton therefore seem to have remained in the Tower unsentenced, Zas until the end of the war, and Arton until he escaped in the autumn.

Du Moulin had received reports from London telling him of the danger in which his friends stood,[2] and seems to have been genuinely afraid for his friend Arton. We possess drafts of two letters written on his account to an unnamed peer.[3] The first of them, written in all probability in March 1673, is highly characteristic of its author. He argued that, though Arton had no pass, as a mere messenger to a principal minister of state he had committed no offence: 'how long since is the bringing of a letter to a Chancellor grown a crime? and would his Lordship be ranked so far amongst suspected persons as to have it a capital offence to come to him in private with a very honest message?' His language about Shaftesbury is indeed bitterly sarcastic:

as to my letter [to him] it is such that I'll never be ashamed of it except it be the first part wherein I must needs confess nothing but the excellency of the end I proposed to myself, can justify in any degree my hyperbolical compliments. *Nay, my Lord, I'll go further and I dare say his Lordship would not have been so angry if my said letter had come first of all and privately to his hands, there being some expressions in it which I fancy would have wrought much upon his good nature* [this passage is crossed through]. . . . As to the rest I am ready to sign it with my own blood, and could I have a fair trial for't I dare boldly lay my life there is no true English jury but would think the proposals I had to offer both honourable and advantageous to England. But . . . all I do beg is that my pretended crimes may not be laid to Arton's charge . . .',

and he concluded by threatening that the Dutch States-

---

[1] *C.S.P.D. 1673*, p. 144; For. Ent. Bk. 177, 13 Apr.
[2] Letters from Ch. Innes (4 Mar.) and J. Bromfield (10 Mar.) to Mr. Chadbourne, also Bromfield to Mistress Sonius, 10 Mar., in R.A. Fagel, 244.
[3] Ibid. 253.

General would be prepared to take reprisals. The second letter, written in the following week to the same unnamed peer, is chiefly interesting for its quotation of a remark by one of Arton's judges, who 'swore by all the blood and wounds, even before he was examined, that they would certainly hang him': an indication that Du Moulin was fairly well informed from London of what was going on. It is noteworthy that neither letter mentions Zas, whose position was far less tenable, and who was perhaps not as friendly with Du Moulin as was Arton.

As we have seen, the two Dutchmen finally escaped with their lives, but their mission was a failure, at any rate in that it certainly did not achieve its direct aims, whatever their precise nature may have been. The length at which this episode has been treated is, however, justified by its indirect importance. Though it failed, it provided confirmation for Charles of the existence of attempts by the Dutch to form relations with discontented elements in England, and even among his own ministers. This is worth bearing in mind, as the tide of suspicion and distrust mounted steadily during the rest of 1673.

VI

ENGLAND'S APPEAL

THE long-awaited Parliament, on which the King depended for supplies to prosecute the war for another
year, and which the Dutch were hoping would refuse
supplies and so force the King out of the war, met at last at
the beginning of February 1673. Every possible preparation
for this all-important session had been made by Charles and
his ministers. It has been seen that the question who was to
be Speaker of the House of Commons had been discussed
as much as three months before it was due to meet: the Committee of Foreign Affairs finally decided that Sir Job Charle-
ton was to have the post offered to him, 'though it's certain
he will not accept of it', but he did in fact agree to take on the
onerous duty.[1] (He soon asked to give it up, on the pretext of
ill health.) The new Lord Chancellor, Shaftesbury, put the
Great Seal to the Declaration of Indulgence to forestall complaints that that Declaration had been issued without the
necessary formalities; during the month of January he issued
writs to fill the thirty-six vacancies in the House which had
been produced during the long recess, and most of these
seats were filled by members who could be expected to vote
the right way; and the speech with which he intended to
follow the King at the opening of Parliament was submitted
to his colleagues and the King, and 'allowed with one or two
alterations'.[2] Even Thomas Blood claimed to be doing his
best to produce a favourable climate of opinion:

Mr. Kiffin and others [merchants] have writ into Holland to stir
up their interest there to close with the mediation of the Swede. I am
at present very busy meeting with friends in order to the next session
that draws near, I hope things may answer expectations by what I
find and my friends that I employ. I am something weakened in that
I am not so able to be at suitable expense in treats, in which as with
persons that I do maintain to look to the main chance, I am at considerable expense, but now almost aground. . . .[3]

---

[1] For. Ent. Bk. 177, 1 Dec. 1672.　　　　[2] Ibid., 30 Jan. 1673.
[3] 11 Jan. 1673, S.P. Car. II, 332, f. 68.

And so he asked from Arlington the same 'instant supply' that Charles was to ask from Parliament. Finally, on Sunday, 2 February, all those Privy Councillors who were also members of the Commons were summoned to a meeting of the Committee of Foreign Affairs to settle the final arrangements. Charles was to meet the House on Tuesday to ask them to select a Speaker, after which there was to be a further meeting at Arlington's house of such M.P.s as he, Shaftesbury, and Clifford thought fit; on Wednesday the Speaker was to be confirmed; and on Thursday, Charles and Shaftesbury were to make their speeches at the opening of Parliament, 'and to send them down to make some brisk resolution upon his speech'.[1]

By a late change in these arrangements, the opening speeches were actually made on Wednesday, 5 February. Charles's speech, the shorter of the two, called for money for the war; tried to reassure his hearers that the concessions made to the Papists in the Declaration of Indulgence in no way affected his support of the established Church but said 'I will deal plainly with you, I am resolved to stick to my Declaration'; and similarly maintained that his army was not intended 'to control law and property', but must be increased in numbers by the summer. Lord Chancellor Shaftesbury then developed these points at greater length in a remarkable speech in which it is sometimes difficult to remember that what reads as irony was in fact spoken in all seriousness. It recites all the usual grievances against the Dutch, from the offensive medals to the question of the flag, but the reasons for the war are really shifted on to a broader basis, in the famous theme of *delenda est Carthago*: irrespective of minor pretexts, 'the States of Holland are England's eternal enemy, both by interest and inclination'. Shaftesbury actually argued that this aggressive policy of war to the death against the Dutch was that of Parliament, because they had called for the previous Anglo-Dutch war of 1664: 'you judged aright, that at any rate *delenda est Carthago* . . . and therefore the King may well say to you, This is your war. He took his measures from you, and they were just and right ones; and he expects a suitable assistance to so necessary and expensive

[1] For. Ent. Bk. 177.

an action, which he hath hitherto maintained at his own charge.' He even tried to use the episode of Zas and Arton to brand those who refused to vote taxes as disloyal: 'At this day, the States support themselves by this only falsehood, That they are assured of the temper of England, and of the Parliament, and that you will not supply the King in this war; and that if they can hold out till your meeting, they will have new life, and may take new measures. There are lately taken two of their principal agents, with their credentials and instructions to this purpose, who are now in the Tower. . . .' Finally, he concluded a remarkable peroration on the subject of the harmonious relations between King and Parliament by saying:

Let us bless the King, for taking away all our fears, and leaving no room for jealousies; for those assurances and promises he hath made us. Let us bless God and the King, that our religion is safe; that the Church of England is the care of our prince; that Parliaments are safe; that our properties and liberties are safe. What more hath a good Englishman to ask, but that this King may long reign; and that this Triple Alliance of King, Parliament and People, may never be dissolved.

Quite apart from the fact that the Triple Alliance of 1668 was with Holland against France, one wonders what the Shaftesbury of the later Exclusion Bill crisis thought of this speech: though of course he did not know of the Secret Treaty of Dover when he made it.[1]

This appeal to the patriotism and loyalty of the members of the House of Commons failed in its object of eliciting an immediate vote of supplies while the mood lasted. It failed, however, not because there was as yet any criticism of the government's foreign policy, but rather because the House, quite unmoved by foreign considerations, persisted in discussing domestic grievances. Supply was held up, not from any dislike of the French alliance against Holland, but in order to secure the revocation of the Declaration of Indulgence and the passing of a Test Act designed to exclude Roman Catholics from office by imposing a sacramental test on all holders of civil and military posts. The feeling that the French alliance and the government's religious policy were

[1] *L.J.* xii. 524–6.

connected was not yet widespread, and so the necessary taxes were eventually voted.

The pattern of the session was clear in the very first week. Even before the King's Speech, on the day previously (4 Feb.), Colonel Strangways, Shaftesbury's local Dorsetshire rival from civil war days, protested against the Chancellor's action in issuing writs for by-elections during a prorogation without waiting for a certificate from the Speaker. On 6 February the House adopted this view, and ordered that new elections should be held; Sir Edward Dering, a courtier M.P. with a great interest in parliamentary procedure, recorded his opinion that it was usual to refer such questions to committees for investigation of the precedents, that the precedents seemed to lie rather on the Chancellor's side, and 'that all the discourse against this thing went upon the consideration of inconveniences which might arise upon this power in the Chancellor' and not on the rights and wrongs of the matter. The House, in fact, clearly feared that in such ways as these the government might be able to influence its composition.[1]

So far as the King's Speech, and particularly his demand for money, were concerned, the usual motion that thanks should be voted to the King was made on the same day, Wednesday, 5 February; but the addition of a clause that the Commons would assist him against his enemies was opposed on the ground that time for consideration was needed, and after the House had 'sat full four hours by one candle till there was not one inch of it left', debate was adjourned until Friday, 7 February.[2] It was then made clear, however, that the House's reluctance was not the result of criticism of Charles's foreign policy. Sir Thomas Doleman moved a grant of £70,000 per month for eighteen months, and his proposal was well received. It is true that Sir Thomas Meres alluded to the Declaration of Indulgence, and even went so far as to say that kings usually consulted with their parliaments before they engaged in a war, but a speech made by Secretary Henry Coventry setting out the reasons for the war, and incidentally making use of the two Dutchmen in the Tower in the same

---

[1] *Dering*, pp. 103–10; Grey, ii. 2–8; *C.J.* ix. 248.
[2] *Dering*, pp. 106–7.

way as Shaftesbury had done, won the full approval of the House. The proposed grant was supported in grand committee of the whole House even by such members as Garroway, Powle, Strangways, and Meres who were most critical of other aspects of policy; it was carried unanimously, and indeed 'the House was so zealous that this supply might be speedy and useful to the King that they would give no ear to anything that might obstruct or delay it' on that particular day.[1] The government's satisfaction at this vote was, however, shortlived; for, though the *principle* that taxes should be voted to support the war had been duly adopted, the passing of the money bill through all its stages was then delayed until the House had won its own way over the Declaration of Indulgence. It is possible, indeed, that between the debates on Wednesday and Friday the leaders of the opposition had decided on the tactical plan of offering the money as an inducement to Charles to give way.

The Declaration of Indulgence was first debated on Saturday, 8 February. The unanimity of the House was not so complete as it had been on the grant, for Waller, in a 'long, premeditated speech', the Attorney-General Finch, Seymour (a follower of Buckingham), and Sir Robert Howard (a follower of Shaftesbury) all supported the King's right to suspend penal laws in matters of religion; but a majority of the House took the opposite view, both from fear of Popery and from the fear that this suspending power might be extended to any civil statue as well, and (in Powle's case) because 'the King by this may change religion as he pleases; we are confident of him [Charles], but knows not what succession [James] may be'. The weight of opinion on this side was so great that the debate very soon turned from the matter of the principle of the Declaration to the best way of securing its revocation, whether by a flat vote that it was illegal, or by the more respectful method of a petition to the King. Finally, it was definitely resolved 'that penal statutes in matters ecclesiastical cannot be suspended but by Act of Parliament', and a committee ordered to draw up an address to the King.[2] And while a reply was awaited, the majority declined to make further

---

[1] *Dering*, pp. 111–12; Grey, ii. 8–11.
[2] *Dering*, pp. 114–16; Grey, ii. 13–26; *C.J.* ix. 251.

progress with the money bill, for, as Buckingham pointed out in the Committee of Foreign Affairs, 'they know every man there, that as soon as the Bill is passed, their time is over'.

In this situation the unity of Charles's ministers began to break up. The French ambassador reported that one of their meetings lasted four full hours. For each of them attached a different importance to the Declaration and the money bill. James, Duke of York, and Lord Treasurer Clifford, being zealous Catholics, wanted to maintain the Declaration, and Shaftesbury, a keen supporter of toleration for Protestant Dissenters, held equally strongly 'Rather lose money, than lose rights'. On the other hand, Prince Rupert as a sailor, and Henry Coventry as the government's leading representative in the Commons, were both preoccupied with the necessity to get the money bill through and prevent 'a second Chatham attempt' by the Dutch; Arlington's temperamental timidity where the possibility of parliamentary attacks existed combined with his sense of reality to induce him to take the same view; Buckingham pointed out some of the difficulties attendant, both on giving way to the Commons and on resisting them. Charles, as one might expect, asked, 'What is the discretion for a man to be angry to his own hurt?' and in the long run was more concerned at the possibility of losing his money.[1] And indeed the government's need for money was so great that in the last resort the Commons held the whip hand.

One or two expedients were, however, tried first to avoid having to give up the Declaration. On 24 February, in his answer to the Commons' address, Charles tried to maintain his prerogative powers as Supreme Head of the Church, while asserting that he did not intend to alter anything in the Church of England, 'but his only design in this was, to take off the penalties inflicted upon the Dissenters . . . and if any Bill shall be offered him, which shall appear more proper to attain the aforesaid ends ["the quiet of the kingdom"] . . . he will show how readily he will concur in all ways that shall appear good to the kingdom'.[2] And indeed such a bill, for the ease of Protestant but not Papist Dissenters, had already

[1] For. Ent. Bk. 177, 12, 14, 16 Feb. 1673; Colbert to Louis, 10/20 Feb. 1673.
[2] *C.J.* ix. 256.

been discussed in the Commons, and had already revealed dissensions in the majority which had voted against the Declaration of Indulgence: old Cavalier and Puritan feuds dating back to the time of the Civil War were revived, and Secretary Coventry was doing his best to exploit them. The hope that the Commons would be divided in this way, was however disappointed, for the general view of the House was that of Meres, 'Let us take care that, whilst we dispute the indulging the Protestant subjects, the third dog does not take the bone from us both.'[1] Cavalier members like Sir E. Dering were so afraid of Popery that they were even prepared, with many misgivings, to countenance some measure of toleration for the ease of Protestant Dissenters. On 26 February 'the Court side' were outvoted and a new address to the King was passed, which included the assertion that the King had been 'misinformed' about his powers to suspend penal laws in ecclesiastical matters—a phrase reminiscent of the days of James I and Charles I at which the Attorney-General Finch was duly shocked—and petitioned Charles to 'be pleased to give us a full and satisfactory answer to our said petition and address' against the Declaration. Two days later a committee was appointed to bring in a Test Act incapacitating all persons who did not take the Anglican sacrament from holding civil and military offices: this was directed at the numerous Papists who were reported to hold commissions and places at Court.[2]

On 1 March Charles made a last desperate attempt to stave off the inevitable by appealing to the House of Lords for advice in the hope that they could be set against the Commons. A suitable vote was obtained three days later,[3] but this brought him no nearer to getting his money, and indeed on the same day in the Commons several voices were raised for further delay over the money bill until the religious question was settled, and further debate was postponed until the 8th.[4] After a month's session no progress had been made with the money bill, the campaigning season was approaching, and even Louis XIV was secretly adding his voice to those in

---

[1] Grey, ii. 33.
[2] *C.J.* ix. 256, 259–60; Grey, ii. 62–69, 74–78.
[3] *L.J.* xii. 539, 543.   [4] Grey, ii. 82–83.

favour of dropping the Declaration of Indulgence in order to get the money which was indispensable to carry on the war. According to the French ambassador Colbert, Charles at one time meditated a dissolution of Parliament, but after seeing him on Friday the 7th he changed his mind and determined to revoke the Declaration. According to the Venetian ambassador, he had a six-hours' meeting with his ministers before this was agreed, but on the morning of the 8th Secretary Coventry was able to inform the Commons that the Declaration had been cancelled. The House promptly voted its thanks, and went into committee on supply.[1]

Even so Charles did not immediately get his money. On 15 March Secretary Coventry was still urging the desperate necessity of voting supply, but the reply of Sir Thomas Meres was 'The motion is good in relation to the King's affairs [but] . . . would not have this bill sent up to hinder them [the Lords], to make a parenthesis in business there to interrupt them'. In other words, the Lords must first pass the Test Act before the money bill was sent up to them; and the Commons postponed passing the money bill through its final stage to the 21st to see what the Lords would do.[2] In the meantime, Lord Treasurer Clifford almost imperilled everything. Acting, so he told James, Duke of York, under divine inspiration, he made an unpremeditated attack in the Lords on the Test Act, which meant the downfall of his hopes as a Catholic. Protesting against this attempt by the House of Commons to impose a sacramental test, he went so far as to describe the bill as 'monstrum horrendum', and to say that it 'ought to be spurned out of the House as a dirty Bill'. This reckless speech was quite unavailing to procure the rejection of the Bill in the Lords, and in the Commons it immediately led to strong protests and proposals that an address should be drawn up petitioning the King to dismiss him.[3] Attacks on other 'evil counsellors', especially Lauderdale, were also rumoured, lists of fresh grievances were being drawn up, and the inexhaustible topic of Ireland was raised. Charles

[1] Colbert to Louis XIV, 10/20 Mar. 1673; Venetian ambassador, same date, *C.S.P.Ven. 1673–5*, pp. 27–28; *C.J.* ix. 265–6.
[2] Grey, ii. 108–15; *Dering*, pp. 139–40.
[3] Colbert to Louis XIV, 22 Mar./1 Apr. and 24 Mar./3 Apr.; Grey, ii. 146–54; *Dering*, pp. 148–9.

and his ministers must have been thankful that on 29 March he was able to sign both the supply bill and the Test Act (the Bill for the Ease of Dissenters being incomplete) and so dismiss his Parliament until the autumn.

So ended a remarkable and stormy session in which the handful of members who remained loyal to the government in all circumstances were heavily outnumbered by a resolute and determined opposition, which had secured the reversal of the King's religious policy. The Cavalier Parliament of 1661 had divided into a Court Party and a Country Party which included both members with a Puritan background and discontented Cavaliers. The growing party cleavage had been expressed by Sir Thomas Meres on 22 February:

> Some heat began to grow in the House by Sir Thomas Meres saying they were plain country men and could not speak so smoothly as the fine men about the town, but they meant as well to the King as they did; and that he loved to speak plainly, and as they did; . . . This speech was something sharply reflected upon by Secretary Coventry, as if Sir Thomas Meres had now and often heretofore laboured to make a distinction in the House between the country gentlemen and the courtiers, whereas there was none, nor ought to be none; and often used the words 'of this side of the House, and that side', which were not parliamentary. . . .[1]

Though Coventry might maintain that such expressions were still to be regarded as unparliamentary, there was in being a Country Party whose main preoccupation was fear that the King's religious policy would lead to Popery: they saw the increase in numbers of the Catholics at Court, and were beginning to suspect that the heir to the throne, James, was a Catholic too. Charles and James, of course, maintained that the outcry on religious matters was only a pretext for an attack on the royal authority; they regarded many members as seeking to follow the example of Littleton and others in forcing their way into office; and the leaders of the opposition they described to the French ambassador under the simple and convenient term of *les malintentionnés*. No doubt all these categories were to be found in the Country Party as in any other opposition party at any time; but in any case it was fear of Roman Catholicism and its political implications that gave

---

[1] *Dering*, pp. 128–9; cf. Grey, ii. 52.

them such unity as they possessed, and it was against the King's religious policy that they had been so strikingly successful.

In one respect, however, Charles and his ministers could congratulate themselves on this stormy parliamentary session. Not only had they emerged safely with their grant of £1,260,000, but their foreign policy had not been challenged. Shaftesbury's description of Holland as England's natural enemy had not been contradicted by anyone, the Dutch intrigues in Parliament of which the government had been so afraid had failed to materialize, and the Dutch had entirely failed to exploit the disharmony between King and Parliament to their own advantage. The French alliance remained unchallenged, and a second campaign against the Dutch was now possible which, if successful, would immeasurably strengthen Charles.

Indeed, the Dutch seem even to have made little attempt to take advantage of the existence of a party of critics in the Commons until the session was nearly over. The only indication of intrigues which survives occurs in an information against a Dutchman, naturalized in England, named Abraham van den Bemde, who was said to be frequently in the lobby of the House of Commons talking with members and particularly with Colonel Richard Neville, M.P., to try to persuade them to break the French alliance, and reading letters of news contrary to the news commonly received by H.M. ministers. It was alleged that he knew that a peace congress was to meet at Cologne a week before that news was public. If van den Bemde was in touch with Du Moulin, his efforts were soon stopped, for he was promptly apprehended by Williamson's agents.[1]

It may be argued that if more of Du Moulin's correspondence for these months survived, we might find that more intrigues were being carried on; but it would still be necessary to explain why the publication of the pamphlet *England's Appeal from the Private Cabal at Whitehall to the Great Council of the Nation, The Lords and Commons in Parliament Assembled* was delayed. It was this famous pamphlet which did more than anything else to identify the French alliance in foreign

---

[1] *C.S.P.D. 1673*, p. 108.

affairs with the danger of Popery at home, and consequently to lead public opinion and the Country Party in Parliament to turn against the war. As far back as 17/27 January Howard had reported to Arlington that 'Monsr. Fagel was preparing an elaborate Manifest and Remonstrance which should be ready to come forth at the first session of the Parliament. To keep time with this there is another Tractate (under the pen, and almost finished) by an anonymous author, intended to be addressed to the Parliament, entitled England's Appeal. . . .' Yet the 'Manifest and Remonstrance' did not appear at all, and *England's Appeal* was not distributed until about the second week in March when the parliamentary session was almost over. The reason for this inaction during February can only be conjectured. It may be that the arrest of Zas and Arton had disrupted the Dutch plans, and that fears were entertained for their safety if other underhand activities were undertaken. Or it may be that William originally hoped that the House of Commons would refuse Charles supplies for other reasons without his interference, which might easily make Charles an irrevocable enemy. If that was William's calculation, he may have waited until it became likely that the Commons would grant money in exchange for the revocation of the Declaration of Indulgence, and only then agreed to release the pamphlet appealing to Parliament. Whatever the reason, distribution of *England's Appeal* did not begin until the beginning of March, though it could have been ready when Parliament met.

Du Moulin and his colleagues then took up the task of smuggling copies into England. On 2/12 March, from on board a 'skuyt' (Dutch vessel) between Delft and Maeslandsluys, 'T. Phillips' wrote to William Medley at the sign of the Indian in Cornhill, requesting him to receive and warehouse nine small packs of fine goods sent by this ship, directed to Mr. John Philipps, merchant, near Aldgate, till Mr. Philipps calls for them. 'The skipper knows nothing of the contents.'[1] Perhaps if the skipper had known what the contents were, he would have refused to take them, for in the jargon of this correspondence a package of 'fine goods' is invariably a parcel of pamphlets.

[1] S.P. Car. II, 334, f. 81.

The English government had received advance warning that some such attempt would be made. Quite apart from what they had learned through Howard, it seems possible that they had received from W. Carr (as usual running with the hare and hunting with the hounds) the first two copies printed off.[1] So a warrant was drawn up on February 21 :

Whereas we have received information of several seditious books, papers and pamphlets now lately printed in Holland and thence transmitted into this kingdom, with design to disorder and disturb our affairs here in this great conjuncture, our will and pleasure is that immediately upon receipt hereof you repair to the Saracen's Head in Aldgate, and there watch in the wariest and most private means [the arrival?] of all such carriages, coaches, wagons or other carriers as usually come in there from Harwich, Colchester, Ipswich, or other towns on the Harwich Road, and that further as they shall arrive, and at their full unloading, you do with the assistance and in the presence of a constable make diligent and thorough search in their several packs, bales, hampers, boxes, bundles etc. for all such books, papers and pamphlets. . . .

Other servants of the government were sent to Bow, Romford, and other places on the Harwich road to undertake a similar watch,[2] apart from the normal procedure at Harwich itself, and we can imagine a series of men busily searching every wagon of every kind for smuggled Dutch propaganda. As one might expect, Colonel Blood hit upon the most picturesque method of smuggling of all, if an undated note in his handwriting is to be assigned to this period :

The pamphlets from Holland may be expected this next week. Let the seamen of the packet-boats be searched for them, for 12 of them is to be sent that way to our friend [identity unknown]. The bulk of them were to be sent to the Spanish ambassador, whose goods are to be searched by appointed persons of the Customs House. They intended to put them in some small casks in barrels of butter (but that is uncertain) to the Spanish ambassador. Let all things to the Spanish ambassador be inspected as it will here.[3]

We do not know whether the Customs searchers who poked into the Spanish ambassador's butter found anything or not. The letter from 'T. Philipps' to William Medley was

[1] Carr to Arlington, undated, S.P. 84/195, f. 202.
[2] S.P. Car. II, 333, ff. 182, 183.   [3] Ibid., f. 181.

intercepted, and Samuel Medley was arrested, perhaps in mistake for William, and spent some time in the Gatehouse of the Tower on a charge of corresponding with persons that sent over seditious books.[1] But even if these consignments were seized, there were many others that were not. Whether smuggled by packet-boat, or in small boats, or by favour of the Spanish ambassador, copies were successfully distributed in London: and there were printers in London who were prepared to take the risk of running off further copies to satisfy the demand for them. One of Du Moulin's correspondents later spoke of a printer who produced '4 or 6000 copies', as though this was only one of several impressions. This is some indication of the very large number that must have been available. The demand was so great that some even wrote to their friends in Holland for copies: we possess one interesting reply from Rotterdam, which states that:

As to the book named an *Appeal from the Cabal* which you order me to send you, 'tis very hard to be got here, and by this time they will be more plentiful in London, for our very good Mr. Moulijn and Capt. Broadnecks [Broadnax] has sent a parcel by the last billinders [a small Dutch vessel] for London, which will be given to our friends; they went from hence this day 3 weeks by Josif Vreake or François van——. What success they will have with them God knows, but here it is in great esteem and the friends that distribute them also; Mr. Moulijn will get an office under the Prince and Capt. Broadnecks stands fair for command. If you cannot get one of the books in London I believe Monsr. Papillon who is Capt. Broadneck's brother in law may help you to one, for I dare say he is one of our friends.[2]

Broadnax was a member of a Kent family whose most prominent member, Sir William, had been a major in Cromwell's army, and a patron of conventicles even after 1660; and he had entered the service of the States-General. His sister Jane's husband, the rich Huguenot merchant Papillon, had been a friend of Du Moulin's in 1669, and it is reasonable to suppose that he shared Du Moulin's outlook, particularly as he was later a prominent Exclusionist: on the other hand, in

[1] *C.S.P.D. 1673*, pp. 93, 106, 139.
[2] Thomas Johnson to Sir Jacob van Galen, 21/31 Mar. 1673, S.P. 84/194, f. 48. The reference to '4 or 6000 copies' is from a letter of 20 Jan. 1674, in R.A. Fagel 244.

1673 he had a profitable contract as Victualler to the Navy, and there is no confirmation from other sources that he was in communication with William at this time.[1]

Thus the *Appeal* immediately attracted much attention, which was not confined to England. In the same month of March Lisola reported that a French translation was being made[2] in addition to the English and Dutch editions. In view of its undoubted importance it is now necessary to examine its contents, to account for its influence, and to discuss the problem of its authorship.

Like Du Moulin's two memorials described in Chapter III, the pamphlet is so closely reasoned that a summary in a short space cannot be expected to do it full justice. The author begins by dividing his subject into three sections: the first, 'a short account of the Crown with which His Majesty is entered into league. 2. The necessary and unavoidable consequences of this war. 3. Some general reflections upon the whole, with some account of the manner and steps by which this war was both promoted and begun.'

The account of France and French policy which is contained in the first section includes a preliminary examination of French resources, and then goes on to argue that 'all these advantages meeting together, they have in all ages had aspiring thoughts'. Examples of France's unbounded ambition are drawn from her history, and it is argued that 'this ambitious humour of theirs, supported by the greatness of their power would long before this time have brought all Europe under their subjection, if their own division and private quarrels had not from time to time put back their designs for many years. . . . And lastly as a consequence of the three former, that it was ever, and will be still, the true interest of Europe to oppose the French designs.' The French cannot be trusted. Mazarin's motto that 'an honest man ought not to be a slave to his word' is quoted, and a long list of examples of deceit is given. These include French underhand assistance to Portugal after the Treaty of the Pyrenees, 'all which with

---

[1] For the Broadnax family, cf. G. L. Turner, *Early Records of Nonconformity* (1911–14), iii. 466, 776–7; for Papillon, see *D.N.B.*

[2] Lisola to Hocher (from Brussels), 15/25 Mar., printed by Grossman, *Lisola im Haag 1672–3 (Archiv für österreichische Geschichte,* li, 1873), p. 177.

many other particulars may be seen more at large in the incomparable books of the Baron de Isola, intituled the Buckler of State and Justice', and French secret support for the Prince of Condé in the Polish election of 1669, contrary to their engagements to the Duke of Neuburg. In regard to the naval rivalry between England and Holland, France's true desire has always been to see the two sea powers exhaust one another for her advantage. The section concludes with two examples of French dishonesty in the present war:

I suppose His Majesty will not thank them [the French] neither for giving out in all Roman Catholic princes' courts, That this is a war of religion, undertaken merely for the propagation of the Catholic faith, and as the French minister at Vienna expressed it in a solemn speech to the Emperor's Council . . . that the Hollanders being heretics, who had forsaken their God, all good Christians are bound to join and unite to extirpate them and to implore God's blessing upon so good a work. . . . How far now this may be agreeable to His Majesty's interest, or to the 39 articles, let any unprejudiced man judge.

And lastly, the allegation was repeated that while Charles had refused to negotiate with the Dutch deputies at Hampton Court, the French had had no such scruples, and had offered separate terms which the Dutch refused.

In the second section of the pamphlet, the probable consequences of the present war are analysed. There are four possible results to it. As to the first of them, the absolute conquest of the Netherlands by the French, 'the very thoughts of it must needs raise the blood of all true Englishmen, and there is hardly any remedy too violent for so desperate a cure or means that could be called unjust, if necessary to prevent so great an evil'. Absolute conquest by the English is unlikely; joint conquest by English and French would provide no permanent solution since the French were not to be trusted and the British share would be difficult to defend. That left the fourth possible result, a victory for the Dutch, as the most desirable. Moreover, other Powers were now concerned. Spain was likely to declare war against France and England, and this would be ruinous to English trade: merchants' estates in Spain would be seized, the valuable trade with Spain lost, the Levant and plantation trade interrupted by privateers, and revenue from Customs duties decreased. Apart from this, the growth of a coalition against France would mean that, should France beat all her opponents, there would be a danger of French 'universal monarchy'.

Let those that have advised His Majesty to this war speak, they must now pull their vizard off, they must appear in their true shape, and tell us plainly whether they are paid for making the French King the universal monarchy, and whether to bring down new golden showers into their laps, England must at least be made tributary to the French. Some few hackney writers will not serve the turn now, and twenty silly stories against Holland cannot make it advisable for us to join with the French King against the greatest part of Europe. . . . I grant the Dutch have offended us, and that our war against them is not unjust: but is it just therefore to destroy so many princes who cannot subsist without them . . . the French King must needs be master of the best part of Europe before we can have to our share either the Brill or Flushing.

I might add several other considerations (and perhaps of no less weight than the former) to evidence the fatal consequences of this war. But by reason they do relate to the safety and preservation of our laws (as well ecclesiastical as civil) I forbear, lest it should be thought I go about (or intend in the least) to raise a jealousy between His Majesty and his people; leaving it wholly to the care and wisdom of the both Houses to provide against it, by those means, and ways as to them shall seem meet and necessary, and as the importance of the thing itself requireth.

This ingenious disclaimer of any disloyal intentions, while clearly pointing to the influence of despotic and Catholic France on English political and religious policy, leads on to the third section of the pamphlet, opening with a profession of objective examination followed by an accusation of bribery:

We ought to have a great care not to pass a rash verdict upon persons whom His Majesty hath irradiated with so many illustrious beams of his princely favour. The safest way then not to wrong neither the Cabal nor the truth is to take a short survey of the carriage of the chief promoters of this war, leaving the judgement of either their innocency or their guilt to the unprejudiced reader.

1. I will not insist too much upon some whispers (come to loud talking of late) of the wonderful effect the French King's liberality had almost four years since in converting the strongest opposers of his interest. . . . But however whether all that is reported of this be true or not, I suppose it is not usual to see so great a familiarity as hath been observed long since between foreign ambassadors and first

ministers of state. Continual treatings and frequent goings to country houses, there to stay several days and weeks, is a new thing in the world. And an ambassador using so noble a house with so much freedom [Arlington's house at Euston], gave a just cause to all observing men to conclude he had paid dear for it. . . .

Having drawn this preliminary picture of corruption, the author goes on to discuss the evolution of foreign policy since 1668. If the Triple Alliance was necessary then to stop the progress of the French, how had the situation altered since? Yet the Cabal had made English policy more and more subservient to France—numerous instances are given —and the only reason why the Triple Alliance was allowed to fall, was that the French King's influence over the English ministers was increased. The Cabal's pretexts for the declaration of war against Holland—medals, East India trade, Surinam, and 'their great masterpiece', the sending of the yacht *Merlin*, are all pulled to pieces most convincingly. Further, if the Cabal's intentions were honourable, why did they 'advise His Majesty to prorogue so often upon the French King's desire?'

Parliaments (I speak it with due reverence) are now and then peevish things that will not be satisfied with fair words, and pry too far into secrets that are not to come to public view. Our Grandees were afraid, if so many clear-sighted men came together; some one or other would spy out the Snake that lay in the Grass, and if their mine had once taken vent, the whole design had miscarried. No, no, we'll do better (saith the Cabal), we'll be wiser than to run that hazard; we are resolved to make war, and will not be crossed in it by any Parliamentary clamours. If for want of a Parliament, we can have no English subsidies, we'll make a shift with French supplies: and if that doth not serve the turn (observe the gradation) we'll shut up the Exchequer. . . .

Then follows an account of Buckingham and Arlington's embassy in June 1672, telling how Buckingham was indignant when told at The Hague that the French were engaged in separate negotiations, how he and Arlington even undertook to co-operate with the Dutch if the French were not content with Maastricht and some Rhine towns, and how all this was reversed when the two ambassadors arrived in Louis XIV's camp at Utrecht. Eight searching questions are put on the conduct of this embassy, the last of which is 'how far their instructions will justify their standing in the behalf of the French, upon a public exercise of the Roman Catholic religion in the United Provinces, the Churches to be divided, and the Romish priests maintained out of the public revenue? As is set down more at large in the second head of the French demands?'

The author concludes by summarizing the pamphlet under twenty headings, and touching a Biblical note, 'Now I call Heaven and Earth to record this day that I have set before you Life and Death, Blessing and Cursing: therefore choose life, that both you and your seed may live.'[1]

In its immediate object of influencing the Commons against the foreign policy of the Cabal, *England's Appeal* appeared on the scene too late to be successful, for the Test Act and the supply bill became law together on 29 March and Charles thereupon promptly prorogued Parliament, preventing the expression of further grievances and possible attacks on Clifford, Lauderdale, and others of his ministers. The *Appeal* had not been in London for more than three weeks at the most, and its arguments had not yet had any echo in parliamentary debate. In his dispatch of 22 March/ 1 April 1673, however, Colbert reported to Louis XIV the growth of considerable anti-French sentiment in both Houses, and in the next few weeks the pamphlet's influence was very great in contributing to the steady change in public opinion on foreign policy which was evident long before Parliament again met at the end of October. Until the spring of 1673, commercial jealousy of Holland had predominated to such an extent that any misgivings about the French successes had found no public expression either inside Parliament or outside, and there had been no serious criticism of the justice of the war. Now, however, the realization gradually grew that France was potentially a greater danger as an aggressive power with the largest and best army in Europe, as a protectionist commercial competitor, and not least on account of the political and religious consequences which French dominance in Europe might produce. For the pamphlet was not merely effective as a discussion of international

[1] See Deuteronomy xxx. 19.

politics: it came at the right time to accord with the domestic situation. Many people who had welcomed the Restoration in 1660 (and *a fortiori* those with a Puritan background) were alarmed at the growing favour shown at Court to Roman Catholics and at the use of the royal prerogative in the Declaration of Indulgence to try to help them—for it was generally thought that the Declaration's real purpose was to aid Papists rather than Dissenters. What more convincing explanation of this religious and political trend could there be than that put forward in the *Appeal*, that some of the King's ministers were acting in the interest, and perhaps in the pay, of Louis XIV, the greatest Roman Catholic despot in Europe? It fitted in with many well-known facts, for it was common knowledge that the French ambassador Colbert was on excellent terms with Arlington, and that the King's latest mistress, Mlle de la Quérouaille, was a Frenchwoman supported by him. The arrival of French subsidies for the war could not be entirely concealed, and it was natural to suspect that French money might be used for other purposes too.

　　Such fears were by no means allayed by the passing of the Test Act, excluding Catholics from civil and military posts. Indeed, the operation of the Test Act served to strengthen them. In addition to the Irish priests and army officers, the Catholic courtiers and mistresses, there were now revealed two far more important Catholics close to the King. One of these was Clifford, who as Lord Treasurer held one of the two greatest offices in the country. The story soon spread how his coach, with its blinds drawn, overturned in the street to reveal him with a priest in full robes on his way to mass at Somerset House. But at any rate Clifford retired from his office rather than take the Anglican sacrament, and withdrew to his house in Devon, there to commit suicide some months afterwards: the Lord High Admiral also abandoned his post, but he remained at Court, for he was none other than James, the King's brother and the heir to the throne. The suspicions that he was a Catholic, which had long been prevalent, were now confirmed; and the strict view which he took of the royal prerogative was also well known. Some politicians who knew James's character and opinions had already made attempts to induce Charles to divorce his child-less Queen, Catherine of Braganza, so that he could marry again and provide an heir. According to James, Shaftesbury had suggested this in 1667, and there had been a more determined attempt at the time of the divorce of Lord Roos by Act of Parliament in 1670. Now in March 1673, according to the French ambassador, some members of Parliament offered to Charles to annul his marriage for the same purpose, again with Shaftesbury's support.[1] Charles refused to have anything to do with the offer, and as a result the central fact of English politics for the next sixteen years was that James was a Catholic. In these circumstances the French alliance took on a more sinister appearance, and the arguments of the *Appeal* about undue French influence over English ministers fell on fertile ground. The demand for the breaking of the alliance therefore grew, along with the desire to attack Charles's ministers and to exclude James from the throne or limit his authority; and William of Orange was the gainer in every way.

In view of the influence which the *Appeal* had, this chapter may fittingly be concluded by an attempt definitely to establish that Du Moulin was its author, as suggested by Miss Barbour and others.[2] The first contemporary suggestion about its authorship was that it was written by Dr. Richardson, the notorious Fifth Monarchist exile who had taken refuge in Leyden, and by William Carr,[3] but it seems certain that it must have been written by someone with a wider knowledge of international politics, and closer to the centre of affairs both in England and Holland than either of these men. One more well-known politician to whom the pamphlet has been attributed is Sir William Coventry, whose name is still to be found pencilled on some of the copies in the Bodleian Library. Sir William Coventry, who was brother of Henry Coventry and uncle of Halifax, had rendered good and loyal service to Charles II, particularly for the navy, until he was dismissed on the pretext of a quarrel with Buckingham, in reality because his character and independent outlook

---

[1] Colbert to Louis XIV, 27 Mar./6 Apr. and 7/17 Apr. 1673.
[2] Barbour, *Arlington*, p. 213, n.
[3] T. H. to Samuel Cottington, 14/24 Mar., S.P. 84/194, f. 27.

made him an awkward colleague, and one who might not readily accept the change from the Triple Alliance to a French one. He then became one of the leading and most respected members of the House of Commons, joining in the criticisms of the government and yet adopting a more responsible attitude than many other leaders of the Country Party. The attribution of the *Appeal* to him rests largely on the fact that some of its ideas were reproduced in his speeches in Parliament in the winter of 1673–4; but as we know from Howard's letter of 17/27 January that the *Appeal* was actually written in January 1673, it is not easy to explain why, if Coventry or any other M.P. was its author, no attempt was made to attack the government's foreign policy in the session of February–March 1673 instead of waiting until the following winter. Moreover, there is no indication that William Coventry was in communication with William of Orange at this time, and from what is known of his character it would seem that he was not the man to enter into disloyal intrigues; yet from Howard's letter we know that the *Appeal* was composed in The Hague, along with a manifesto prepared by Fagel, and from Du Moulin's correspondence it is amply clear that the latter, then in great favour with William, was responsible for the *Appeal*'s distribution.

Another claim has been made by Lisola's biographer, Pribram, for that great ambassador's authorship of the pamphlet.[1] Lisola was one of the greatest living opponents of the French, had devoted his career to an attempt to build up a coalition against Louis XIV, had been in England within the previous six years, and was the author of several famous anti-French pamphlets, especially *Le Bouclier d'État et de Justice*. He probably had both the knowledge and the ability to write the *Appeal*, he was ambassador at The Hague in 1672–3, and Pribram claimed that the style of the *Appeal* was his. On the other hand, the author of the *Appeal* claimed to be an Englishman, 'a true lover of his country', and his pamphlet was written in good, sometimes colloquial, but always trenchant, English prose; whereas the *Bouclier d'État* and others of Lisola's were printed in French. Moreover, we know from one of Lisola's own dispatches that, although the

[1] p. 668, n. 2. Cf. D. Ogg, *England in the Reign of Charles II* (1934), ii. 526, n. 2

Appeal was written in January, there was no French translation yet available in March for Lisola to send to Vienna;[1] this could scarcely have been the case if Lisola himself had been the author. Nor does the reference in the *Appeal* to the 'incomparable books of the Baron de Isola' read as though Lisola were himself the writer.

More positive arguments are available in favour of Du Moulin than for any other possible author. Being a naturalized Englishman, he could claim to be 'a true lover of his country'; his analytical method of dividing his subject into sections and headings, each of them closely argued, is characteristic of his other memorials; so too is the quality of his prose, which was, if anything, better in English than in his native French. He combined the necessary knowledge of European and English conditions, and many of the author's illustrations are taken from episodes on which Du Moulin concentrated at other times; for example, as an instance of French deceit, he quotes the underhand support of the Prince of Condé in the Polish election of 1669, a subject which had bulked large in his letters from Paris in that year. He refers to an English agent, Marsilly, whose seizure by the French had also attracted his attention in the same year. He is exceptionally severe on the relations of his personal enemy, Arlington, with the French ambassador Colbert; he knows that the application of the Emperor to join the Triple Alliance was taken out of the hands of Secretary Trevor, into whose province it should have fallen, and given to the other Secretary, Arlington; in referring to a dispute between England and France over the West Indian island of St. Christopher's he quotes 'the narrative my Lord Willoughby delivered to the Council of Plantations, which is entered in their books'; he mentions the course of a petition of London traders to the Council. Who but Du Moulin, with his past in Arlington's service and on the Council of Trade, could have drawn upon all these references? Again, the treatment of the English pretexts for war is similar to that in other pamphlets which will have to be examined later, and of which drafts, with corrections, exist in Du Moulin's papers.[2] Lastly, the account of the embassy of Arlington and Buckingham in June 1672

---

[1] Dispatch quoted, p. 101, n. 2.   [2] See Chapter VIII below.

shows such knowledge of their conversations with William that it can only have been derived from him or Grand Pensionary Fagel, and it is reasonable to suppose that the writer was someone closely in their confidence. The final quotation from the Authorized Version also squares with authorship by Du Moulin rather than Lisola.

In short, the author of *England's Appeal* was in all probability an Englishman, close to William of Orange, with a detailed knowledge both of recent European developments and of the workings of English policy and a hatred alike of France and of Arlington. These are all qualifications possessed by Du Moulin, who in any case organized the pamphlet's distribution. When we find his authorship asserted by de Vic, a well-placed English correspondent in Flanders, it seems overwhelmingly likely that he was indeed the person responsible.[1]

It remains possible, however, that others made suggestions and supplied information for incorporation in the pamphlet as it appeared in print; and it is certain that others saw it and approved it before publication. William Howard was in The Hague when it was being composed, and may have had a hand in it: there were later some rumours that he was its author. More important is the likelihood that William of Orange and Fagel themselves exercised some general supervision over its contents, and supplied information about Arlington and Buckingham's embassy. Certainly they approved of the pamphlet's publication. Howard in his letter of 17/27 January had definitely asserted that the *Appeal* was a part of official Dutch policy, and not merely a pamphlet written by an anonymous author; and this statement has ample confirmation from other sources. We have seen that as soon as the pamphlet appeared there were rumours that Du Moulin and a colleague, Captain Broadnax, were to be rewarded for their part in distributing it: Du Moulin shortly afterwards became one of William's confidential secretaries and Broadnax became a colonel. It is significant also that when various unauthorized pamphlets purporting to be continuations of the *Appeal* appeared in Holland, they were

[1] De Vic to Southwell, 25 Mar./4 Apr. 1673, Add. MSS. 34342, f. 67 (quoted by Barbour, p. 213, n.).

immediately and effectively suppressed by William's order as being too extreme,[1] but no such official action was ever taken against the original *Appeal*, which was still being distributed by Dutch agents in London in January 1674.

The fact that the pamphlet was secretly approved by William probably accounts for its singular moderation in some respects. In general the author's points are very forcibly urged, but it is noticeable that care is taken to eschew any uncomplimentary references to Charles and James. Even the point that French influence over English policy was endangering England's civil and religious institutions was not elaborated in any detail, but left as a hint to escape the accusation of deliberately fomenting rebellion. The aim was to break the Anglo-French alliance and even to ruin the ministers responsible for negotiating it, but not to foster revolt or permanently to embitter William's uncles against him. William still had the long-term objective of bringing England over into the coalition against France, which could hardly be done if Charles were made irreconcilable: perhaps also he remembered that he too was a Stuart, not far from the succession to the throne, and so it was no part of his policy to weaken permanently the royal authority. In William's eyes the objective was the strictly limited one of inducing, or forcing Charles to make a separate peace, and the *Appeal* was restricted to that purpose. Indeed, for that purpose it was probably more effective than a more scurrilous general invective would have been, and its results became apparent when Parliament met again in the autumn and winter following.

---

[1] Pierre Du Moulin to William of Orange, app. 12/22 July 1673, in R.A. Fagel 291 (printed by Japikse, *Corres.* II. i. 270); Knuttel's Catalogue of pamphlets in the Koninklijke Bibliotheek, Nos. 10912 et seq.

VII

THE SUMMER OF 1673

THE campaigning season of 1673 opened with the Anglo-French alliance against Holland still unshaken, and the two kings determined to renew their efforts to overwhelm their small, but plucky, opponent. In comparison with the spectacular campaign of 1672, however, this second campaign proved to be something of an anti-climax in which the superior forces of Louis XIV and Charles II failed to bring the Dutch to a decisive battle and in which events of note were comparatively few. This was especially true on land, where the renowned French armies continued to find the flood-waters which separated them from the troops of William of Orange an insuperable obstacle. An army with which Louis XIV travelled in person did succeed in capturing the Dutch fortress of Maastricht on the River Meuse (21 June/1 July) after a siege in which the small English contingent with the French army, led by Monmouth and including the young John Churchill, distinguished themselves; but the provinces of Holland and Zeeland which were the heart of the Dutch Netherlands remained untouched, with William holding on in the knowledge that time was on his side. By the end of the autumn of 1673 Louis XIV was forced to admit that he could not compel the Dutch to surrender, and to turn his attention elsewhere. At sea, also, De Ruyter continued to hold his own against the combined navies of England and France, and after the battles of Schooneveld in June and the Texel in August his fleet remained formidable enough to prevent the accomplishment of Charles's cherished project of landing an army in Zeeland.

Thus the fighting of 1673 reached no decision. The peace conference which opened at Cologne in June under the mediation of Sweden was equally abortive. For some months previously the three Powers had all professed a desire to restore the peace of Christendom, and though negotiations for a truce had broken down, they had agreed to attend a conference, which, after much discussion on where it was to take place, was finally fixed at Cologne. But though all three powers agreed to negotiate, there was never the slightest chance of agreement. The French ambassador, Courtin, began by maintaining substantially the same impossibly harsh terms as the Dutch had rejected in June 1672 and which they could hardly be expected to accept now; and in any case he wanted to delay matters as much as possible until his hand had been strengthened by the capture of Maastricht or some other striking military success.[1] Courtin also dominated the English delegation, which, after Sunderland's illness had prevented him from being the ambassador, was led by Sir Joseph Williamson and Sir Leoline Jenkins, of whom the former was the more influential partner.

Charles and his ministers had agreed on the terms for which their ambassadors were to ask: that Dutch ships should strike to the English flag; that the Dutch should pay a total of £600,000 as war indemnity and in return for Dutch fishing in English waters; that William should be appointed perpetual Stadholder; that Englishmen should be evacuated from Surinam; that East Indian trade should be satisfactorily regulated; and, most important of all, that the Dutch should cede some 'cautionary towns'. 'I had rather part with all my money than lose the towns', Charles told his ministers on April 28; and when they met again on May 4, and discussed 'As to the best terms upon which to make peace', Williamson noted, 'Answered, abate anything. Everything but towns. . . . Any one town rather than none.'[2] This rather desperate optimism was possible before the opening of the campaign, but only a great military success could have secured 'the towns', and that success did not materialize. Even when the demand for towns was abandoned by Charles in the face of military failure, his ambassadors at Cologne were no more likely to reach a settlement with the Dutch, because the settlement between England and Holland was made dependent on one between France and Holland. Williamson and Jenkins had strict instructions to maintain 'that inseparable tie which our master is resolved to keep in towards France in every step of

[1] See Williamson's Journal for June 1673, in S.P. 105/229.
[2] For. Ent. Bk. 177, 31 Mar. and dates given.

the treaty':[1] Charles would not and probably could not make
a separate peace, and, acting on his orders, his ambassadors
always took care to act in close concert with Courtin. No
sooner had they arrived in Cologne than Courtin became
their mentor, and outlined the situation to them: he even
gave Williamson and Jenkins a full picture of their principal
opponent, the Dutch diplomat, Beverningk: 'seems harsh,
but that only, a Republican complexion, is frank, only a little
hot, especially upon wine, ergo to be dealt with in the morning
only, apt when drinking to drink high, then to be hot and to
embroil. But on the other side when a little fuddled, apt to
talk and even to drop his own senses, much may by this way
be got from him.'

Williamson solemnly noted down these and other tips,[2]
but they proved to be of little use to him in the face of the
intransigence of his allies, and also of the Dutch. For the
Dutch never showed any willingness to cede territory either
to France or to England, and as time passed by without any
serious defeats, and with ever-growing hopes of securing
allies and obtaining a separate peace with England when
Parliament next met, they became steadily more intractable.
For them, the Cologne conference rapidly became something
of a side-show, to be allowed to continue while the decision
was reached by diplomacy and intrigue elsewhere. And so
Williamson accumulated a mass of notes and correspondence,
and in later years retained some nostalgic memories of social
occasions at the conference, but the practical results of his
stay of nearly a year at Cologne were nil. A detailed account
of the negotiations would be as barren as they were.

More important were the building-up of a coalition against
France, and the organization of Dutch propaganda and intrigue in London to force Charles to make a separate peace.
The former aim was achieved when on 20/30 August a treaty
of alliance between Holland, Spain, and the Emperor was
signed at The Hague, binding them to joint action if the
negotiations at Cologne had no result.[3] As a direct result of
this treaty, the Emperor Leopold declared war on Louis XIV

---

[1] Williamson to Clifford, 13/23 June, in S.P. 81/61, f. 63; and cf. Williamson's
Journal for June.
[2] Journal, 5/15 June, S.P. 105/229, f. 20.   [3] Mignet, iv. 206.

a fortnight later; and Spain's declaration of war became an imminent threat to the merchants of the City of London. The negotiation of this alliance has been described before, and our present purpose is rather with the second Dutch aim and the intrigues which have not previously been brought into the light of day.

As early as the beginning of June, Colbert had reported to his master Louis XIV, in a dispatch from London,[1] that prominent M.P.s could be expected to attempt to break the French alliance in their next session in the autumn—a striking indication of the way in which opinion had developed since the *Appeal* had appeared only three months previously. Moreover, Colbert also wrote that some of Charles's ministers were suspected of entering into relations with these M.P.s, and that Arlington had admitted to him that the Lord Chancellor, Shaftesbury, had for a time been involved, but had been won back to the view that the French alliance in which he had taken part was a matter for the King and his Council alone, and must be maintained. At the same time Arlington tried to fill the French ambassador with distrust of Sir Thomas Osborne, who on Clifford's retirement received the White Staff of the Treasury which Arlington had coveted for himself; and conversely Buckingham and Lauderdale, who were reputed to be Osborne's friends, told Colbert that it was really Arlington who was less loyal to the alliance. The plain fact was that the unity of the Cabal was rapidly breaking up. They were all realists and could see that the war had failed in its aim; they were all keen observers of the political situation and the trend of opinion, and could foresee stormy weather ahead when Parliament next met; in varying degrees they all wished themselves well rid of a war which might lead to their ruin, and looked for a way out; and the instinct of self-preservation made each of them ready to seek his own safety at the expense of the others, and created mutual distrust between statesmen who had never been cordial friends. This disunity obviously suited the Dutch interest admirably; but it is less easy to determine whether, as the French ambassador and Charles suspected, the instinct of self-preservation led some of his ministers into actual intrigue

[1] 12/22 June.

not only with the Country Party, but with William of Orange.

The cloud of suspicion hangs most heavily over the head of Shaftesbury, whose latest biographer has summed up the situation by saying that, in default of definite evidence, 'the most that can be said . . . is that there is probability in the statement' attributed to a confession by Howard (to which no clear reference is given, and which it has been impossible to trace), that Shaftesbury was implicated in intrigues with William of Orange.[1] Temple, in his memoirs, described how Shaftesbury 'was believed to manage a practice in Holland for some insurrection here' in terms which indicate that he thought it not unlikely;[2] and the well-known secretiveness and taste for intrigue of 'the false Achitophel', and the constant atmosphere of mystery and conspiracy which surrounds him, make it natural to harbour such suspicions. We have seen that he may have been approached in September 1672 and that in January 1673 Du Moulin made an attempt through Arton to reach him, which Du Moulin thought might have found favour if that envoy had not been arrested. Perhaps the very vehemence against the Dutch of the *delenda est Carthago* speech was partly inspired by a desire to remove Charles's distrust.

It is certain that in March and April 1673 rumours began to spread that Charles and his Chancellor no longer saw eye to eye. Such rumours were partly the result of the support which Shaftesbury gave to the Test Act in contrast to Clifford's denunciation of it in the House of Lords. It is true that Shaftesbury's reply to Clifford was defended by Arlington as being intended to conciliate the Commons and get the money bill safely passed, and even Charles and Colbert thought that Clifford's attack on the Test Act was most inopportune; but from then onwards Shaftesbury began to be regarded as the one member of the governing circle who shared the popular desire to exclude Papists from office at the Court and in the army. It is perhaps unnecessary to assume that Shaftesbury had actually got wind of the terms of the Secret Treaty of Dover, or even to assume that his

---

[1] Miss L. F. Brown, *First Earl of Shaftesbury* (American Historical Association, 1933), p. 213.   [2] Temple, i. 206–7.

support of the Test Act represented a complete reversal of his policy of religious toleration; for in his eyes that policy had always been primarily intended to benefit, not Catholics, but Dissenters, who had little desire for political office in 1673 so long as they were allowed to worship in peace, and had no objection to a Test Act against Catholics. As the theme of politics changed from indulgence to Dissenters and only incidentally to Catholics, to a general fear of Popery, Shaftesbury's political position changed too, and in particular he revived his old plan of enabling Charles to divorce his childless Queen so that he could remarry and have Protestant heirs to exclude James from the throne. By the end of June a pamphlet purporting to be 'a letter from the Chancellor to the Duke of York dissuasive from Popery is showed about town and very much praised', and Shaftesbury was steadily becoming the champion of Protestantism against James and Popery.[1]

The problem is whether this hatred of Popery extended to the French alliance in Shaftesbury's case, as it was now beginning to do for many people, and secondly, whether it extended even to entering into underground relations with William of Orange. Some confirmation is available for the theory that Shaftesbury would have liked to bring the war to an end in May 1673 by reaching a secret arrangement with Holland. He and some other Englishmen (said to include the Duke of Ormond), commissioned one 'Colonel Alexander' to go over to Holland. This 'Colonel Alexander' was one Augustus Coronel, a financier who had handled the payment of the dowry brought to Charles in 1662 by his Portuguese Queen, Catherine of Braganza, and who had afterwards got into difficulties and transferred his operations to the Continent. Coronel's instructions are unknown, but he crossed the Channel, and saw Lisola and through him the Pensionary Fagel, claiming to have Charles's permission for his errand. It was arranged to send him back to England with an offer of the flag, a war indemnity, payment for fishing rights, the cession of Surinam and St. Helena, and 500,000 guilders for the ministers who brought about peace, and he was also

---

[1] Colbert to Louis XIV, 7/17 Apr. 1673; H. Ball to Williamson, 26 June, in *Letters to Williamson*, i. 67.

to carry a letter from William of Orange to Charles. The intrigue was, however, cut short by Coronel's untimely death, and it was not taken up again through another intermediary, perhaps because Charles made clear his disapproval of negotiations behind the back of Louis XIV. Coronel's claim that Charles was aware of his mission is corroborated by a reference in a letter from Williamson to Clifford, where it is even regarded as being quite reconcilable with a close French alliance.[1]

This episode is evidence of Shaftesbury's desire to end the war at this time, but not that he engaged in underground intrigues unknown to Charles for the purpose; and Arlington told the French ambassador in June, that Shaftesbury, after considering combining with M.P.s to work against the French alliance, had been persuaded not to do this. Following Arlington's advice, Colbert went to see the Chancellor, told him that as one of the promoters of the French alliance he expected him to do his utmost to perpetuate it, and returned well satisfied with Shaftesbury's protestations of loyalty. Charles described these protestations as being as knavish (*fourbes*) as all the actions of a minister who was the weakest and worst disposed of men,[2] and evidently suspected him of treachery. But there is no convincing evidence of any treasonable activities: Du Moulin's correspondence contains hardly so much as a reference to Shaftesbury after Arton's failure, and when in October 1673 Du Moulin was discussing what the speeches at the opening of the next session might be like, he referred to the *delenda est Carthago* speech and its author in terms so disparaging as to make it highly improbable that they were then co-operating.[3] If Shaftesbury had really been 'managing a practice in Holland for an insurrection' some sign would surely have been left. The most likely conclusion seems to be that William benefited indirectly

---

[1] P. L. Muller, *Nederlands eerste Betrekkingen met Oostenrijk, 1658–78* (Amsterdam, 1870), pp. 65–66, based on a dispatch from Lisola to Hocher, 1/11 June 1673; Klopp, i. 339–40, citing a dispatch of 11/21 July; Japikse, *Prins Willem III*, i. 323; Hop en Vivien, *Notulen*, p. 430; Williamson to Clifford, 13/23 June, in S.P. 81/61, f. 63.

[2] Colbert to Louis XIV, 12/22 June and 30 June/10 July 1673.

[3] Du Moulin to an unknown M.P., 26 Oct. 1673 (? N.S.), in R.A. Fagel 253; see pp. 127–8 below.

from Charles's distrust of his greatest minister, but that there was no direct connexion between them.

The same is also true with regard to Charles's other ministers. At the end of June Buckingham was observed to have long and suspicious conferences with the Spanish consul in London, Fonseca, but as Charles pointed out, Buckingham was now largely discredited and powerless to harm, and the opportunity was taken to imprison Fonseca for a time, for 'dangerous practices and correspondencies tending to the disturbance of the government', as a reprisal for the imprisonment of the English consul at Cadiz.[1] But, surprisingly enough, the only one of the ministers against whom there is serious evidence of having secret relations with any of Du Moulin's agents in London was Sir Robert Carr, who held the minor post of Chancellor of the Duchy of Lancaster.

The Du Moulin papers contain a letter dated from London, 17 May 1673. It has no address or addressee's name on it, and is the only letter in the collection signed by the initials 'R. C.', which probably stand for the printer R. Crouch or possibly for Richard Chadbourne, a Protestant schoolmaster friend of Du Moulin's. The letter opens:

> Cousin, I received yours of the 5th instant and according to your design I have done my uttermost for my cousin your wife, but it so fell out that we waited our great cousin at a very unseasonable time, for he was going to the cabal, but since that, I have discoursed at large with him, as to that affair and also to news. I find him a little uneasy, things do not go right, the Dutch have lost the best opportunity that ever they are like to have; had they come to the river the city had mutinied, and knock [*sic*] the cabal on the head. . . .

The original letter bears no clue to the identity of this 'great cousin' who was so sympathetic to the Dutch cause, but in the margin of a translation into French which was made for the benefit of William or Fagel, there is a note opposite the equivalent of 'great cousin', identifying him as Sir Robert Carr, Chancellor of the Duchy of Lancaster and Arlington's brother-in-law.[2] (As Carr's initials are also R. C. as in the

---

[1] Colbert, dispatch of 30 June/10 July; *C.S.P.D. 1673*, p. 408; *Letters to Williamson*, i. 111, 136.

[2] The original letter, in English, is in R.A. Fagel 244; the translation in the Archives of the State of Holland, folder 2925 g. Note, however, that in this document Carr is erroneously given the title of Comptroller of the Royal Household.

signature, it is perhaps necessary to say that this is a coinci-
dence: the letter is not in Carr's handwriting and the marginal
note clearly refers to the 'great cousin' and not to the writer.)
Carr was a good orthodox Cavalier and Anglican, and there
is no other evidence that he was intriguing either with the
Dutch or with the parliamentary opposition; but it would seem
from this reference that he at least sympathized with the
Dutch in secret. As Chancellor of the Duchy of Lancaster he
had little influence on the formation of foreign policy and
did not normally attend meetings of the 'Cabal' (Committee of
Foreign Affairs), but we know that it so happened that at this
date Arlington was out of London, and Carr was in temporary charge of Arlington's duties as Secretary of State.[1]

From this letter (though it is necessary to emphasize that
there is no corroborative evidence), it looks as though Sir
Robert Carr may have been an important source of information for Du Moulin's agents in London, and we may have
here the explanation why the latter were so well informed of
what went on at Court in the months of January and February
1674 which are covered by most of the correspondence that
survives. The rest of 'R. C.'s' letter of 16 May is not sensational, but it does read like the news of a man who is well
informed of what is going on behind the scenes:

The interest of the cabal diminisheth, there is a cabal setting up
against the cabal. Some hope, and believe too, that the King is weary
of the French, and fears the design will not take. Ormond and Angle-
sey's party thrives, especially since Bedford and others are come in,
and the honest party begins to appear. The French promise daily
payment [of the subsidy] but not yet performed . . . now the Dutch
are to fight with a Prince [Rupert] that never was fortunate in battle.
He lost and ruined his uncle [Charles I] and so I am apt to believe
he will do his cousin [Charles II]. This I can assure you, that if our
fleet be baffled this year, 'tis as impossible for the King to raise more
money, as to build Paul's in a day. . . . Here is a prophecy come out,
that tells us that this year our fleet shall perish by storm, God defend,
and that the King shall suffer the same misfortunes his father did
before next Easter, save losing his head, and that Holland shall be
saved by England['s] means (you know I do not mind prophecies).
Here is many observation made by some concerning the misfortune
of our plenipotentiaries [to Cologne], one falling sick, and the other

[1] *C.S.P.D. 1673*, pp. 236, 241.

dangered of perils by sea, in a month of May. 'Tis not good dissembling with God, for they have no design of making peace. You may assure yourself and friends, that no meeting shall be, and then if a meeting no proposals but such as cannot be consented to, and all for delays, until they can try if they can master Holland by force; and this pray satisfy some of the Dutch that if they depend on the Spaniards, they shall be deceived, for our cousin [Carr?] saith that the Queen of Spain hath given leave for the French, and also for the English, to march through her country for Holland [Louis's advance on Maastricht] . . . you may let Peter Mullin know that his friend [Arton] is still in prison, and like to suffer. I have spoken to Sir Joseph Williamson in your concern [?]. I would advise you to be as quiet as you can and rest on the same rock of salvation waiting for the glorious appearance of our Redeemer with your friend and cousin, R.C.

It is natural to ask whether, if Sir Robert Carr was in secret communication with the Dutch, the same may not also have been true of his brother-in-law, Arlington. By the summer of 1673 he had grave misgivings about the advisability of continuing with the 'design', and Colbert had some suspicions of him; he was especially apprehensive of being attacked in the next parliamentary session, and prepared ultimately to form some relations with the opposition to avoid it. But he had always been in bad odour at The Hague: William had conceived a dislike for him at their meeting in 1672, and he objected to Arlington's tendency to try to patronize him. Du Moulin, on whom William and Fagel relied for their opinions of English politicians, was Arlington's enemy, had always depicted him as the very man with most responsibility for forming the French alliance, and had made him the principal butt of *England's Appeal*. The likelihood of a reconciliation seems very remote, and we shall find that when Arlington did go to The Hague after the end of the war, the welcome which he received was anything but that which would have been given to someone instrumental in procuring peace.

In general it may be said that William must have been very much encouraged by the knowledge that Charles's ministers were no longer united and determined in their efforts to partition his country, but that, with the minor exception of Sir Robert Carr, he was not engaged in any plot with any of them: his agents were rather concerned in influencing private members of the House of Commons. In the summer of 1673, however, the hesitations of the English government led William to make one last effort to achieve his object of a separate peace with England by means of a negotiated settlement with Charles. In conjunction with Lisola, van Beuningen, and Monterey, the Spanish governor at Brussels, it was decided that the Spanish diplomat, Don Bernardo de Salinas, should travel to London to see the Spanish ambassador, the Marquis del Fresno, carrying with him a letter from William to Charles (a draft of which survives in Du Moulin's handwriting), and proposals for a separate peace. At the same time the two abusive continuations of the *Appeal* which had appeared anonymously in Holland were suppressed, in order not to embitter Charles at a critical moment. This mission, however, was as unsuccessful as the previous attempts in 1672 had been; for when Don Bernardo had an audience with the King, Charles would not hear of a separate peace, and Don Bernardo was summarily dismissed from the country on 24 July lest Louis XIV should entertain any jealousy of a longer stay. The only favourable result, from the Dutch point of view, was that his visit served to increase Charles's distrust of Shaftesbury, who was reported to have had an interview lasting three hours with Don Bernardo before he left. Charles even went so far as to ask his Chancellor how much money he had been offered by the Spaniards, and when Shaftesbury protested, Charles told him that the Spaniards were not treating him properly, since they had offered Arlington £40,000. There is no clue to the actual subject of the conversation.[1]

A partial explanation for Charles's rejection of these offers out of hand may be that he had some lingering hopes that the sea battle which was imminent would at last lead to a successful invasion of Zeeland; but that these hopes were now very small is shown by the fact that Charles was even prepared to give up his claim for 'cautionary towns' to secure peace before Parliament met.[2] The obstacle to a peace between England

[1] R.A. Fagel 252, ff. 1455, 1465; Japikse, *Corres.*, II. i. 257–60; Japikse, *Prins Willem III*, i. 323–4, and references; Arlington to Williamson, 11 July 1673, in S.P. 81/61, ff. 91–93; J. Richards to Williamson, 25 July, *C.S.P.D. 1673*, p. 458; Colbert to Louis XIV, 31 July/10 Aug.

[2] Colbert to Louis XIV, 31 July/10 Aug.; Arlington to Williamson and Jenkins, 28 July, S.P. 81/61, ff. 221–6.

and Holland was not now any great difference over the precise peace terms, but William's insistence on a separate peace and Charles's refusal or inability to abandon his French ally. This deadlock could only be broken by bringing parliamentary pressure to bear on Charles and demonstrating that it was absolutely impossible for Charles to continue to fight in 1674.

Even while the results of Don Bernardo's mission were still unsettled, the Dutch had other irons in the fire for their purpose. On 7/17 July 1673 William sent for Du Moulin to come to his room, and they had a conversation lasting about an hour. Perhaps as a result of this talk, Du Moulin wrote to his old friend William Howard (of whose activities since his return from Holland in February nothing is known) inviting him to cross the Channel to Nieuport to see him. Howard, adopting the pseudonym of 'Richard Andrews', agreed to come, 'not having the power to resist the tempting force of your kind invitation'. Charles later admitted to the French ambassador that Howard had shown him Du Moulin's letter, and that he had seen no harm in allowing Howard to go to Nieuport, but had not authorized him to go on into Holland. Perhaps he hoped to use Howard to discover the Dutch plans. No confirmation is available of French suspicions that Shaftesbury and Arlington, or Buckingham, were using Howard as an intermediary.[1]

'Mr. Andrews' boarded the packet-boat with his 'foot-boys' in the first days of August, and when he landed at Nieuport he was met by 'Mr. Hunt', a name which conceals the identity of Du Moulin. These aliases, however, did not deceive the English spies, and when, instead of talking matters over at Nieuport, they proceeded to travel into Holland, their movements were noted. We can trace their progress to Bruges—Howard

a very shrowd fellow, went by the name of Mr. Hull formerly [Jan. 1673] in The Hague, and as I hear was the man that writ the Appeal, a short man about 40 years old . . . he talked discontentedly of the affairs of England, also seemed little affected. He spoke not a word of any language but English but had another young man [Du Moulin]

[1] R. Bulstrode to Williamson, 8/18 July, S.P. 84/194, f. 177; Du Moulin's letter not extant; 'Rich. Andrews' to Du Moulin, 21 July, R.A. Fagel 244; Colbert to Louis XIV, 15/25 Sept. and 20/30 Oct. 1673.

with him that spoke good French and some Dutch. By their discourse
. . . expressed little kindness towards Your Excellency [Arlington].

From Bruges they went via Rotterdam to The Hague where
Howard stayed at Du Moulin's lodging except when they
paid a short visit to army headquarters about 19 August.[1]

It is to be presumed that the purpose of this trip to army
headquarters was to enable Howard to report personally to
William on political conditions in England. News of his
activities caused anxiety to Courtin at Cologne and Colbert
at London, for, when taken in conjunction with rumours that
Don Bernardo de Salinas was to pay a second visit to England,
and that Sir Gabriel Sylvius might be on a secret visit to
Holland, Howard's journey might mean that Charles was
considering abandoning his French alliance. Williamson had
to reassure his French colleague at Cologne that Charles had
prohibited Don Bernardo's return, and that Howard could
not possibly be on an official errand. Charles had to face
representations from Colbert and to promise not to undertake any negotiations directly with Holland and to do all in
his power to prevent the Spaniards and Dutch from being
able to offer terms before the meeting of Parliament.[2]

At the same time Charles had his own reasons for fearing
the plots of Du Moulin and Howard. It is a measure of his
alarm that he began to encourage Louis XIV to intrigue with
the Dutch Republicans against William, and even described
his nephew as his greatest enemy. This desire for revenge on
William represented a complete reversal of Charles's former
patronage of him, as against De Witt and the Republicans.[3]

Conversely, Howard's reports must have encouraged the
Dutch and their allies, and confirmed the view of English
politics which Du Moulin had put forward. Williamson
reported from Cologne that Lisola and the Spaniard Lira
were confident enough to declare 'that the Parliament at its
first meeting will most certainly oblige the King (for in that
style they presume to speak) to abandon the French', and at

1 Puckle to Arlington, 8/18 Aug., S.P. 84/195, f. 26; S. Lynch to Arlington,
same date, S.P. 77/43, f. 18; R. Bulstrode to Williamson, 8/18 Aug., 19/29 Aug.,
and 22 Aug./1 Sept., S.P. 84/195, ff. 22, 44, 47.

2 Williamson to Arlington, 12/22 Sept. and 19/29 Sept., S.P. 81/64, ff. 106,
173–4; Colbert to Louis XIV, 15/25 Sept.

3 Colbert to Louis XIV, as in note 2, also 18/28 Sept. and 13/23 Oct.

the beginning of October, Williamson and Jenkins, in reporting that the outcome of the Cologne negotiations must
depend on events in Parliament, declared that

Holland and Spain [have] for these 3 or 4 months in the most
express and presumptuous terms imaginable undertaken in a manner
to all this part of the world, that the Parliament at their meeting will
not only peremptorily refuse all manner of supplies to the King, but
proceed to the obliging His Majesty (for in that indecent style they
speak) forthwith to change all his foreign alliances and interests, and
we have great reason to believe this single expectation into which they
have thus deluded the world has contributed more to the reputation
of their affairs in the Empire . . . than any other consideration whatsoever. . . .[1]

The Dutch, however, did not confine their 'indecency'
to words, but strove by equally obnoxious actions (from
Williamson's point of view) to do all in their power to foster
this favourable attitude among members of the House of
Commons. Their agents continued at work in London,
though the hopes which were placed in Howard were disappointed. He did not leave on his return journey to England
until late in September, the reason being (according to
Tucker, an English agent at Rotterdam) that Howard

would not go back to England on the general errand of that party
without £100 down. The other [Du Moulin] promised it in the
general as from the States, but Howard would have his money, which
kept him so long there, that at Whitehall it was smelt out, and so all
the rest of that business followed, Howard was clapt up, etc. The
business was Moulin would have cousened Howard of the £100, but
at last Moulin was forced to pay Howard the money down.[2]

Howard was evidently unaware how much was known of his
activities at Whitehall, for he would hardly have returned
if he had thought it possible that he would be immediately
arrested. He left Nieuport on 20 September, and, after a
report that the packet-boat was lost at sea had proved to be
false, he was promptly apprehended as soon as he arrived in
London. On 2 October Arlington wrote with some satisfaction
to Williamson that 'this morning Mr. Howard, His Majesty's

[1] Williamson to Arlington, 12/22 Sept., S.P. 81/64, f. 106; Williamson and
Jenkins to Arlington, 7/17 Oct., S.P. 105/221, f. 312.
[2] Williamson's Journal, 6/16 May 1674, in S.P. 105/222.

pretended envoy to the Prince of Orange, was sent a close
prisoner to the Tower for having been busy at The Hague
under that character without any colour of authority from
His Majesty or any of his ministers'.[1]

Howard at first tried to justify himself by putting the
blame in some way on his servant for running away in Holland and betraying him, but he soon provided himself with a
more effective defence from punishment by making his
escape 'by the folly and negligence of the messenger in whose
hands he was'. The English government thought so much of
Howard that the officer who was nominally in charge of him
was sent to the Gatehouse for the escape of his prisoner.
Rumours spread that Howard was the true author of the
Appeal; Charles promised that everything possible would be
done to seize him; but he was able to get away safely back to
Holland. There we hear nothing of any further political
activities, but plenty of gossip to the effect that, together
with William Carr, he turned his favour with the Prince of
Orange to good account financially. By selling passes giving
immunity from Dutch privateers they were said to have
earned 7,000 guilders from one merchant alone in the five
months which the war had still to run.[2]

It is impossible to tell what Howard proposed to do when
he returned to England on this occasion, but perhaps his
plans were not very different from those of two other agents
of whom it was reported that 'the day before the two gents
came from The Hague, there was a sum of money brought to
their lodging, judged not less than 2,000 guilders. I confess,
as I hinted to your Excellency before, I doubt they are employed to do hurt amongst the Parliament men.'[3] From now
to the end of the reign there are constant reports of M.P.s
receiving money from Holland or France or Spain. These
'bribes' should be regarded with caution: it does not neces-
sarily follow that, when offered, they changed votes and opinions in the crudest possible way, and it is far more likely
that the money was used to reward people who would have

[1] S.P. 81/65, f. 10.
[2] R. Yard to Williamson, 3 and 8 Oct., *Letters to Williamson*, ii. 31, 33; Colbert
to Louis XIV, 13/23 Oct.; Williamson's Journal, as on p. 125, n. 2.
[3] R. Bulstrode to Williamson, 17/27 Oct., S.P. 84/195, f. 88.

been supporters in any event, and perhaps to confirm the waverers.

In regard to the two sessions which we shall now have to consider, it is impossible to tell how much Dutch money went into the pockets of M.P.s—or indeed, to prove with absolute certainty that any did. It may be confidently asserted that opinion would have been strongly anti-French in any case, and probably more money was spent, and to greater effect, on the printing and distribution of Dutch propagandist pamphlets.

In addition, direct appeals were made by letter to M.P.s who it was thought might be sympathetic to the Dutch alliance. The draft of one such letter exists, and it is reasonable to suppose that it was not the only one of its kind. It is written by Du Moulin to a member of the House of Commons whose name unfortunately is not given. We gather that he was an old acquaintance to whom Du Moulin had not written during the previous year, and it may well be that Du Moulin was writing to every member with whom he could claim any acquaintance to enlist his support in the coming critical session. In the following extract it will be noticed that skilful use was made of the fact that on 5/15 October Louis XIV had declared war on Spain.

You must needs resolve, now you are together, either to run the fortune of His Most Christian Majesty and help him as far as in you lieth to enslave all Christendom, or else to advise His Majesty to shake hands with his old friends and not to break with the House of Austria upon no other ground but because the Spanish counsels are not Frenchified. It is true the English Court doth think that flower de luces set up at Amsterdam and all other places would be a very gallant sight, but the Dons [Spaniards] are of another mind, and in very sober sadness I am not able to understand what you might propose to yourselves by lending your helping hand to the war. I need not tell you what strict alliances have been made here of late and how strengthened we are now by the confederacy of so many potent Princes. You see already the French are everywhere *sur la défensive* and it is not very probable some few regiments new raised, though under the command of Monsr. de Schomberg, can turn the scale, by being transported either to Dunkirk or Calais, or their noble achievements make amends for the infinite losses the merchants and the whole nation with them are to expect as soon as Spain breaks, and that, you know, will be as soon as they'll find their endeavours and friendly applications fruitless. In the meanwhile for a last trial the States have again sent to the King to beg once more peace of him, and if the wind had been more favourable I doubt some of the grand Speakers might have been somewhat disappointed and forced to *delere* some of their new *delendas*. But however it will appear, before the King can resolve either way, that prosperous success as well in the campaign as in the cabinet, hath not made them less desirous of peace than before, or less willing to grant to His Majesty all what he may rationally expect. The issue is in the hands of God, who either in peace or war doth never want means to protect and deliver from opposition those that are unjustly persecuted. Before I end I must beg of you to send me what prints will be worth reading, especially the Speeches [of the King and Chancellor at the opening of Parliament] concerning which last, I can't but tell you that if the next doth this country as much good as the *delenda Carthago* hath done, my Lord Chancellor will be the best friend they have ever had. I hope you will give me leave also to trouble you oftener with my scribbling, and if you desire it I'll send you our public news, but then I'll write gazetteer-like, not intending to meddle any more with politics, which I fear may make this very letter less welcome to you.[1]

In this way Du Moulin appealed to fears of the political, commercial, and religious results of the French alliance, and argued that, while the Dutch were now in a stronger position than before, they were still ready to grant reasonable peace terms if Charles could be induced to offer them. The letter from the States-General to Charles to which reference is made was intended to be the public counterpart of Du Moulin's private letter, and was drafted by him as well, according to the history written by de Wicquefort who was in a position close to him at The Hague. When Charles received it, he remarked that it was more like a manifesto than a letter, and indeed it was plainly intended to be printed and distributed in London (as was duly done), and, being dated 15/25 October, was timed to coincide with the opening of Parliament on the 20th.

The first section of the letter puts forward the idea that before the outbreak of war in 1672 the Dutch had done everything possible to conciliate Charles, down to the sending of Meerman as Ambassador Extraordinary in that year, but no conference was granted 'upon the point which might have

[1] Dated 26 Oct. 1673 (? N.S.), in R.A. Fagel 253.

ended all our differences, till an hour after Your Majesty's
Declaration of War had been read and approved in Your
Council'. The second section goes on to argue that after the
outbreak of war the Dutch had continually made overtures
of peace, but their deputies had been confined to Hampton
Court without any audience with Charles, and the representations of the Spanish ambassadors and others had been ignored,
even when Charles's own nephew the Prince of Orange had
come to power in Holland; and at Cologne the Dutch had
been told that they could expect peace only on 'such conditions as never were demanded of a free people, and . . . [such]
that they can only be the consequences·of an absolute conquest, the subversion of the Reformed Religion, of which
Your Majesty and the kings your most illustrious predecessors have been the strongest support and defenders, and
which carried with them at once the utter ruin not only of
us, but also of the Low Countries belonging to the King of
Spain'. The conclusion states that the Dutch had therefore
been obliged to make alliances with Austria and Spain,

but before the evil be past remedy, we thought fit to make one final
essay, and to assure Your Majesty that whatsoever change hath happened in Europe, our deference and respect for Your Majesty is still
the same; and that how considerable and how potent soever our allies
are, we are not the less disposed to give Your Majesty all the satisfaction which you can reasonably pretend; . . . we presume therefore
to hope that Your Majesty will not refuse at our request and inter-
cession, what we have not been hitherto able to obtain. . . . Your
Majesty cannot continue a war, which hath already been so ruinous,
without declaring it against those who are united with us, and without
hazarding the safety of all Christendom, if the arms of the King of
France should be victorious through the succours given by Your
Majesty to him. And Your Majesty can no longer take it ill that we
yield not what Your Majesty might demand of us for France, since
by an indispensable necessity we can no longer do it but with the
agreement of our Allies. So that as the general treaty appears accompanied with many difficulties. . . .

The implication is that Charles should agree to make a separate peace, and the intention of the whole letter is clearly to
saddle Charles with the responsibility for continuing a war
which would be disastrous to England and to Europe. No
one can have thought that such a letter would convince

Charles of the error of his ways, but it was a convenient way
of appealing to public, and especially parliamentary, opinion.[1]

Unfortunately for the Dutch, the letter was delayed some
days by contrary winds before a special herald or 'trumpeter'
arrived at Harwich with it together with a large bundle of
letters addressed to the Spanish ambassador, which were
suspected of containing instructions for the Dutch agents
and sympathizers in London.[2] Every publicity was then given
to it, copies being plentifully distributed in London.

As the meeting of Parliament on 20 October drew nearer,
feeling mounted steadily. The letters which Williamson received at Cologne give a striking picture of the development
of public opinion in these months. On 1 August Sir Nicholas
Armourer, a courtier and old crony of Williamson's, wrote:
'I hope you will bring us peace against October; if not, look
to it; my friend Sir Eliab H[ervey], Sir Lewis, and Robin
Thomas will belt you all.' The failure of the French admiral
D'Estrées to obey Prince Rupert's signals at the sea battle
off the Texel lost the English fleet a great opportunity of
victory, and made the French violently unpopular in consequence as reports of the battle were spread. Prince Rupert
himself was known to be disgusted with the conduct of the
French admiral; his coach was often seen at Shaftesbury's
door, and the two men were looked on as 'the great Parlia-
ment-men, and for the interest of old England'. On 1 September Robert Yard, one of Williamson's clerks, wrote to him
that 'the generality of the people are very inquisitive concerning the negotiations at Cologne, and not a little troubled to
hear of the small hopes there are of the success of the treaty.
The truth is, all sorts of people seem weary of the war, and
would look upon him as a very welcome messenger, who
should bring the news of the conclusion of a peace.' On
3 October another correspondent reported that attacks were
being planned on members of the Cabal: 'October being
now began, we already (men of all sorts) are condemning and
acquitting several persons (and those of no mean quality) as

[1] See *The Letter sent by the States-General . . . to His Majesty, together with His Majesty's Answer to the said Letter, translated out of French into English*, 1673. Cf. A. de Wicquefort, *Histoire des Provinces-Unies*, ed. 1874 (Amsterdam), iv. 580. (For de Wicquefort, see pp. 197–99 below.)
[2] Colbert to Louis XIV, 27 Oct./6 Nov. 1673.

if the next meeting of the Parliament should be nothing but an High Court of Justice, and a gaol delivery. The members begin to flock up to town, and are met at the very stirrup to be engaged in cabals against this or that great man.' And matters were made worse than ever by the outbreak of war between France and Spain. Henry Ball, reporting his forebodings about the meeting of Parliament, said that 'the fears of a war with Spain are so great in the City that it's their common cry, We shall be ruined if we do; the merchants thinking it as bad a mischief as can possibly come to them'.[1]

Charles had long foreseen this state of affairs. At the end of June he had anticipated that bills would be produced to exile York and exclude Roman Catholic princes from the throne, and that money would be given only on condition that peace was made with Holland. He had used this argument to press on Colbert the necessity of an early peace. Louis's reaction had been to tell Colbert to urge Charles not to call Parliament for a few months more in order to disappoint the hopes of the Dutch, but Charles had rightly pointed out that postponement would only embitter Parliament more, and that the war could only be carried on by parliamentary subsidies. Perhaps to prevent the French ambassador from continuing to urge a prorogation or a dissolution, Charles began to profess to him a surprising optimism about Parliament. He declared that Shaftesbury had been brought back to loyalty, and that the worst hot-heads in the Commons had been convinced that he could not honourably desert Louis XIV: only Sir William Coventry and Garroway were still capable of perverting the others, and he had hopes that the former would not speak against the French alliance while the latter could be threatened with the loss of his commissionership in the Customs. At the same time he complained bitterly about the conduct of his brother James, as being the cause of the principal difficulties he would have to surmount.[2]

As Arlington told Colbert, people were very apprehensive of James's succession to the throne, and the policy of Catholicism

---

[1] *C.S.P.D. 1673*, pp. 475 and 525; *Letters to Williamson, passim*, especially ii. 21–22, 29–30, 45.

[2] Colbert to Louis XIV, 30 June/10 July; Mignet, iv. 206; Colbert to Louis XIV, 1/11 Sept., 22 Sept./2 Oct., 25 Sept./5 Oct., 20/30 Oct.

and despotism which James might pursue. Moreover,
James's succession might come at any time. Less than a
fortnight before Parliament met, Henry Ball, one of Williamson's clerks, wrote to him that Charles 'has had lately 3 sad
fits of an apoplexy, the first whereof took him in the Duchess
of Portsmouth's presence, who has since begged he would
not come to her at nights. . . . On Tuesday, they say, he had
a third fit in the Privy Garden, so that many people are much
concerned and have begged His Majesty to be advised by
his physicians, who tell him he must a little refrain company,
&c. . . .'[1] For people who heard such rumours as this of the
state of Charles's health, the succession problem was urgent.
And at this juncture James was making his second marriage,
to Mary of Modena—a Roman Catholic and a French protégée. When Parliament met, a proxy marriage had been
celebrated abroad, and Mary was about to cross the Channel
to consummate the marriage.

In most men's minds fear of James's Popery and fear of
the alliance with the Catholic despot Louis XIV were now
combined. The Dutch propaganda fell on fertile soil, and we
shall not be surprised to find the same M.P.s attacking the
French alliance, the ministers who had made it, and James's
marriage.

This was the situation which Charles had to face; and, if
the French ambassador and others are to be believed, he did
not even have the support of united ministers behind him, for
Arlington and Buckingham were at loggerheads, so were
Shaftesbury and Lauderdale, and each of the first three was
fostering his own group in the Commons. Only Lauderdale
was absolutely reliable, and he was the most unpopular of
all, excepting James. As Colbert wrote to Louis on 20/30
October, giving Charles's optimistic view of the attitude
which Parliament would take to the French alliance, the
House of Commons met and dealt the first blow to their
hopes.

[1] *Letters to Williamson,* ii. 35.

VIII

CHARLES IN DIFFICULTIES,
OCTOBER–DECEMBER 1673

THE parliamentary recess which had lasted from March to October 1673 had followed on an adjournment of the two Houses, and not on a prorogation, so that the meeting on 20 October did not mark the beginning of a new session. For this reason Charles decided that on that date he would prorogue Parliament for a few days so that a new session could begin on 27 October. This would prevent the opposition from raising the objection that two money bills should not be passed in the same session, and it would have the incidental advantage that in the meantime Mary of Modena could arrive in the country, and her marriage to James could be consummated, without fear of parliamentary addresses against it.

It was therefore intended that the proceedings on 20 October should be purely formal in character; and

it was ordered (as it was said) that to prevent any occasion of discourse Mr. Speaker should not take the chair till the Black Rod were ready to come to the door. Accordingly he came not till half an hour past ten. As soon as he was come, and sat down by the table, the House with some earnestness called 'to the chair, to the chair'; which he not taking notice of, it was said if he would not take the chair, some other should. Then he said it was the constant custom to go to prayers first, and after that, he would take the chair.

Sir Robert Thomas said that prayers was but a ceremony, and might be dispensed with [a remarkable statement, considering the period].

Then Mr. Powle said if he would not take the chair, he would speak to him where he was; whereupon he was forced to take the chair, for those that did not desire it could not well speak against his taking the chair, being present and a full House.

Powle briefly argued that 'we had been very careful to prevent Popery, but it was in vain to suppress it elsewhere if it got footing so near the throne', that the Duke of York was going to marry an Italian lady, 'kin to two cardinals', and that the House should make an address to the King that the match should not be consummated. This was seconded by Birch, a former colonel in Cromwell's army, of plebeian origin and blunt opinions, 'who said that from the first intention of the Spanish match to this day, all our troubles had had their rise from these Popish alliances'; and Henry Coventry and the Court's other supporters could say nothing to prevent the address from being carried.[1]

In the meantime the arrival of Black Rod had been delayed. There were several peers who were to take their seats in the House of Lords for the first time, and Shaftesbury, who as Chancellor controlled the proceedings there, insisted on admitting them with all the due formalities, however long it might take. James immediately suspected that Shaftesbury's dilatoriness was deliberate, in order to gain time for the 'violent party' in the Commons to pass the address against his marriage, and as a result he renewed his representations to Charles to dismiss his Chancellor.[2]

Thus the temper of Parliament was evident from the outset, and the prorogation for a week was not likely to help matters much. James was able to marry Mary of Modena, but the marriage naturally did not make the members of the House any more tractable: indeed, as it proved, it made them less inclined to vote money to continue the war in alliance with Louis XIV.

We possess an interesting analysis of the political situation written during this week by Sir William Temple, which shows clearly the attitude of various groups in the Commons towards the war. He divides the House into four 'parties'. The first of these 'would run up to the height and fall upon the ministers, especially Buckingham, Arlington, Lauderdale, and their carriage, particularly in the business of the war, so as absolutely to break all the present set both of men and business at Court, and bring some of themselves in their room'.

This group, according to Temple, included Garroway, Sir Robert or Robin Thomas, Sacheverell, Lord Cavendish, and William Russell, and was supported by Halifax. It can be seen that this group included several of the later leaders of

---

[1] *Dering*, pp. 149–51. [2] Clarke, *James II*, p. 485; Burnet, ii. 36.

the Whig Party, and it is to be presumed that among their ranks are to be found those members who were in touch with Trenchard, Medley, and other Dutch agents—for, needless to say, no names are mentioned in their correspondence.

Temple's second group 'is more moderate, would only secure the business of religion, break the war with Holland, both these with all the good measures that can be to the King, and no violent ones to the ministers, and of this Strangways and Powle seem the heads, but strong in the numbers of the House'. The strength of this group, which included ex-Cavaliers like Strangways of unimpeachable loyalty, is perhaps the best testimony to the efficacy of Dutch propaganda and the way in which moderate public opinion had swung against the war. Temple's third party also bears the same witness, but in a different way: they were for voting money on pretence of not exasperating the King, but also 'with pretence of not perfecting it unless peace be made, though this be understood to be a way of securing the business of money under a show of moderation and popular aims, and of this Sir John Holland is the head'.

The fourth group is led by Shaftesbury in the Lords, and by Sir Robert Howard, Secretary to the Treasury, in the Commons. Nothing is said about their attitude to the war: the party 'is made chiefly to carry on the business of the divorce', i.e. to induce Charles by a mixture of persuasion and parliamentary pressure, to divorce Catherine of Braganza and to marry again. Charles had not openly discouraged them.

The King seems sometimes very earnest in it, and sometimes cold, and in all these matters is either so uncertain or disgusted that those who are nearest him know not yet what will be the issue. But hitherto seems resolved to go on with France, will not receive overtures from Spain or Holland, and talks of setting out the fleet next year without money from Parliament if it fails, and in this mind none seem now to be left but the Duke [of York] and Arlington.

Arlington's private opinion was, however, less encouraging than Temple could know.

Lastly, according to Temple, there was the small group of members representing the government in the House.

The Court's business in the House seems to be much wanting in point of men to manage it of credit and ability, for besides Mr. Secretary

[Henry] Coventry and Mr. Attorney [Finch], who are reckoned to speak as from their places wholly, there is none of much talk that undertake it but Sir Ro. Carr and Sir Rich. Temple, who are the worst heard in the House, especially the last. My Lord Treasurer [Danby] seems to be yet but discovering the coasts, and not resolved what course to steer. . . .[1]

The accuracy of Temple's judgement of the situation was soon revealed when Parliament again met in the following week. Charles opened the new session on Monday, 27 October, with a short speech to the two Houses, in which he said: 'I thought this day to have welcomed you with an honourable peace; my preparations for the war and condescensions at the treaty gave me great reason to believe so; but the Dutch have disappointed me in that expectation, and have treated my ambassadors at Cologne with the contempt of conquerors. . . .' This skilful attempt to suggest that the Dutch were intransigent at Cologne, while ignoring their readiness for a separate peace, was the basis for a request for a further supply of money to make them climb down, and was accompanied by renewed assurances of Charles's zeal in preserving the established religion and laws. These points were then developed at greater length by Lord Chancellor Shaftesbury in a speech which had also, presumably, been approved by his fellow ministers. It enumerated the terms required for a peace with Holland (flag, fishery, trade treaty in the East Indies, but no mention now of cautionary towns); went on to limit the term 'Carthaginian', which he had applied to the Dutch in February, to the Republican Party only, and argued that the Dutch negotiators, while openly pretending to be conciliatory, were secretly quite uncompromising and refused to make any concessions at Cologne. Having asked for supply, he concluded his official speech by asserting the King's devotion to 'religion and property'—'he hath not yet learned to deny you anything; and he believes your wisdom and moderation is such, he never shall' [sic]—and by reminding the Commons of the widows and orphans, affected by the Stop of the Exchequer, who would be aided by a supply of money to pay the King's debts. He then added a curious postscript of his own, praying

[1] Temple to Essex, 25 Oct. 1673, in *Essex Papers*, i. 130–3.

that this session may equal, nay exceed, the honour of the last; that it may perfect what the last begun for the safety of the King and kingdom; that it may be ever famous for having established upon a durable foundation our religion, laws, and properties; that we may not be tossed with boisterous winds, nor overtaken by a sudden dead calm; but that a fair gale may carry you, in a steady, even, and resolved way, into the ports of wisdom and security.[1]

Some saw in this postscript a *double entendre*, concealing an invitation to the Commons to continue the anti-Catholic policy of the Test Act by other steps to secure the nation from its Roman Catholic heir presumptive: on the other hand, his *delenda est Carthago* speech, and others, had been equally fulsome.

When the Commons had returned to their own chamber, it was immediately moved, and carried without opposition, that consideration of the King's Speech should be postponed until Friday, the 31st. An attempt by Henry Coventry to get immediate thanks voted for the King's observations on religion and property was prevented, Garroway arguing that if thanks were returned 'so suddenly, we shall be thought, without doors, teized and corrupted'. There followed an attack on the Speaker, Edward Seymour, as being a Privy Councillor and Treasurer of the Navy; because 'you expose the honour of the House in resorting to gaming-houses, with foreigners as well as Englishmen, and ill places . . . [you are] . . . an unfit person to be Speaker, by your way of living'; and because 'he had used opprobrious words of the whole House, having called them a company of curs'. The real grievance, of course, was that Seymour was less a servant of the House than a minister and political opponent; and the Country Party found it impossible to persuade the House to take the unprecedented step of removing the Speaker.[2]

The postponement of the debate on the King's Speech, and therefore on the French alliance and the war, gave members time to digest the letter from the States-General which had just been brought over by the 'trumpet', and particularly its implication that the King's references to Dutch

[1] *L.J.* xii. 589.
[2] Debates for 27 Oct. in Grey, ii. 182–8; *Dering*, pp. 151–4.

intransigence had been false.[1] On Wednesday night, the 29th, we learn that 'there was a great meeting of Parliament men about uniting', but there is no detailed account of what was discussed.[2] On the 30th the Commons heard Charles's reply to their address against the marriage of James to Mary of Modena, in which, besides saying that the marriage had now been completed, Charles pointed out that there had been no opposition in the previous session to a proposal for James to marry an Austrian—and Catholic—archduchess: but the point was precisely that Mary was much more dangerous as being the protégée of Louis XIV. In her person fear of Roman Catholicism and of the French alliance were combined, in spite of Coventry's denial that Louis XIV had paid her dowry. The Commons replied by voting a second address against the marriage, and Garroway proposed that the Test should now be extended to apply to all members of both Houses.[3]

These were, however, only preliminaries to the great debate on the King's Speech on the 31st, when the question would be decided whether money would be granted to enable Charles to pursue his foreign policy. The attack on the French alliance began on that day, in grand committee of the whole House. Russell opened by proposing that the House should flatly refuse to vote any money:

> . . . Would not vote things hand over head; let us consider what we give this money for, and consider that what we give is destructive to the nation (by maintaining this war) and the Protestant religion—The French King calls this war 'a Catholic war'; and seeing we are upon so wrong a bottom, and if betrayed by those about the King, let us tell him plainly of it; former Parliaments have done it. . . .

He was supported by others, including Lord Cavendish, who pointed out that they had never been consulted about the war, 'and what we have given is turned to raising of families, and not paying the King's debts'. We may say that this view was that of the first of Temple's groups. It was, however, too extreme for the moderate members of the second group, the ex-Cavaliers like Strangways and Sir Henry Capel, who,

[1] See pp. 128–30 above.
[2] Sir T. Player to Williamson, 3 Nov., in *Letters to Williamson*, ii. 55–56.
[3] Grey, ii. 189–96; *Dering*, pp. 155–6.

while they were equally opposed to the war, were reluctant to vote a flat refusal of all money for the King. They preferred to take the old line that redress of grievances should precede supply, though Sacheverell argued that 'giving of money' was itself one of the greatest grievances. On the whole the third group and the few supporters of the Court found it expedient to fall in with this view that grievances should be discussed before supply, as being a lesser evil than uncompromising refusal of all money; and Sir Robert Howard from the fourth group, agreed, while laying special stress on the danger from Popery in high society as the greatest grievance —'Seek ye first the kingdom of Heaven, settle religion, and all things will be added. . . . Go in a parliamentary way for "Grievances" and "Religion", and think of this Vote last.'

The general opinion was that Russell's original proposal was too severe, and it was accordingly amended to read that no money should be given until the end of the eighteen months which the previous grant in March had been nominally intended to cover. On this basis the debate continued all day until after four o'clock in the afternoon—an unusually long debate for the period. The length of the debate was, however, due rather to the desire of members to expatiate on their grievances against the government than to any disagreement about the French alliance, which was condemned by almost all. The French ambassador, indeed, went so far as to report to his master that there were not four people in the entire House who did not think that the sole means of maintaining the Protestant religion was to make peace with Holland, and in every way possible to oppose the plans of Louis XIV. Compared with the complete silence on the French alliance in the previous session, this almost unanimous condemnation is most striking: it is reasonable to ascribe it to the combined effects of *England's Appeal* and the realization that James was a Catholic. The general feeling that the danger to English trade and religion was much greater from France than from Holland was perhaps most effectively expressed by Sir William Coventry, and most movingly put by Sir Henry Capel, whose father had been beheaded in 1649 for his efforts for Charles I in the Second Civil War. 'If this war was for the maintenance of the Crown and nation, would venture all he has, life and fortune, for it: He is descended from one that lost his life for maintaining of both.'

The debate was brought to an end by a skilful stroke by Sir William Coventry, whose opinion always carried great weight in the House. After an attack on the inadequate assistance which the French navy had given off the Texel, which he regarded as ample justification for England making a separate peace, he suggested that to the motion that no money should be given until the end of the eighteen months covered by the previous grant (i.e. until the autumn of 1674), there should be added the words 'unless it shall appear that the obstinacy of the Dutch shall make a supply necessary'. To an impartial observer these words seem those of a responsible leader desiring to prevent the Dutch from using the Commons' vote to insist on unreasonable terms, but Colbert characteristically regarded it as merely a trick to make Parliament the judge of Dutch obstinacy. At all events, this addition enabled all parties to agree on the motion without more ado. If Henry Coventry and the small body of ministerialists would have liked some more positive assistance, they realized that this was the most for which they could hope from the House in its present mood.[1]

The debate had satisfied the greatest hopes of the Dutch. As Colbert reported on 10 November, the House had shown itself convinced that the purpose of the joint attack on Holland was to be able to restore Catholicism to the country the more easily and this opinion was so widespread that it was no longer questioned. Copies of the Commons' vote were immediately printed, and some of the Prince of Orange's household were reported to believe that the people of England wished William were their king, 'that the Duke of York nor any of his shall ever be able to succeed; that the Parliament would wish he were already upon the throne; and those about him hope great fortunes upon these expectations . . . and that some in England think on the carrying on of this design, being enemies to the King of England's person and family. . . .'[2] To many people it seemed a golden opportunity

1 Grey, ii. 197–213; *Dering*, pp. 157–8; Colbert to Louis XIV, 3/13, 17/27 Nov.
2 de Vic to Arlington, 25 Nov./5 Dec. (from Cologne), S.P. 81/67, f. 232. Cf. a previous letter, 15/25 Aug., S.P. 81/63, f. 125.

for the Dutch to make a definite offer of peace to Charles II: Charles might be induced by his difficulties with his Parliament to accept a reasonable offer, or, if he did not accept it, public opinion would become even more hostile. As a matter of fact, the Marquis del Fresno had already before the debate written to say that it was time to offer peace by yielding 'the flag', a war indemnity both for England and France, and the surrender of Surinam. When Don Bernardo passed on the contents of the Marquis's letter to the Pensionary Fagel, he added that this was not the Marquis's own idea but had been suggested to him 'from elsewhere'—from someone whose identity is unknown. There is no definite evidence that the Dutch had decided to make such a peace offer, but in the early days of November it was 'confidently diffused' among members of the House of Commons that the Spanish ambassador was actually in possession of proposals from the Dutch which would shortly be made public.[1]

If that was the case, the plans of the Marquis del Fresno and the Dutch were forestalled by Charles. On hearing what had happened in the Commons on 31 October, Charles realized that there was no hope of getting the House to vote new taxes in the immediate future, and in order to deal with this situation he decided on measures rather more drastic than was his wont and confided them to the French ambassador.

His first decision was to prorogue Parliament until shortly after Christmas to give members time to cool off a little. Rumour said that there was a long discussion in Council on whether to prorogue Parliament or to dissolve it,[2] but Charles knew well enough that in the prevailing state of public opinion new elections would produce a more hostile House and not a more favourable one. As the House of Lords had adjourned until Tuesday, 4 November, the prorogation could not take place until then, and this gave the Commons the time, on Monday, to resolve to address the King on the subject of the standing army which had been raised for the long-planned invasion of Zeeland. Behind the usual complaints about

---

[1] Huygens den zoon, *Journaal*, printed in *Werken van het Historisch Genootschap*, Utrecht, 2ᵉ serie, IV (1881), p. 18; Arlington to Jenkins and Williamson, 17 Nov., S.P. 81/67, 162–3; Colbert to Louis XIV, 10/20 Nov.

[2] T. Derham to Williamson, 5 Nov., in *Letters to Williamson*, ii. 61.

billeting and military law, and that 'this army has the youth
of the nation; it debauches them, and fills them with such
principles, that towns by them are debauched', there lay the
fear that this army might be used inside England for purposes
that no one knew. Arlington was afraid that that same afternoon he would be the first of the King's counsellors to be
denounced by name, but he was mistaken.[1]

On 4 November the members assembled at 8 a.m. as
arranged, but the Speaker, Seymour, did not arrive until 10.
Having been 'called to the Chair by a great voice, he at last
took the Chair', and Sir Robert Thomas moved to consider
'the business of evil counsellors, as a grievance', and named
Lauderdale. 'The word was no sooner out of his mouth, but
the Black Rod knocked at the door', and the Commons
flocked up to the other House, to find Charles there waiting
to prorogue them, after a few short words:

> I think it necessary to make a short recess, that all good men may
> recollect themselves against the next meeting, and consider whether
> the present posture of affairs will not rather require their applications
> to matters of religion, and support against our only competitors at sea,
> than to things of less importance; and in the meantime, I will not be
> wanting to let all my subjects see, that no care can be greater than my
> own, in the effectual suppressing of Popery. . . .

What these words meant would appear before the House sat
again on 7 January: in the meantime the prorogation came
as a surprise, for it had been thought that Charles's need for
money was urgent.[2] All the opposition could do was to take
a full part in the following day's proceedings, celebrating the
anniversary of Gunpowder Plot. M.P.s met in St. Margaret's,
no longer as a House, but as individuals, to hear Stillingfleet
preach to them. At six o'clock, in the Poultry, a play called
The Burning of the Whore of Babylon was acted, 'with great
applause', 'with a relation of their matchless devilish Gunpowder Plot and their oath of secrecy; also the Priests' and
Jesuits' prayer for the good success of this damnable plot':
copies were later printed by 'R. C.' And after dark there were
more bonfires than in thirty years previously, more than two

---

[1] Grey, ii. 215–22; *Dering*, pp. 159–61; Colbert to Louis XIV, 3/13 Nov.
[2] Grey, ii. 222–3; *L.J.* xii. 593; Arlington to Jenkins and Williamson, 4 Nov.,
S.P. 105/221, f. 387.

hundred between Temple Bar and Aldgate, and 'the young fry made the effigies of popes, carried them in procession, and there burnt them'.[1]

In this way there was a great demonstration of anti-Papist opinion, but no more action was possible now that Parliament was no longer sitting. Within a week of the prorogation there followed a second shock in the dismissal of Shaftesbury from his position of Lord Chancellor. Charles had probably never trusted him, but by skilful handling he had been able to make good use of his abilities, hoodwinking him on the Secret Treaty of Dover and employing him in preparation for the war. By November 1673, however, Shaftesbury was believed to be intriguing with the parliamentary opposition both in England and in Scotland, and perhaps with the Spaniards and Dutch as well, and he was now no longer an asset but a liability. By dismissing him Charles would show that he intended to punish disloyalty of any kind, and he would also make it clear that he disapproved of Shaftesbury's pet scheme of a divorce for him to exclude James from the succession: and perhaps it was also necessary to get rid of Shaftesbury so that Charles could adopt a new policy of strict Anglicanism, against the Dissenters whom Shaftesbury patronized, as well as against the Catholics.

On 9 November, therefore, Charles sent for the Great Seal from Shaftesbury, and instead promoted the Attorney-General, Sir Heneage Finch, to be the Lord Keeper. During the month that followed there were several rumours of a reconciliation between Charles and Shaftesbury, who was even offered a large French bribe to rejoin Charles's service; but though Charles may have had some misgivings about his action, for Shaftesbury might be a dangerous opponent, he had now determined to put his confidence in other men and in other measures.[2]

From November 1673 onwards Charles depended on an alliance between the Lord Treasurer (whom we shall call by the title he received in 1674, Earl of Danby), the Lord

[1] Sir T. Player to Williamson, 10 Nov., *Letters to Williamson*, ii. 67; Charles Hatton to L. Hatton, 6 Nov., *Hatton Correspondence*, i. 119; *C.S.P.D. 1673–5*, p. 8.

[2] Colbert to Louis XIV, dispatches of Nov. 1673, also those of the Venetian ambassador (based on James) in *C.S.P.Ven. 1673–5*, pp. 175–7, 183.

Keeper, Finch, and the Speaker, Seymour (who had great influence with many west-country M.P.s). Through them he hoped to win back the support of the body of moderate ex-Cavaliers who had been alienated by the favour he had shown to Roman Catholics, by means of a return to a policy of strict Anglicanism which would show that their fears of Popery at Court were unfounded. The 'Catholicizing' clauses of the Secret Treaty of Dover were abandoned for the rest of the reign in an endeavour to build up Cavalier and Anglican support in the House of Commons.[1] On 20 November a proclamation forbade all Papists and Recusants, excepting the Queen's servants, to come to Court, and ordered that the laws against them were once more to be enforced.

Charles hoped that these measures would make the House of Commons more amenable when it met again in January. At the same time he sought to play William and Du Moulin at their own game of influencing public opinion by means of judicious propaganda. Du Moulin had written the letter from the States-General to Charles, dated 15/25 October, with the deliberate intention of distributing copies in London to foster anti-French sentiment: Charles now reprinted the letter, and added his own reply, dated 7/17 November, hoping that he could thus show up the deceitfulness of the Dutch by answering them point by point, also for the benefit of public opinion.

The letter begins by pointing out that the original Dutch letter was rather a manifesto, as was indicated by its means of delivery by a 'trumpeter' at a time when ambassadors of the two countries were having daily meetings at Cologne: perhaps the Dutch did not really want a reply, but a reply is necessary to maintain Charles's honour and undeceive those who might have been taken in. Charles's letter then follows the same plan as the Dutch, claiming to answer all its arguments one by one. There is a long section on the disputes over Surinam, the East Indies, and the flag, designed to prove that in 1670–2 the Dutch had made no serious attempt to satisfy his just grievances: the arguments are specious enough for those who did not know that Charles had planned war

[1] For the building up of this alliance see Conway's letters to Essex at this time, in *Essex Papers,* vol. i.

earlier in 1669–70, but, in view of our knowledge today of the Secret Treaty of Dover, it is scarcely necessary to discuss them in detail. One feels that even in 1673 they must have shown how attenuated were the issues dividing the two countries.

There follows a similar section designed to show that the Dutch efforts to secure peace since the outbreak of war had also been insincere. The deputies who were sent to Hampton Court had had no authority to make proposals, but only to hear what England wanted: it was all a device to try to gain time while the Dutch tried to negotiate a separate treaty with France. (This was an ingenious attempt to turn Du Moulin's argument that France had then been ready to desert England and make a separate peace.) The Dutch had delayed the opening of a peace conference for several months until their choice of Cologne for it had been accepted. The Spanish ambassadors had never made any peace proposals on their behalf, but had only uttered general hopes of peace, which Charles shared. Nor had the Prince of Orange made any overtures (Charles knew that he could safely pass over William's unofficial emissaries). The whole letter of 15/25 October had been deliberately manufactured to deceive the Dutch and English peoples, as was indicated by the fact that while the States-General were urging Charles to make a separate peace, they were saying that they themselves could not leave their own allies. While the English ambassadors had abandoned many of their demands at Cologne, the Dutch had made no reply save on the question of the flag, which they were disposed to grant in very ambiguous terms. The letter of 15/25 October itself had made no firm proposals, but had merely expressed a very general desire for peace. If there was a genuine Dutch desire to bring the war to an end, let them send to their representatives at Cologne authority to draw up equitable articles of peace.[1]

Charles certainly made the best of a bad case, but he was too late to destroy the powerful feeling against Louis XIV which had grown up in the previous nine months, and it was becoming daily more probable that he would be unable to continue the war in 1674. At the end of November 1673 he

[1] See p. 130, n. 1.

told Ruvigny, whom Louis XIV had sent over to assist Colbert, that he, James, and Arlington were the only three people in the country who still sincerely wanted an alliance with France. He went on to say that he realized that his crown and his safety depended on the French alliance, and that he would do all in his power by cutting down expenditure to continue the war, doing without the assistance of Parliament if necessary. But shortly afterwards the Lord Treasurer Danby, and Samuel Pepys and others from the Navy Office, demonstrated that it would cost £1,400,000 to fit out the fleet for a year, and that all the revenue for 1674 had already been anticipated; so that on 25 November Charles had to confess to Colbert that it would be quite impossible to continue the war unless the House of Commons voted him more money. Colbert, in reply, attributed this to evil counsellors who wanted to persuade Charles to be guilty of a disgrace (*bassesse*) unworthy not only of a great King, but of any gentleman or man of honour, by falsely arguing that it was impossible to fight on. Nettled by these aspersions on servants whom he knew to be loyal, Charles insisted that he had not the money to equip even twenty ships, and went to the length of suggesting that Danby and Colbert should go through the accounts together to prove it—a remarkable offer to admit a foreign ambassador into the most intimate secrets. Finally, Charles went away to play tennis, saying that he would do all in his power to fight another campaign, and that only the sheer impossibility of doing this would make him default on his obligations to Louis XIV: and this, with the implication that it might well prove to be impossible, probably represented Charles's attitude at the end of November.[1] In the next fortnight there was much clutching at straws, but the general mood of Charles and his ministers, Louis and his ambassador, was one of pessimism.

In the meantime, the Dutch and the Spaniards had also been considering the situation created by the debate of 31 October and the prorogation of 4 November. No sooner had that prorogation taken place, than messengers hastened away to report to The Hague and Brussels. The first of these messengers was 'a tall lean man, goes by the name of Mr.

[1] Colbert to Louis XIV, 27 Nov./7 Dec.

Freeman': according to the information which Arlington received he had come over to England with Howard at the end of September, ready for the parliamentary session, and returned to Holland in November with two more in his company (probably 'Nic. Smyth' and another), 'which gives jealousies that they do pass to and again, carrying on Dutch designs'. 'Mr. Freeman's' business in Holland may have been more than simply to describe what had happened in London, for at the beginning of December the English agent in Brussels, Bulstrode, reported that the Spanish governor, Monterey, 'sticks not to say and affirm in confidence, that some deputies have been underhand sent from the leading members in Parliament, to assure the Hollanders, they will induce His Majesty to break his alliance with France, and this is the main thing they depend on here'.[1] Whether or not 'Mr. Freeman' carried such specific assurances from leaders of the opposition in the Commons, it can safely be inferred that he did predict to Du Moulin that Parliament would act in that way; and, having given his information to Du Moulin, he and his two companions remained in The Hague until the time came for them to return to London with their instructions at the beginning of the January parliamentary session.

By now the English government was well aware that a group of exiles at The Hague was plotting against it in combination with the Dutch, and one of its spies, James Puckle, was specially sent to The Hague to keep watch on them. He reported that William Howard was there, 'and is frolic', and 'the other three persons . . . as busy as bees'; and in a later and longer letter expanded the group to include Howard, Carr, 'Mr. Freeman', Du Moulin, 'with 2 more whose names are so often changed as I can't advise you certainly'. But beyond the facts that their business was 'to carry on the designs of the States in bringing about a peace by the Parliament' (which was already suspected) and that Howard and Carr were rewarded by passes permitting English ships to enter Dutch ports without molestation (giving the 'ill-affected' subjects of Charles II the opportunity to cross and

[1] James Puckle to Arlington, 25 Nov., in S.P. 84/195, f. 104; Bulstrode to Arlington, 4/14 Dec., in S.P. 77/43, f. 187.

recross the Channel) Puckle was not able to supply more precise information of what these men were doing or indicate how they could be prevented. Arlington could only wait and see what happened.[1]

In the meantime, however, the Marquis del Fresno had also sent his messenger over to report what happened in the autumn session. The English agent Bulstrode was travelling through Flanders early in November, when he was

overtaken by a Spanish gentleman who spoke very good English and came in great haste express from the Marquis del Fresno to his Excellency the Count Monterey. I rode some miles with him, and he told me he brought the welcomest news to his Excellency that could be imagined, which was that the Parliament would give the King no supply till they were satisfied the obstinacy of the Dutch should make it necessary. . . .

Looking over the shoulder of this 'black man with pockholes in his face', as he wrote a letter to the Marquis del Fresno, Bulstrode saw him sign himself Fonseca.[2] This was the Spanish consul in London, a man known to be friendly with members of the House of Commons and with merchants in the City who feared the disruption of the valuable Spanish trade. Some years later, when a suitable opportunity came Charles's way, he was actually expelled from England on a charge of holding undiplomatic conversations with members of the parliamentary opposition.

When Fonseca returned to London a fortnight later the Spanish ambassador sent him to give an account of his journey to Arlington, nominally to reassure him that no plots were being hatched, but also with another purpose which will shortly appear. According to the account which Fonseca gave, he reported to the Spanish governor in Brussels, Monterey, that Parliament was favourable to them, and urged Monterey to get the Dutch to seize the opportunity to offer peace terms sufficiently advantageous to separate England from France. Monterey sent him to press his case in person at The Hague, where he had conversations with Don Bernardo de Salinas, Fagel, and van Beuningen, but (said Fonseca) the Dutch were now so pleased with the way events were

---

[1] James Puckle to Arlington, 29 Dec. and 1 Jan. (? O.S.), in S.P. 84/195, ff. 118, 121.   [2] 9/19 Nov., S.P. 77/43, f. 134.

developing that they were not now prepared to make any concessions at all: the entry of Spain into the war had led at last to the withdrawal of the French army from its exposed position in the Dutch territory which it had seized, Charles II had no money to continue the war, and so the Dutch no longer needed peace so urgently. Nevertheless, Fonseca went on, Spain would use her influence with Holland to secure a favourable peace offer, if Charles would do his best to get Louis XIV to return to the frontiers of the Peace of the Pyrenees (giving up his conquests in 1668).[1]

This was altogether an extravagant hope, but it served to emphasize the confidence of the Dutch as a preliminary to another offer of peace. On 10 December the Marquis del Fresno presented certain proposals to Charles, to which he undertook that the States-General would be prepared to consent. They comprised principally the recognition by the Dutch of England's claims regarding the saluting of her flag, mutual recognition of conquests, and the payment by the Dutch of a war indemnity of 800,000 patacoons. Charles's reply was not an immediate refusal of these terms; instead, he claimed in addition 'an equal and reciprocal regulation of trade in the East Indies', permission for Englishmen in Surinam to leave, and an admission by the Dutch that they could not fish off the British coasts without a British licence.[2] But more important than the addition of these extra terms was the fact that Charles referred them all to the Cologne peace conference for discussion. That meant that peace with Holland on these terms could only come as part of a general settlement, for which neither the Dutch nor the French were eager: and indeed Arlington told Colbert that the purpose of the King's answer was simply to defeat the Spanish ambassador's object of embroiling the King with his Parliament by evading his proposals.[3] Charles was still clinging to his French alliance, determined not to make a separate peace with Holland until he was absolutely forced to relax his hold by the sheer inability to fight on; and between his view that there should be a general peace including his ally Louis XIV

[1] Colbert to Louis XIV, 27 Nov./7 Dec. 1673.
[2] Printed in T. Bebington, *Arlington's Letters* (1701), ii. 450–7.
[3] Colbert to Louis XIV, 15/25 Dec. 1673.

or none, and William's desire for a separate peace to enable him to concentrate against Louis XIV, no compromise was possible, however slight the difference between the actual proposals put forward by each. Sir William Temple summed up the situation when he wrote that 'the answer to the Spanish ambassador's memorial came out in the style which is by all interpreted to signify no peace but in conjunction with France. . . . The short of our present story seems to be that the Court will upon no terms fall out with the French alliance, and the Nation will upon no terms fall in with it. . . .'[1]

Certainly to refer the Spanish ambassador's proposals to Cologne meant in effect that they were shelved, for a complete deadlock had now arisen there on the question whether representatives of the Duke of Lorraine, whose territories had long been occupied by French troops, should be admitted into negotiations there. Williamson considered Dutch support of the Duke to be 'a studied obstacle . . . to keep us all here at a bay' while they endeavoured to bring about a separate peace with England at London; on the other hand, the Dutch were able to argue that as they were in alliance with the Duke of Lorraine the French insistence that Lorraine was a matter solely between him and Louis XIV was unreasonable. The obstacle could easily have been circumvented if there had been a genuine desire for peace on both sides, but Louis XIV, having failed in Holland, was determined now to secure compensation from the Spanish Netherlands, while the Dutch were determined to yield nothing and wait for events to develop in London. As Williamson saw clearly, nothing of importance was likely to happen at Cologne until Parliament met. 'God Almighty give us good news of the 7 Jan. for that is looked upon by all the world as the great crisis to all our business here. I beseech God put it into the hearts of the House of Commons to be wise. . . .'[2]

In the meantime, however, human agencies were also at work influencing the hearts of the House of Commons. The propaganda continued steadily on both sides. As has been seen, Charles had adopted the same methods as his oppo-

---

[1] Temple to Essex, 25 Dec., *Essex Papers*, i. 154.
[2] Williamson to Arlington, 5/15 Dec. 1673, S.P. 105/221, f. 440; Williamson to Coventry, 19/29 Dec., S.P. 105/225, f. 24.

nents, in causing his letter of 7/17 November to the States-General to be printed, and Arlington had expressed the belief that this had brought some of the most reasonable members back to their duty. The States-General did not immediately reply, but a report (false as it turned out) reached London that the States had 'voted that the King was very sharp and obstinate', and this was promptly printed in the official *London Gazette*, and, in the words of the clerk in the office of the Secretary of State,

what I did was not without order, and without any design further than to show the insolence of the Dutch according as our advices gave it us from abroad, without adding or diminishing . . . yet it seems we have a great many people here amongst us that will by no means be brought to have the opinion of our enemies they deserve, and seem to believe that this story was coined here at Whitehall to injure these good people. The Parliament storm at no rate, and pretend to be highly offended, and that the business shall be fully examined at their next sessions, they thinking themselves very much concerned because it was said in the Gazette that the Dutch would draw up propositions for peace, and send them to the principal members of the Parliament and endeavour what they could do that way.

Evidently the Dutch propagandists had so long a lead that the insinuations of their opponents were not believed, and recoiled upon their authors.[1]

Both the Spanish ambassador's proposals of 10 December and Charles's answer to them rapidly became public property. The first public reaction to the proposals seems to have been favourable, especially on the part of 'the Parliament men, who daily discourse of no longer continuance of the war', and some even thought that it ought to be regarded as a grievance if they were not accepted. Charles therefore took care that his answer should be immediately 'communicated to all the Spanish merchants, public ministers, and persons of note in town . . . and therefore they say, that it may give the general satisfaction, it shall be printed . . . it makes now the talk of peace grow very hot again and is a very pleasing sound in most people's ears'.[2]

In the meantime, Du Moulin's pen had not been idle. It

---

[1] R. Yard to Williamson, 12 Dec., *Letters to Williamson*, ii. 94–95.
[2] 17–19 Dec., ibid. 99, 101, 103.

had never been intended to leave unanswered Charles's letter of 7/17 November to the States-General. A draft reply exists in Du Moulin's papers and in his handwriting, consisting almost entirely of a detailed treatment of Charles's statement of the disputes about Surinam, the flag, East Indies trade, and so on;[1] but for some reason this plan was abandoned in favour of a change of tactics. Only a few sentences of the actual letter of the States-General, dated 9/19 December, correspond with Du Moulin's original draft.

The letter opens by thanking Charles for the honour of his letter of 7/17 November,

but we cannot but let you know at the same time, how much we are troubled to see Your Majesty so prepossessed against us; and that those Ministers whom you most trust have hitherto had the skill to influence Your Majesty so far, as we see they have done, by persuading you to aver so many things which they supposed were out of your memory, and which they knew in their consciences to be contrary to all truth.

For this reason, Sir, we do not think fit to give a particular answer to all the heads of the letter Your Majesty hath written to us, that we may not give a new occasion to those that have so possessed Your Majesty to exasperate you further, but . . . we shall satisfy ourselves with declaring here unto Your Majesty, that as we have alleged nothing in the letter we had written to Your Majesty, whereof we have not in our hands authentic and undeniable proofs, so we shall be ready at all times to produce them before Your Majesty wheresoever you will be pleased to give us a fitter opportunity for it. And withal since Your Majesty (supposing that what information you had received from your ministers, was more faithful) hath complained to your Parliament of our obstinate averseness to peace . . . to let Your Majesty and all the kingdom see that we do not affect to speak of peace (as is laid to our charge) without really desiring the same, and that we are far from intrenching ourselves within general words without coming to any particular overtures [as Charles had alleged], we are ready to renew with Your Majesty the treaty which you concluded with us at Breda in the year 1667. . . ,

with a favourable amplification of article 19, relating to the flag. In regard to allegations that 'various injustices' have been committed, the Dutch are prepared to send ambassadors, 'to give you a more faithful account of the truth than you have received from our enemies', to examine these complaints, with a promise that satisfaction is to be given for all injuries; and in order that peace shall not be delayed in the meantime, this promise is to be guaranteed by Spain.

After this preliminary offer of a renewal of the Treaty of Breda, the greater part of the letter is devoted to showing that there would be nothing dishonourable in England making a separate peace with Holland without caring about any obligations to Louis XIV. Whereas the Dutch could not forsake their allies without being guilty of the highest ingratitude, Charles could, because the war, from being an attack on Holland alone, had become a general one, involving especially the Spanish Netherlands 'for the preservation of which Your Majesty hath always appeared so zealous'. Moreover, Louis XIV had never sought anything but his own private advantage, and had himself been prepared to negotiate separately, especially just when Charles was refusing to deal with the Dutch deputies at Hampton Court (a favourite argument of Du Moulin's). 'For a final proof of the obligations your Allies have laid upon Your Majesty' (equally characteristic sarcasm) reference is made to the disloyal behaviour of the French fleet at the battle of the Texel, as represented by Prince Rupert himself. A last argument in favour of a separate peace, taken almost word for word from Du Moulin's original draft, is that the Cologne conference is at an 'absolute stop' owing to the obstinate refusal of the French to grant passes to the ministers of the Duke of Lorraine, a Dutch ally, and to admit him into the negotiations.

We conceive hopes that if Your Majesty will never so little reflect upon [our offer] you will own that nothing beyond it can be demanded of us with any justice, not being able to persuade ourselves, neither that Your Majesty would without need, as well as without advantage, countenance any longer the arms of the French . . . nor to endanger still both all Europe and the Protestant religion. We'll expect with great impatience Your Majesty's resolution, upon which the rest and prosperity of so many nations doth depend.[1]

This letter may be regarded as the third speech in a public debate following which a vote was to be taken when the

---

[1] *A Letter from the States-General . . . to the King of Great Britain: Dated 9/19 December 1673.*

House of Commons met in January. There can have been no hope that the proposal to return to the Treaty of Breda would satisfy Charles, and the tone of the letter throughout was polemical rather than conciliatory. Circumstances made its purpose even clearer. The original letter was sent from Holland to the Marquis del Fresno for him to deliver to Charles or his Secretary of State, Arlington; and simultaneously Du Moulin and his colleagues began to smuggle over printed copies for distribution in London. The Marquis, however, was dissatisfied with the letter when he read it. As a diplomat of the old-fashioned school, he disliked it: it seemed to go far beyond the ordinary language sanctioned by diplomatic convention. For other reasons also he desired more moderation from the States-General, for it was to be expected that Louis XIV, having completed the withdrawal of his troops from Holland, would turn his attention to the Spanish Netherlands in the next campaign and burst upon it with tremendous fury. No inundations could save Flanders from the French armies, as they had saved Holland, and it was therefore important not to embitter Charles too much and destroy any chance of his support in the traditional English interest of keeping Flanders out of French hands. So the Marquis withheld the letter, and instead of delivering it he wrote back to The Hague suggesting certain modifications in its language. But the Dutch agents in London began to distribute their printed copies, being quite unaware of this; and the result was that these copies were being passed from hand to hand in London, 'given up and down here to such persons as they fancy are discontented with the present posture of affairs', about Christmas, some fortnight before the original reached the King. The letter was actually delivered to Arlington on 8 January, the day after Parliament met, many copies in the meantime 'having been sent in packets to several members of the House of Commons'. Sir William Coventry, having opened his packet, took it straight to the Lord Keeper to indicate his disgust at such methods on the part of the Dutch, and his refusal to be involved in anything disloyal: but other members were not so fastidious.[1]

[1] W. Bridgeman to Williamson, 26 Dec. 1673, *C.S.P.D. 1673–5*, p. 69; Arlington to Jenkins and Williamson, 29 Dec., S.P. 81/69, f. 123; J. Richards to William-

Williamson's clerk Bridgeman gave it as his opinion that 'I do not find any great smartness in it, nor do I believe it will or can have any effect among wise and sober men, not pretending so much as to answer any part of the King's reply'. He was soon to be disillusioned about the effects of Dutch propaganda; but others more exalted than he were hoping against hope that the House of Commons would prove more amenable when it met on 7 January. One of the purposes for which Louis XIV had sent over the Huguenot Ruvigny to assist and soon to supersede his ambassador Colbert, was so that he could utilize his English family connexions and French money to form a pro-French party in the House; and Ruvigny hoped to have the support of a powerful faction led by Lord Ogle (son of the Duke of Newcastle) and Lord Berkley. Colbert's dispatches also show that both Charles and Arlington thought that the House might be better disposed as a result of the new religious policy adopted in November. Charles was equally optimistic about his chances when he chatted at Court to an old acquaintance of ours, Sir Gilbert Talbot, who had now given up his diplomatic career but retained a place at Court and a seat in the House. On the eve of the meeting Sir Gilbert wrote to Williamson describing the situation as he, a courtier and friend of Arlington's and Williamson's, saw it—though there is no hint that he knew that his former subordinate on the Copenhagen embassy was now organizing Dutch propaganda.

His Majesty hath good hope that the satisfaction which he hath given in point of Popery (by banishing all recusants from his Court, except the Queen's servants), and in securing the property of the subject, which were the two great grievances, will allay the spirits of the malicious; but for my part I fear the ill humours will break out when we embody. . . . Some few well-meaning people of us do cabal as formerly to try if we can find a way to divert the storm that threateneth, but there are so many cabals of the malicious to countermine our counsels that my fears far exceed my hopes. . . . Yet neither would our condition possibly be so desperate, did not some of His Majesty's own intimates help to blow the coal . . . at our last meeting the Duke of Bucks' name was started as a pernicious minister, since which time he hath so personally courted all the Members in town, the debauchees

son, 9 Jan., *Letters to Williamson*, ii. 107; R. Bulstrode to Williamson, 5 Jan., S.P. 77/44, f. 8*b*; del Fresno to the States-General, 9/19 Jan., in R.A. Fagel 252, f. 155.

by drinking with them, the sober by grave and serious discourses, the pious by receiving the sacrament at Westminster, that he thinketh he hath gained a strong party of friends; and because he is of opinion that the Parliament must have a sacrifice to appease them, his greatest endeavour with all men (next to the clearing of his own innocency) is to characterise the Lord Arlington for the most pernicious person in His Majesty's counsels; but I hope we shall spoil his design, for we have a petition to be presented against him in the Lords' House for the death of the Earl of Shrewsbury and the scandalous cohabitation with his wife, and at the same time, an impeachment against him in our House for none of the meanest crimes. . . .[1]

At this crisis in the King's affairs the old rivalry between Arlington and Buckingham flared up again. The influence of both men was fast declining, but this last round in their rivalry might well prove to be the most dangerous for Charles. Buckingham was trying to save himself from attack in the Commons by using Arlington as a scapegoat; on the other hand, Talbot and Arlington's other friends proposed to retaliate by appealing to dislike of Buckingham's morals as well as his political past. Not content with committing adultery with the Countess of Shrewsbury, he had fought a duel with her husband and killed him (with the Countess present, so it was said, disguised as a page, holding Buckingham's horse), had openly lived with the Countess while his own wife was still alive, and had buried their infant son in Westminster Abbey. The morals of the Restoration were easy, but this was going too far.

While most of the blame for this rivalry between Arlington and Buckingham can probably be placed on the latter, the same could not be said about the rivalry between Arlington and Danby. Arlington never forgave Danby for taking the post of Lord Treasurer which he had himself coveted, and lost no opportunity of telling the French ambassador that Danby was hostile to the French, and was not telling the truth when he said that another campaign could not be waged because even parliamentary assistance could not come in time. In short, the ministers' disunity was so great, and their fear of taking action for which they might be held responsible was so lively that, so the Venetian ambassador

---

[1] 2 Jan., *Letters to Williamson*, ii. 105–6.

reported, 'the government is brought to such a state of confusion that the King calls a cabinet council for the purpose of not listening to it; and the ministers hold forth in it so as not to be understood'.[1]

It was a situation in which Charles would need all his political skill to enable him to ride the storm; but events were to show that he was still not entirely without resources.

[1] 12/22 Dec., *C.S.P. Ven. 1673–5*, p. 187.

IX

THE CLIMAX: THE SIGNING OF THE TREATY OF WESTMINSTER, JANUARY–FEBRUARY 1674

IN the opening days of January 1674 all the statesmen of western Europe waited eagerly for news of the meeting of Parliament in London. On its decisions the course of the war and of diplomacy in 1674 would depend. At the end of November 1673 the French army had withdrawn from Utrecht and the centre of the United Provinces; Orange flags were hung out in the streets to welcome the troops of William III, and the great Domkerk reverted once more from the mass to Calvinism. Yet French garrisons still remained in Arnhem, Nijmegen, Maastricht, and other Dutch towns; and if the withdrawal of the French from Utrecht represented an admission by Louis XIV that he could not conquer Holland, it also foreshadowed a vigorous attack on the Spanish Netherlands in the spring. After all, the ultimate object of Louis XIV's invasion of Holland had been to make easier his encroachments on Flanders without Dutch interference; but perhaps now that that invasion had failed, it would be simpler to make a direct attack on the Spanish Netherlands, and also more effective, since the superior French army could not be handicapped here by inundations. Here and in Franche-Comté Louis XIV could retrieve his failure in Holland, and conversely the anti-French coalition could fear that this would be the next step towards French domination of Europe. Much therefore depended on whether Louis could still count on English support, for even if the English could not make a landing from the sea, the very fact that the English navy was at sea would prevent the Dutch from concentrating on giving full support on land to the Spaniards. If Charles II were forced by his Parliament to make peace, it would prevent a serious diversion of Dutch resources from the main struggle.

In December there had been so many rumours in London

that Parliament would be prorogued again on 7 January, that Charles had issued a special proclamation to disprove this, commanding all members to be present at the session. After this, rumour still persisted in saying that the French ambassador was employing every possible method to induce Charles to dissolve Parliament in the belief that a new one would be less hostile to the French alliance:

> Before the meeting of the Parliament Madame Carwell [Louise de la Quérouaille, best known as Duchess of Portsmouth, Charles's mistress] sat upon him in the most efficacious manner with her coats up, for a dissolution, and he swore by Christ and by her —(his new Sacrament) that it should be done. The next morning, she comes to him with an instrument ready drawn, which he refused to sign, alleging that he was drunk when he promised. But afterwards she came to him as he sat in his chair, took up her coats, and fell into his lap, and then again he swore to her as aforesaid to do it, but as before he was drunk with wine so now with his lust, and they have not yet been able to screw him up.[1]

There is no corroboration in the French dispatches of any such attempt 'to Delilah' Charles in this way to secure a dissolution, and we can only regard it as an indication how and for what purposes contemporary gossip thought French influence was being exercised on Charles. Still, it is perhaps worth noting that even the dirty stories of the day were anti-French.

Certainly Charles could not afford either to prorogue or to dissolve Parliament. If he was to retain the friendship of Louis XIV for which he had staked so much, he must make one final effort to get the parliamentary supplies necessary to carry on the war, and either succeed or show Louis that it was quite impossible. (Incidentally, the attempt might also qualify him for another French subsidy instalment.) This meant that he must face Parliament, and the present Parliament, elected in the enthusiasm of 1661, critical as it had now become, was less so than a new one would be, elected in the prevailing discontent and hostility to France.

He relied greatly on the effects of his proclamation of 17 November against Popery, on the reductions which he had made in the strength of the army, and on the efforts of

[1] Unsigned (? 'J. T.' to ? Du Moulin), 20 Jan. 1674, in R.A. Fagel 244.

Danby, Seymour, and Finch to build up on this basis a Court Party of Cavaliers and Anglicans in the Commons. In addition Charles intended to take advantage of the amendment in the previous session, which refused money 'unless the obstinacy of the Dutch shall make it necessary'; he hoped to show that the Dutch had been obstinate, and had made him no serious proposals in the meantime. And lastly he had adopted a suggestion that he should try to win the confidence of the two Houses by showing them the treaty binding him to France, and proving that there were no harmful secret political and religious clauses attached to it. This suggestion had been pressed on him separately by Buckingham (ever anxious to exculpate himself), Danby, and the new French ambassador Ruvigny, none of whom knew of the original Secret Treaty of Dover and its 'Catholic' clauses:[1] it was a very embarrassing suggestion for Charles, who knew of those Catholic clauses only too well, but he finally agreed to offer to produce the later treaty providing only for an attack on Holland, in the hope that his deception would never be discovered. It was a dangerous game to play.

Wednesday, 7 January, duly arrived, and the members of the two Houses assembled to hear the opening speeches of the King and his Lord Keeper. It was estimated that not less than 400 members of the Commons were present, or roughly four-fifths of the House—a remarkably large proportion for the first day of a session in the seventeenth century.[2] Charles's speech was on the lines sketched above: reassurances about religion and property, the argument that as 'no proposals of peace have yet been offered, which can be imagined with intent to conclude, but only to amuse', the only way to a good peace was to fit out a strong fleet, and lastly,

I cannot conclude, without showing you the entire confidence I have in you. I know you have heard much of my alliance with France; and, I believe, it hath been very strangely misrepresented to you, as if there were certain secret articles of dangerous consequence; but I will make no difficulty of letting the treaties, and all the articles of them, without any the least reserve, to be seen by a small committee of both Houses, who may report to you the true scope of them: and

[1] See the French dispatches of 22 Dec./1 Jan. and following dates.
[2] Conway to Essex, 10 Jan., *Essex Papers*, i. 161.

I assure you, there is no other treaty with France, either before or since, not already printed, which shall not be made known.

One observer reported that Charles 'fumbled' in delivering this last part, 'the consultation of many days and nights', and 'made it worse than in the print';[1] however that may be, having uttered this outrageous lie, Charles had sufficient self-possession to end by saying that, 'having thus freely trusted you, I do not doubt but you will have a care of my honour, and the good of the kingdom'.

According to Ruvigny, Charles was heard with great attention, and his speech was received with more applause than had been heard for many years; even Du Moulin's correspondents wrote that it was so much to the satisfaction of members that Charles was 'humm'd up'. He was followed by his Lord Keeper, Finch, the most notable part of whose speech was a skilful account, worthy of the most prominent lawyer of the day, of the Dutch intrigues and propaganda. After criticizing the delaying tactics of the Dutch at Cologne, he said that they hoped to profit from the impatience of the English for peace:

To increase this as much as was possible, they prepare a letter, which they send by a trumpeter, sitting the Parliament, or very near it [that of 15/25 Oct.], and cause it to be given out, that nothing could be more desired than they had offered. His Majesty quickly made that letter, and his answer to it, public; and for that time, defeated the design of this paper stratagem. Their next recourse was, to such proposals as they could procure the Spanish ambassador to deliver on their behalfs.

Not only were these proposals inadequate, but

the Dutch themselves have, since, departed from those very proposals, which they procured the Spanish ambassador so earnestly to recommend: for they afterwards sent the ambassador a reply to His Majesty's answer to their letter; wherein they abate much of what the ambassadors had offered, and seek to reduce things to the state they were in at Breda . . . yet this reply, besides the disrespect it carried to Spain, whose proposals it shrunk from, was so offensive to His Majesty, that the ambassador, like a wise and great minister, that is, like himself, thought it became him to send it back again, without offering to present it. Nevertheless, this paper hath since stolen into the press,

---

[1] Ibid.

and is printed at The Hague, as a letter delivered: and hath since been sent hither, under covers, to several members of the House of Commons, whom they libelled in the former war for their zeal, and now pretend to reverence for their deliberation. . . .

The Commons ought obviously to vote money to fit out a fleet, and so bring the Dutch to their senses and force them to deal fairly.

This address also seems to have found favour, for according to Ruvigny, the Lord Keeper spoke with such eloquence that he was admired by the whole assembly; but when the House of Commons returned to its own chamber, the hopes which the Court Party entertained from such a good beginning were disappointed. Sir Thomas Meres moved that the House should adjourn until the following Monday, 12 January, so that members could have time to consider the speeches, 'being of great concernment'. As Ruvigny foresaw, this gave time for the opposition to plot and strengthen those members of it who had been shaken by the speeches; but still, the Court could expect that the effect of the speeches would not have entirely worn off in five days, and could afford to be more optimistic of getting money for the war than at any time previously.[1]

These intervening five days before the Commons next met, were, however, to be fatal to Charles's hopes. The House of Lords had not adjourned like the Lower House, and, indeed, no sooner had Charles left it after the opening speeches than the attack on Buckingham's immorality began; and on the following day Shaftesbury began once more to stoke up the fires of anti-Popery feeling. He was reported as saying that there were in the neighbourhood more than 16,000 Catholics determined on desperate measures, that no one could be sure of his life as long as these people were at liberty, and that the House should think seriously about the means to prevent a massacre which might take place any day. Almost unanimously the House voted to petition the King to remove all Papists from the neighbourhood of London. On 12 January the peers had a second foretaste of the Popish Plot, when a boy of thirteen was interrogated in their

---

[1] For the opening of Parliament, see *C.J.* ix. 286–9; Grey, ii. 225; Ruvigny to Pomponne, 8/18 Jan.; Conway to Essex, 10 Jan., *Essex Papers*, i. 161.

House. He handed in a paper which he said he had found in the street, and which declared that King and Parliament were in danger of dying by gunpowder or massacre: the writer claimed to be a Catholic belonging to a Catholic household.[1]

The effect of all this was naturally to support those who argued that more effective steps should be taken against Popery before more money was voted; but probably more effective in preventing the passing of a vote for money for the war was the arrival in London of Dutch agents, with instructions and fresh supplies of pamphlets from The Hague to support their case.

Arlington had had warning to expect that some of Du Moulin's coterie at The Hague would be crossing over to England in time for the parliamentary session. His spy in The Hague, James Puckle, had reported this, and himself had crossed by packet-boat to try to waylay them at Dover, and to seize the letters they were bringing.[2] French spies had also informed the French Secretary of State for Foreign Affairs, Pomponne, that a Dutchman was on his way over from Middleburg, bearing letters of exchange, the proceeds of which were presumably intended to corrupt M.P.s. Pomponne immediately dispatched a messenger, de Granville, to carry this news to Colbert in London, so that he could arrange for the man to be intercepted. de Granville seems to have travelled by way of the Spanish port of Nieuport, where on Tuesday the 6th he saw the man in question, and, crossing by the ordinary packet-boat, left him there on the Tuesday evening. Calculating that the man would try to find a ship to take him from Nieuport to Gravesend (as being safer than the packet-boat), but that he would not be able to embark before Wednesday, de Granville hastened on to London and delivered his message to Colbert on the Thursday morning. Colbert immediately went off to tell the King at midday, and he on the spot ordered Arlington's clerk, Bridgeman, to issue the necessary orders for the Dutchman's arrest at Gravesend. That same evening Ruvigny and de Granville went to see Arlington and met him on his return from the House of

---

[1] Ruvigny to Pomponne, dated 11/21 Jan. but probably written early on the 12th (Shaftesbury's name is wrongly written Shrewsbury); *L.J.* xii. 600.
[2] 1 Jan. (? O.S.), S.P. 84/195, f. 121.

Lords. They found to their dismay that Arlington had heard nothing from Bridgeman, whom they put down as 'a great supporter of Spain', but Arlington gave orders to write to the 'Governor' at Gravesend, and de Granville and a servant of Bridgeman's went down to Gravesend with the letter.

de Granville stayed at Gravesend until Saturday the 10th and then returned to London very dissatisfied. He alleged that after Bridgeman's servant had delivered the order to the 'Governor', he had seen him pass another note which he believed to be a counter-order, and said that the examination of travellers who landed had been very slight. The Dutchman had escaped him, so he thought, by the treachery of Charles's servants.

This conclusion, however, was not justified. The truth was that de Granville had been mistaken in several of his calculations. The Dutchman in question was probably Arton, whose imprisonment in the Tower for carrying Du Moulin's letter to Shaftesbury had not modified his political views: he had escaped from the Tower in October 1673 and returned to Holland to join his friend Du Moulin once more. He dared not set foot in England again, however, for obvious reasons, and his journey to Nieuport was not made so that he could cross the Channel himself but only to accompany three English colleagues there and see them safely embarked. While de Granville was concentrating on Arton, 'J. Turner', 'Nic. Smyth' (Trenchard and Medley), and Williams were unnoticed. They went on board some vessel, possibly that of 'Captain George', on the Tuesday, and, sailing 'as if the heavens had designed to blow me home', they were in London on Wednesday evening, the same day as Parliament opened and actually the day before de Granville.[1]

On Friday the 9th, while de Granville was waiting impatiently at Gravesend, the first letters were being sent back to The Hague. Three letters of this date survive, one from 'J. Turner' to Dr. Arton, one from 'J. T.', and one from 'J. Nicholas' to someone unknown;[2] probably the writer in each case was the same, and all three found their way to Du Moulin. Together they give an account of the position in London

[1] Ruvigny to Pomponne, 8/18 and 11/21 Jan.; 'J. Turner' to Dr. Arton, 9 Jan., R.A. Fagel 244.   [2] R.A. Fagel 244.

as they found it: 'my cousin [Charles] is resolved to stick close
to my brother-in-law [James] and Mistress Lloyd [? France]';
'my old neighbour is gone out of town [the House of Commons has adjourned] till Monday next'; people were not sure
whether, when it met again, the House would consider the
King's Speech or fall upon grievances first; and 'that small
parcel of goods which you have consigned to Mr. Speedwell
are come to the best market in the world'. Most of 'J. Nicholas's' letter contains a report of proceedings in the Lords and
an account of an interview given by Charles to some of Lauderdale's Scottish opponents, which shows that the writer must
have had accurate information from someone at Court.

His last sentence is an ironical prayer that 'God keep the
Parliament within due bounds and respect to His sacred
Majesty'. That such a prayer was the very opposite of his
true desires was illustrated by his opening sentence to the
effect that he and his friends had 'disposed of your fine goods
to your old neighbour who is in very good heart and courage,
and I hope he will prove an honest man for all your fears and
doubts'. Indeed, the immediate purpose of their arrival was
this distribution of the contents of 'that small parcel of fine
goods', or in other words copies of pamphlets, to be handed
especially to members of Parliament, 'your old neighbour'.

Foremost among these pamphlets was 'the manifest', or
an *Answer to His Majesty's Declaration of War*. An answer to
Charles's declaration of war and the pretexts put forward in
it had long been a plan of Du Moulin's, and this now appeared
at precisely the critical moment when many M.P.s were uncertain whether or not to accept the arguments of Charles
and his Lord Keeper on 'Dutch obstinacy'. It is a long and
exhaustive statement of the Dutch case on the old grievances
which Charles had brought forward to justify his attack on
the United Provinces: the medals, Surinam, the yacht *Merlin*,
and all the old differences were recapitulated as Du Moulin
demonstrated their inadequacy as *casus belli*, and showed how,
far from the Dutch having been obstinate, it was Charles who
had been unreasonable and (it was implied) determined to
attack whatever the Dutch had done. This comprehensive
reply to the English declaration of war opened the eyes of
many of the London reading public and confirmed the

opinions of others.[1] At the same time there appeared on the scene another pamphlet, a *Relation of the most material matters handled in Parliament, relating to religion, property, and the liberty of the subject* in 1673. This contained a report of the votes of the Houses regarding the Declaration of Indulgence and other controversies and their addresses to the King on these subjects, based on the Journals. The account was linked together by a commentary stressing the danger of Popery and of the French alliance, and was concluded with a set of mock accounts, purporting to describe pensions owing to various ministers and courtiers for their services. From the references to this pamphlet in Du Moulin's correspondence it is not possible to state positively that it was smuggled over from Holland with the manifest, though it appeared at the right moment and fitted in admirably with Dutch policy. It is possible that this *Relation* was written in London; and if, as was suggested in Chapter IV, Marvell was in touch with Du Moulin and writing pamphlets for him, it might conceivably have been his work.

These were not by any means the only pamphlets circulating in London at this time. Older pamphlets were reprinted, sometimes with modifications to bring them up to date; for instance, the famous speech alleged to have been made some years previously by Lord Lucas against the errors and extravagance of the Court was reprinted at Middleburg—with a postscript to show how the French alliance had made matters worse still.

So the 'parcels of fine goods', 'linen', 'tobacco', and other euphemisms for pamphlets multiplied. As Arlington wrote to the ambassadors at Cologne, 'the Dutch libels swarm among us to sow the seeds of sedition; there is a new one dispersed under the title of an Answer to His Majesty's declaration of war, more malicious than all the rest'. Du Moulin's agents were soon writing home glowing accounts of the effect produced and the discomfiture of the King.

'The King was in cabal on Thursday night last, when he said he would give anything to know how or by what means

---

[1] The draft of this pamphlet is in Du Moulin's handwriting, with many emendations, in R.A. Fagel 252, 143; apparently it had been sketched out a month or two previously.

the manifest and the Relation (a terrible new book which he had read, having the same delivered into his hands by a Lord, who had it of a member of the House of Commons but would not say who he was) came out.' Charles was too astute a politician not to realize the importance of this propaganda campaign, and it is significant that in this same week he sent for Evelyn and commissioned him 'to write something against the Hollanders about the duty of the Flag and fisheries'. Evelyn's methods were too slow and scholarly for such a controversy, and his book did not appear until six months later when the issue had long been settled; but the fact that Charles gave him the task is as good an indication as could be wished for that the Dutch were not over-estimating the effect of their pamphlets.[1]

On Wednesday the 7th it had seemed not impossible that the Commons might vote a supply of money to continue the war, at any rate when some of their grievances had been ventilated; but when the House resumed on Monday the 12th after its short adjournment, the supporters of the Court very soon found that the House's temper had become much more unfavourable to them.

There were again more than 400 members present, and their first step was to emphasize their Protestantism in spite of differences and divisions 'chiefly occasioned by the undermining contrivances of Popish recusants', by the traditional method of petitioning the King for a general fast-day. ('How a debauched Court and people relish this you may imagine', remarked Du Moulin's correspondent.) They had then to decide what subject they should next take up, and after a long debate it was resolved that the House would in the first place proceed to have grievances redressed, 'the Protestant religion, our liberties and properties, effectually secured', Popery suppressed, and all counsellors removed who were 'Popishly affected, or otherwise obnoxious or dangerous to the Government'. With regard to the King's Speech, all that the Court Party were able to secure was a resolution of thanks for what had recently been done against Popery, and for the 'gracious promises and assurances' in his speech. This meagre address,

[1] Arlington to Jenkins and Williamson, 12 Jan. S.P. 81/70, f. 122; letter of 20 Jan. in R.A. Fagel 244; Evelyn, *Diary*, 9 Jan. and 19 Aug. 1674.

containing no answer to the demand for money which had been the theme of the speech, was only carried by 191 votes to 139.

Moreover, many of the speeches in the debate made it clear that the principal grievance to be redressed, the principal danger to the Protestant religion, and the principal crime of the evil counsellors, was the French alliance. Sir John Monson derived the Declaration of Indulgence and the favour shown to Popery from Buckingham's diplomatic journey to France in 1670; Russell attacked 'ill ministers [who] have pensions from France, and accuse us of being pensioners to Holland'; Birch 'thinks all in vain, if, by any means, we are incited to carry on this league with France, and war with Holland', quoted the second article of the treaty with France as 'the setting up of the Catholic Religion in every conquered town in Holland', and said, 'we have not had a smile, since the French alliance began'; Clarges advocated 'Religion, after the King's death, secured . . . but the first thing to enter upon, would have "the counsellors"; we have always gracious answers from the King, but they are still intercepted: Proclamation against Papists, and yet Priests are walking in Whitehall in defiance of it; Popish commanders at the head of companies. . . .' When Colonel Roger Whitley and other courtiers finally returned from Westminster 'late and weary', they could anticipate a series of attacks on the King's ministers, based on four points raised by Sir William Coventry:

'1. Who advised the King to break the Triple Alliance.
2. Who advised him to loose the honour of the nation in endeavouring to seize the Dutch Smyrna fleet before war was declared.
3. Who advised him to loose his own honour in shutting up the Exchequer.
4. Who advised him to put out the Declaration for Toleration of Religion.'

The interdependence of foreign and domestic policy was now apparent to all.[1]

The attacks began on the following day, Tuesday the 13th, and were the principal preoccupation of the House for the

---

[1] For 12 Jan. see *C.J.* ix. 291–2; Grey, ii. 225–34; ['J. T.'s'] letter of 20 Jan. in R.A. Fagel 244; *Letters to Williamson*, ii. 108.

rest of the week. Lauderdale was the first to feel their displeasure. An address petitioning Charles to remove him from office as a person proved dangerous and obnoxious to the government was easily carried, for he had very few friends in England, powerful as he was in Scotland. Buckingham was the next to be accused, but he, unlike Lauderdale, was present in London, and planned to save himself by ingratiating himself with the Country Party and putting the blame on his old enemy Arlington as a convenient scapegoat. He offered to waive his privilege as a peer, to come to the bar of the House of Commons to answer questions. This he did on the 13th and again on the 14th trying always to impute the most unpopular decisions of the Cabal to Arlington; but he did not make a very good impression, and an address similar to that against Lauderdale was carried. As 'J. T.' pointed out in his report to Du Moulin, even the Court made little effort to save him, and 'would have been glad to have had him impeached', for it was well known that he had forfeited the royal favour and was approaching the opposition.[1]

From the point of view of the Country Party, the difficulty was that they could only petition Charles to remove the ministers; if Charles chose to ignore their petition there was little that they could do to enforce their wishes. There was a rumour that Lauderdale would indeed be dismissed, and that his authority in Scotland would be taken over by Charles's young illegitimate son, the Duke of Monmouth, as Secretary, 'who though his abilities in the learned art of writing be not so great as some men's, yet out of the store of learned statesmen which the Parliament will I hope mercifully leave us, we shall find him a good amanuensis'. But Du Moulin's correspondent was as wrong here as he was in reporting that Lauderdale had been driven out of Edinburgh by a rising. The truth was that Charles would not give up so reliable a servant as Lauderdale, who had greatly strengthened the royal authority in Scotland.

The only more drastic step open to the Commons would have been to try to impeach the King's ministers before the House of Lords. Impeachment could place even a minister's

[1] *C.J.* ix. 292–3; Grey, ii. 236–70; Ruvigny to Pomponne, 15/25 Jan.; 'J. T.', as in previous note.

life in jeopardy; but the King's influence was naturally stronger in the Upper House, and experience had shown that the peers would find one of their number guilty only on the strongest legal evidence, and certainly not on political considerations. Naturally the Commons could rarely hope to produce evidence of a minister's crimes which would hold good in a law court. Their difficulty was well shown when they came to discuss the case of Arlington, who as the principal architect (outside the royal family) of the French alliance was especially obnoxious to those members of the House who were connected with, or sympathetic to, the Dutch.

Arlington came before the Commons on Thursday, 15 January, to answer the same questions as had been put to Buckingham about his conduct over the past few years. His answers made a much more favourable impression on the House than Buckingham's had done; they seem to have surprised even the friends who hastened to congratulate him afterwards. He contrived to give replies which seemed frank and yet evaded responsibility for acts of policy and advice by ascribing them to the entire Council: here he was on good constitutional ground and he made it very difficult for his opponents to establish any charges against him. One member, Howe, immediately moved that Arlington should be declared innocent. Yet Sir Gilbert Gerrard and Lord Cornbury persisted in their attack, and especially with the most serious of their charges, that he had been guilty of holding correspondence with the King's enemies—a treasonable offence, which would qualify him for impeachment if evidence could be produced to support it. This evidence was to be provided by 'a person beyond sea'.

There were numerous conjectures who this 'person beyond sea' might be, especially one Captain Palden, then abroad, and a client of the Duke of Buckingham. But Arlington's greatest enemy 'beyond sea' was obviously his former protégé with the passion for revenge, Du Moulin. There is no evidence that Du Moulin's name was actually mentioned in the House, as was Palden's, but 'J. T.' says specifically, in a letter of 23 January, that 'some have proposed to the Parliament men that a way may be found out that one Du Moulin may come over with safety to impeach Arlington'. Four months later, when Williamson was passing through Holland on his way back from Cologne, he was told the same by William Carr: Du Moulin was to come to England, with a promise of safety from 'the Parliament men', and testify to 'what Puffendorf told him Koningsmark, the then Swedish ambassador at Paris, had told him (Puffendorf) as said by the King of France, that Colbert the French ambassador had writ him about Lord Arlington, i.e. that having told him the munificences of the King of France his master, he the Earl gave into it'. In order to give this ludicrous piece of hearsay evidence at several removes, to prove that Arlington was a French pensioner, Du Moulin tried (so Williamson was told) to pretend to William of Orange that he was going to England to see some French malcontents: but Gabriel Sylvius 'smelt it out and hindered it' in February. In a letter of 6/16 March from 'J. T.' there is some confirmation that Du Moulin had at least mentioned the possibility of his coming over to London for some unspecified purpose.

If there was in fact such a plan to bring Du Moulin over to give this or other evidence against his old patron, certainly nothing came of it, and the attack on Arlington broke down. Lack of evidence, the efforts of the courtiers and his friends in the House led by his brother-in-law Sir Robert Carr, and possibly the good relations which Arlington had taken care to maintain with Shaftesbury rather than the Duke of York, all combined in his favour. Paradoxically enough, after some days' debate, it was Arlington's clientèle in the Commons who wanted an impeachment (and a triumphant acquittal) and his opponents who wanted only an address on the same lines as those against Lauderdale and Buckingham; and on 20 January the former succeeded, by 166 votes to 127, in getting a committee appointed to examine the charges.[1]

Arlington's successful appearance in the Commons on 15 January gave him a flicker of optimism: he 'did not despair' that the House would, after all, vote supplies for the King. In the same letter as he reported this to Williamson,

---

[1] For this attack on Arlington, see Barbour, chap. xii; *C.J.* ix. 293–6; Grey, ii. 270–328; 'J. T.', letters, 20, 23, 27 Jan. in R.A. Fagel 244; *Letters to Williamson* for this period, *passim*; *Essex Papers*, i. 164; Williamson's Journal, 30 Apr., S.P. 105/222; R. Bulstrode to Williamson, 26 Jan./5 Feb., S.P. 77/44, f. 51.

however, Arlington's clerk, Bridgeman, had to admit that 'I find most people here are possessed with an opinion that the Dutch are content to make the peace upon any reasonable terms, so much have the Dutch arrived by their artifices upon the generality of the people, and some no inconsiderable members of the government....'[1] At the same time the Duke of York was complaining of meetings which, he said, were taking place at the house of Lord Holles, attended by Lords Carlisle, Shaftesbury, Falconbridge, and others, to concert the actions of the opposition in the House of Commons. He was so pessimistic that he wanted an early dissolution of Parliament.[2]

The view of the political situation which was held by the Dutch agents is embodied in a very long letter, dated 20 January, and unsigned, but in all probability written by the same 'J. T.' of the many aliases, whose real name was either Trenchard or Medley (see Chapter IV). After his account of events in Parliament in the previous ten days, he goes on,

. . . it is conjectured by the most intelligent, that he [Charles] is firm and resolved to stick to the French League, and that he will try the utmost with the Parliament to see whether he can get any money of them, and it is said they would be contented with £300,000. And whether the Parliament will, when the King has gratified them by giving up all his ministers to them, and consenting to such good laws against Popery etc. as they shall propose, give him money or not, is a great question, and such as no man can resolve, yet . . . we are of opinion, or at least hope no money will be given . . .,

and in any case he doubted whether a fleet could be equipped in time for the spring.

The letter also contains a variety of information about the parliamentary session and other matters, one or two interesting anecdotes (such as that of the lampoon against King Charles which Rochester handed to him by mistake), and some cases where anecdote and information overlap, as in the story of the death of an illegitimate child of the Duke of York's at Chiswick, from whose venereal disease, communicated to the baby's nurse and her husband, is drawn the important deduction that no issue of James's recent marriage

[1] W. Bridgeman to Williamson, 16 Jan., *Letters to Williamson*, ii. 112.
[2] Ruvigny to Pomponne, 22 Jan./1 Feb.

to Mary of Modena is likely to survive to inherit the crown: an important matter for someone so close to the succession as William of Orange. But the letter contains not merely observations on the situation in London, but an account of some of the activities of the writer and his friends, and their suggestions for the future course of Dutch policy.

The letter does in fact begin with a notification of the arrival of the Dutch agents, and their distribution of the 'manifest', which it is said, 'was timed well, it has also had the good effects proposed and hoped for'; so much so, that they had arranged for 'a good impression' of it to be printed off in London to satisfy the demand for it. There had, however, been some slight criticisms of this and the letter of 9/19 December, and to answer these, Trenchard and Medley and their friends had drafted another letter which, they now proposed, should be sent by the States-General to the King by a special 'trumpeter' to Harwich, while copies of it would be printed in London for publication at the same time according to the now well-worn technique. Their draft still survives in Du Moulin's papers.[1] It explains how the letter of 9/19 December came to be printed ('to let the world see the sincerity as well of our endeavours as intentions, and the justice of our arms') before the Spanish ambassador had handed the original to the King; refutes stories that the 'Manifest' of the States-General was so complimentary to the English Parliament that it could not possibly be authentic; and, lastly, asks for a safe-conduct for an ambassador to cross to London, to negotiate a separate peace, with an immediate truce while the treaty was being finally settled. These last 'candid proposals' (*sic*) would, so it was thought, either break the French alliance immediately, or

if it be not accepted it heaps more coals of fire upon their heads. And as the manifest (as it was intended) has satisfied the parliament men, so this will have a special influence upon the merchant and trading part, who will see plainly that it is not the Dutch but the Court who are obstinate . . . and will also . . . keep the parliament men from giving money, and these are not our own opinions, but we have the concurrence of divers others of consideration, with us. . . .

Here we have the clearest possible statement of the tactics

[1] One of seven documents in R.A. Fagel 252, 1466.

which the 'fifth column' was pursuing, and which were said to be approved by 'divers others of consideration'. Among these there was especially one who made some suggestions of his own, 'your friend . . .'; tantalizingly, the name was actually written by 'J. T.' in his letter, and then obliterated by scribbling over it. It seems to have been a short name of six or seven letters at most; and one might hazard a guess that it began with A, were it not that what can be discerned of the shape of the word underneath the scribbling does not seem to fit any known politician with that initial.[1] All that can be said is that 'your friend' was on good terms with 'some Lords of the Council' with whom he had discussed the manifest; he was in a position to say 'That your cousin [Charles] said that Will Howard, Du Moulin and one Medley, Venner's kinsman, are the Cabal that do all these things', and that ship's passes from the Prince of Orange were produced at the Council board, 'on which were entered at the bottom of each, Solicited by Mr. Howard'. Evidently this mysterious friend of Du Moulin's was well placed at Court.

This letter of 20 January,[2] with its draft of another proposed letter from the States-General to Charles, was duly handed to the invaluable 'Captain George', who was prepared to run the risk of smuggling it out of the country and into Holland. By the time it reached Holland, however, the draft had become out of date, and this repetition of previously successful tactics was not in fact required.

It will be remembered that on 10 December the Marquis del Fresno had made peace proposals to Charles which he guaranteed would be accepted by the Dutch; and that Charles answered them by making some additional demands (especially that the Dutch should pay for fishery rights) and referring the negotiation to Cologne. The Spanish ambassador duly communicated this reply to The Hague, and at the same time suggested to his colleague there, Don Bernardo de Salinas, the lines on which it could be answered in its turn. Don Bernardo consulted with the Dutch Council of State, and

[1] Mr. H. Hardenberg, of the Rijksarchief, suggests that the name is 'Andrews', an alias employed by William Howard. There is no certain evidence that Howard was in London at this time, but cf. p. 194 below.
[2] R.A. Fagel 244.

presumably with William; and all Charles's amended terms were accepted, except that the payment of 800,000 rijksdaalders was not to be named a war indemnity because that would admit the justice of Charles's attack, and that they refused to pay anything specifically for permission to fish, but were prepared to increase the figure of 800,000 rijksdaalders for the general payment if that would content Charles. On these lines a new peace offer was drawn up with an accompanying letter from the States-General to Charles, dated 14/24 January; and that it also had William's approval may be safely inferred, not only from its terms, but from the fact that it was again drafted by his own secretary, Du Moulin. This letter, which was substantially in accord with del Fresno's suggestions, was sent to him to be delivered to Charles in that way, as representing terms backed by Spain; and the Spanish ambassador did actually have an audience at Whitehall for this purpose, on 22 January.[1]

The letter was written in the form of an answer to the suggestion made in the King's Speech at the opening of Parliament, that he had received no sincere proposals from the Dutch; and most of it consists of a commentary on the proposed peace terms, justifying each in turn as a reasonable settlement. Charles's demands regarding the fishery are unreasonable and cannot be entertained, and

we cannot believe that . . . you would stop the conclusion [of peace] upon a motive or consideration of this kind, and oblige us to grant what Your Majesty's predecessors have never stipulated in any treaty . . . and of which Your Majesty yourself has not made the least mention, neither in the Treaty of 1662, nor that of 1667; and seeing also that article was never any part of Your Majesty's complaints. . . .

The matter being thus, nothing remains but the perfecting a work already so advanced . . . hoping that Your Majesty will not suffer the quiet of your people, and the good of your kingdoms, to depend upon particular interests of the Crown of France, which continues entirely to stop the conferences at Cologne, by refusing to give passports to the Duke of Lorraine's ministers . . . without other aim but of engaging Your Majesty further and further in this sad war, so destructive to all Europe. . . .

[1] J. Nipho to Williamson, 12/22 Jan. 1674, S.P. 77/44, f. 22; R.A. Fagel 252, 1466; R.A. St.-Gen. 6923; English translation of the letter in *L.J.* xii. 616–18.

Reference is also made to the 'complaints without ground' made in the Lord Keeper's opening speech, but only to say that, though these *could* be answered, 'we believe it better to forget and pass over whatever there might be of animosities and sharpness, than longer to keep open wounds we desire to heal'. These conciliatory professions may at this stage have been genuine: certainly the tone of this letter is considerably less offensive than that of most of Du Moulin's previous compositions: and yet the letter is still so skilfully phrased as to put Charles irretrievably in the wrong should he decline the offer made and continue to refuse a separate peace. It may also have been a sign of conciliation that printed copies of this letter did not appear simultaneously on the streets of London—or it may have been simply that they could not be published in time. Or perhaps it was more effective to allow Charles to realize that it *could* be printed with great success if necessary.

Ruvigny, who had now succeeded Colbert as French ambassador, was sent for as soon as Charles had read the letter, and the King told him that he was not at all satisfied by it. But it put Charles in a very difficult position: if he refused terms which appeared to be so reasonable, he could anticipate that these terms would immediately be made public by the Dutch, and almost everyone inside or outside Parliament would conclude that he was tied hand and foot to Louis XIV in the French interests. Moreover, on this same day anti-French feeling in the House of Commons had again shown its strength.

The House had now concluded its attacks on Charles's ministers, and its leaders proposed that two days later, on Saturday the 24th, the House should begin to discuss 'grievances'. Powle drew particular attention to 'the business of the foreign war, that hangs over our heads, like a comet, threatening destruction'. Clarges 'would not have it [the debate] confined to the "war"; it may introduce "money"; would have that as the Extreme Unction, and have Saturday for our "Grievances"' in general. Sir Thomas Lee was 'not afraid to talk of the "war" [as the subject of debate] for that is the bottom of all our "grievances"; all these thoughts and talks of Popery are from it'. In the end it was Birch who suggested that 'to the end we may have field-room enough', the House should on Saturday consider 'the state of the nation by reason of the war', and it was substantially his suggestion that was adopted. At last the House was beginning to take up the subject of the war which had been the theme of the King's Speech a fortnight previously; but it was turning to it, not, as the Court Party had hoped, to discuss what money supply should be voted, but to debate it in a hostile spirit, as a 'grievance'. It is not surprising that Arlington now made no secret to the French ambassador of his conviction that the States-General had a very strong cabal in the House, so that he did not doubt but that Charles would be forced to accept peace on the conditions proposed in this last letter.[1]

Charles, however, had one last trick at his disposal, before he would agree to admit defeat. Late on Friday the 23rd, at the Committee of Foreign Affairs, he decided that he would submit the Dutch letter of 14/24 January to the two Houses and ask them for their advice on whether or not to accept the terms offered him. This might lead to disagreements among the Country Party, particularly over the fishery, which he might be able to turn to his advantage; and in any case it would bring matters to a head, either eliciting financial support for an attempt to get better terms, or, if the Commons accepted these, finally convincing the French that he could do nothing more and must make a separate peace with Holland.[2]

So on Saturday, 24 January, the day which the House of Commons had appointed for a discussion of the grievances arising out of the war, Charles went to the House of Lords 'in the most splendid manner, Arlington carrying the sword before him', and sent Black Rod to fetch the Lower House; and then said:

At the beginning of this session I told you (as I thought I had reason to do), That the States-General had not yet made me any proposals which could be imagined with intent to conclude, but only to amuse. To avoid this imputation, they have now sent me a letter by the Spanish ambassador, offering me some terms of peace, upon conditions

---

[1] *C.J.* ix. 297; Grey, ii. 335; Ruvigny to Pomponne, 22 Jan./1 Feb.
[2] Arlington to Williamson and Jenkins, 26 Jan., S.P. 81/71, f. 88, and similar letter to Lockhart, ibid., ff. 85–86.

formally drawn up, and in a more decent style than before. It is upon this that I desire your speedy advice: for, if you shall find the terms such as may be embraced, your advice will have great weight with me; and if you find them defective, I hope you will give me your advice and assistance, how to get better terms. Upon the whole matter, I doubt not but you will have a care of my honour, and the honour and safety of the nation, which are now so deeply concerned.

So saying, Charles dismissed the two Houses with copies of the letter of 14/24 January and other relevant documents, which were then read to the members.

The leaders of the Country Party in the Commons were left in a quandary. They could see that the King's move was designed to divert the debate on grievances arising out of the war which had been planned; and in the King's revolutionary step of asking them to approve or disapprove of peace proposals, they feared a further trick. Perhaps the aim was to manœuvre the Commons into a position where they would be obliged to support Charles in a demand for more concessions: perhaps even the proposals were not genuine, for indeed those M.P.s who were in touch with the Dutch agents had heard nothing of any such letter. Sir Eliab Harvey promptly decided to move that consideration of this 'thing of great consequence' should be adjourned until Monday morning, and this suggestion found general favour, though one or two members took the opportunity of giving their views. Secretary Henry Coventry tried to stress the unsatisfactoriness of the articles relating to Surinam and fishing licences in the hope that these old grievances against the Dutch would once more be taken up; Garroway, on the other hand, declared that 'the King had begun and carried on the war without them, and so let him make an end of it', and this idea that Charles should get himself out of his own mess so far won favour that the House decided for the present not to enter into the Journals the papers submitted to them.

The House of Lords also postponed consideration of the royal message until Monday. The King's supporters managed to pass a vote of thanks for his message; but, on the other hand, the clique of peers who met at Lord Holles's house pressed on with their anti-Popery plans before the House adjourned. The Earl of Salisbury moved for a bill to educate children of the royal family (that is, James's children) in the Protestant religion; the Earl of Carlisle seconded this, and further moved for a bill to restrict the marriage of members of the royal family to Protestants only; Halifax moved that all Papists and reputed Papists should be disarmed, and Lord Mordaunt that all English priests should be removed from the Queen's household. A committee was appointed to draw up such a bill; and it was in this anti-Popery atmosphere that the debate on the French alliance would take place on Monday the 26th.[1]

The intervening Sunday, however, gave an opportunity for consultations on the subject of this debate; and some of those leaders of the Country Party who were uncertain about their attitude went to see the Dutch agents, Trenchard and Medley.

We had a meeting with some Parliament men, who knowing our interest, and looking upon us in a manner as Legates, inquired of us whether we had a copy of the Letter and proposals, and what we knew or thought of it? To which we could only answer that we neither heard nor knew anything of it, till the King communicated the same to the House. Then they moved this point, whether the Parliament should interpose to advise the King upon his speech; if advise, then what?

Trenchard and Medley were now also in something of a dilemma, since they had heard nothing at all from Du Moulin since their landing nearly three weeks previously, and had no instructions to cover this position. So they contented themselves with pointing out that Parliament was only being called upon to give advice when everything else had failed.

That the interests of the French, the Duke [of York], the King's women and his ministers, were become like a tired horse; they could carry the King no further. Now the Parliament must be good-natured, and carry him through this bog,

and they recommended that Parliament should advise the King to make peace, but should not commit themselves to these articles; Charles should 'enter into a treaty, and refer all to that'.

The Dutch agents seem to have been a little aggrieved to be put into this difficult position. They took care to point out

[1] For 24 Jan. see *C.J.* ix. 298; Grey, ii. 338–41; 'J. T.' letter of 29 Jan. in R.A. Fagel 244; *L.J.* xii. 616–18; Macpherson, *Original Papers* (1776), i. 71.

to Du Moulin that their ignorance of the letter and proposals 'has rendered us less considerable in the eyes of those Parliament men we converse with, and so less capable of serving you'. They quoted opinions that the letter was untimely; it hindered the House from giving the 'direct and downright blow' to the French alliance which had been planned; it was unnecessary, and the States need not have offered any indemnity. But if they had known in advance of the letter, Trenchard and Medley argued, they could have advised the Parliament men to vote the articles satisfactory, 'which had put an end to the business at once. For as we proposed in the meeting above remembered, so it passed in the House.'[1]

The Commons did indeed make their decision, on 26 and 27 January, on the same lines as the Dutch agents had suggested. On the first day, Monday, most of the discussion centred on whether the House should address the King, to find out whether he had in mind a separate peace, or a joint one in which France would take part; but the House finally decided that a separate peace between England and Holland was clearly contemplated, and an address would be unnecessary. After another long debate on Tuesday, it was resolved that the King should be advised to proceed in a treaty with the States-General 'in order to a speedy peace'—without any mention of whether the articles put before them were satisfactory or not.

Both debates, as recorded by Grey, seem rather confused. There can be no doubt that the general feeling of the House was against France and in favour of a separate peace with Holland. Only one or two members, like Waller, thought that England should stand by her French ally on the ground that 'if thieves are robbing your house, and you call up your neighbours, and go to bed yourself, will they help you again?' Again, there was hardly any opposition to the view that the articles of 14/24 January would be a satisfactory basis for peace. It seems as though even some of the courtiers, like Sir John Holland, had now formed the opinion that Charles would not be sorry to be advised to make peace on these terms. But in spite of this fundamental agreement on the part of a substantial majority of the members, there was con-

[1] Letter of 29 Jan. previously quoted.

siderable disagreement on the way in which the House ought
to proceed. Some members, including Sir William Coventry,
thought that the House should close immediately with the
Dutch offer, vote that it contained 'matter of peace', and
advise the King accordingly; the very fact that the Spanish
ambassador had sponsored it was a guarantee that it was
genuine, and not a trick in the French interest. Other members, particularly the more extreme critics of the administration, were inclined to hedge as long as possible to make quite
sure that Charles's action in submitting the Dutch offer to
them was straightforward. No doubt those who were in touch
with the Dutch agents thought that the projected address
to find out whether the peace would be a separate one, would
both clarify matters and gain time for information and instructions to arrive from Holland; and even when it was established
that it was to be a separate peace, they were not anxious to
identify themselves with any particular terms, lest by any
chance they should be called upon to vote money in order to
secure them. To this group, Charles's action in asking Parliament for advice was obviously a calculated manœuvre whose
purpose was uncertain, and they wanted to move cautiously
until the way was clearer. Lastly, there were those members
who felt, like Garroway, that the King should be left to get
himself out of the difficulties he had made for himself, and
that the longer he was in those difficulties the better, because
it would give the Country Party an opportunity to press on
with the measures which they were meditating. As Arlington
pointed out, 'One thing was very remarkable in the debates
of each House, That no man opposed the coming to a speedy
peace, but those that had most professedly railed at the war
before, and now saw His Majesty in a fair way, by this
expedient, of breaking through those snares they had laid
for him'.[1] Lord Conway was another who declared that
'Those who thought the French alliance a grievance, do now
think a peace, nay, a separate peace, to be the greater grievance, so that one may see they designed only to fetter
the King and take their advantages. . . .'[2] In their opinion
the opposition in the House of Commons was merely

[1] Arlington to Jenkins and Williamson, 30 Jan. 1674, S.P. 81/71, f. 169.
[2] Letter to Essex, 27 Jan., *Essex Papers*, i. 168.

factious, and there can be no doubt that the element of faction entered into this, as into any other, political struggle; yet it seems difficult to describe this, or any other, political struggle in terms of faction alone. Neither Arlington nor Conway was a neutral observer, and neither did justice to the genuine doubts and hesitations of those who feared that the royal message was only another manœuvre to maintain the French alliance.

At all events, the Commons did resolve that the King should be advised to negotiate for a speedy (and, by implication, a separate) peace with Holland; and on the following day, 28 January, the House of Lords reached a similar decision, after hearing 'the treaty' between England and France read in accordance with Charles's desire. This was not the original treaty of Dover, nor even the treaty concocted later in 1670 for the benefit of all the Cabal, but a third treaty of 2/12 February 1672 known to all the Privy Council. While the House was in committee, Charles handed in a letter from Ruvigny, who, imitating the Dutch, formed a belated scheme for submitting the French side of the case to Parliament: according to the Dutch agent 'Nic. Smyth', Charles 'asked him if he took him for a porter to go on errands', and Ruvigny replied that 'he might without dishonour carry his master's proposals as well as the States' proposals'. All, however, was in vain. The French alliance had very few supporters, and Charles determined to accept the inevitable.[1] Conway thought that Arlington was now advising Charles to break the alliance,[2] and this left James, Duke of York, as almost the only believer in it. In these circumstances the French could have no ground for blaming Charles for deserting them.

Having made up his mind to make peace, Charles acted quickly. On 30 January Arlington informed the English embassy at Cologne that a preliminary treaty was being sketched out with the Marquis del Fresno, based on the Dutch concession of the English claim to 'the flag', permission for British subjects to leave Surinam, the payment of 800,000 patacoons by the Dutch, and the postponement of

---

[1] *L.J.* xii. 622; Historical Manuscripts Commission, IX. ii. 40 (House of Lords MSS); 'Nic. Smyth', letter of 27 Jan., R.A. Fagel 244; and reference given p. 177, n. 2, above.   [2] See p. 181, n. 2, above.

a commercial treaty until later. On 2 February Charles received a request for passports to enable Dutch ambassadors to come over to London; but the prospect of having Dutchmen in London 'managing practices' (though in fact they could not have been more effective than Trenchard and Medley) was so alarming to Charles and his ministers, that that same afternoon they decided it would be preferable to send an English ambassador to The Hague instead. Sir William Temple was the obvious choice, for he could count on being *persona grata* there from the days of his previous embassy there in 1668. On 4 February a warrant was issued for his appointment as Ambassador Extraordinary. On 5 February, however, the Marquis del Fresno sent word that he had received full powers from the States-General to negotiate and conclude a peace on their behalf in London.

The terms of the peace treaty presented so little difficulty that they were signed in the space of only four days, on 9/19 February 1674, on the basis of the Dutch offer of 14/24 January. Charles afterwards protested strongly to Ruvigny that the Spanish ambassador had tricked him at the last minute by insisting on incorporating a clause from the Treaty of Breda to the effect that each nation should refrain from assisting the other's enemies: this, he foresaw, might be invoked to prevent Louis XIV from recruiting volunteer troops from Charles's dominions, especially from Ireland and Scotland. On the other hand, Temple asserted positively in his memoirs that there was a private understanding between the negotiators, to the effect that Monmouth and the existing English contingent with Louis XIV should be allowed to remain, but no new recruits should be sent to join them, so that it looks as though Charles was engaged in a characteristic piece of double-dealing.[1]

The terms of the Treaty of Westminster, as it is generally and appropriately called, gave Charles hardly anything to show for his efforts. The Dutch conceded the barren honour of the flag, and promised once more to make it easier for British subjects to leave Surinam; but they successfully refused to pay for the right to fish off the English coasts, and

[1] Temple, i. 167 et seq.; del Fresno to William, 3/13 Feb., in Japikse, *Corres.* II. i. 331–2.

the fact that a treaty of commerce was postponed until later meant that they preserved their monopoly in the East Indies. Even the payment of 800,000 patacoons was of little advantage to Charles, for the greater part of it was immediately allocated to pay to William of Orange the dowry which Charles I had been prevented by the Civil War from giving to William's mother. It is not surprising that when Sir Gabriel Sylvius crossed to Holland to offer Charles's formal congratulations to William and secure ratification of the peace, he remarked on the widespread joy there at such a satisfactory peace, 'bonfires and being drunk were but two of the least signs of it'.[1]

Another sign is to be found in a letter drafted by the hand of Du Moulin. The pen which had formerly been used for polemical purposes was now employed to send a formal message of congratulation from the States-General to Charles. Among the hopes which are expressed that the friendship between the two nations will be unshakable, is a reference to the marvellous effects of the means used by Divine Providence to bring this great work to perfection.[2] Charles, however, was no believer in a Divine Providence of this kind; he knew only too well that human agencies were at work, and was ready to pursue with his wrath the persons responsible. The best testimony to the importance of Du Moulin's pamphleteering in bringing about the Treaty of Westminster is to be found in the efforts which Charles and Arlington made afterwards to drive him out of William's service and to track down those who had co-operated with him. Ruvigny had also learned his lesson, for within a month we find him recommending to the French Secretary of State that money spent on pamphlets to divert the 'natural aversion' of Englishmen for Frenchmen into aversion for Spaniards and Dutch, would be money well spent.[3]

[1] Orrery to Essex, 21 Feb., *Essex Papers*, i. 179.
[2] Draft in R.A. Fagel 252, 1466.
[3] Ruvigny to Pomponne, 2/12 Mar.

X

THE END OF DU MOULIN

1. *The End of the Session*

IN the Treaty of Westminster Du Moulin and his colleagues had achieved their primary object of driving England out of the war so that William of Orange and his allies could concentrate on fighting Louis XIV, while those Englishmen who had co-operated had also achieved their purpose of bringing the open French alliance to an end. Some attempt to assess the importance and the consequences of this success for Europe and for England will be made in the concluding chapter. But when the peace treaty had been signed, none of those involved regarded it as the final consummation of their hopes, but only as a means towards it. Trenchard and Medley and their acquaintances in the House of Commons saw it as a stage in the struggle against Popish influence at Court, and particularly in the struggle to safeguard England against a Popish succession; and a series of proposals was made for this purpose during the remainder of the parliamentary session. Equally, William had the limited objective of trying to get English recruits for his armies, and to prevent Louis XIV getting recruits for his; while ultimately he aimed at making England not merely neutral but an ally in his lifelong struggle against Louis, and, as he heard reports of James's diseases, he was aware that he stood close to the English succession. There seemed, therefore, to be some advantage in maintaining the connexion between the Dutch and the English opposition which had been formed by Du Moulin and his colleagues; and, conversely, Charles and James were well aware of the dangers of this alliance between discontented subjects and their nephew William, which might well become a serious and permanent embarrassment if nothing was done to prevent it.

The 'fifth column' which had been created during the war therefore remained an important factor in politics for some time after the end of it, and it may be as well briefly to describe how it was broken up, at any rate as it was organized by Du

Moulin—for it is probable that William maintained some English connexions, however obscure they may be, until the Revolution seated him on the English throne.

After the debate on the Dutch peace offer, which took place on 27 January, Parliament sat for another month, during which the relations between King and Commons did not improve, and the prospects of a grant of money did not grow brighter. The situation was described by 'J. T.' on February 10:

> My coz. [Charles] and our old neighbour [Parliament] are yet at law, and although I have taken up all my time of late in endeavours to reconcile them, yet I cannot effect it [ironically]. My coz. [Charles] would bate much of his former claims, but still insists upon a sum of money, which my neighbour [Parliament] will not concede us. To-morrow they are like to have a hearing at the Rolls [a meeting of the Council or Foreign Committee] and I am made to believe by our Councell that my neighbour will be decreed to quit the possession of the house where he now lives to my coz. for a term of time [Parliament will be prorogued]. My said neighbour [Parliament] is so enraged against my brother-in-law [James], that he can hardly speak of him with patience, but is ready wherever he meets him to fly in his face, and I am informed that he is resolved to prefer a Bill against him this week, but I hope if our business goes well tomorrow at the Rolls it may cool his sturdy courage. Some are of opinion that my cozen [Charles] underhand encourages him against my brother [James], but I doubt not but my brother will break the neck of that. . . .[1]

At the beginning of February the three addresses which had been agreed on in principle, urging Charles to dismiss Lauderdale and Buckingham and to make a speedy peace, were drafted and finally passed through the House of Commons. There followed a series of debates on proposals designed to reduce the powers at the disposal of the executive when James became King. A Habeas Corpus Bill to tighten up the subject's protection against arbitrary imprisonment passed its three readings; an address to the King declared that any standing army was a grievance, and petitioned him to dismiss all troops raised since January 1663; another bill proposed that judges should hold their positions during good behaviour (*quam diu se bene gesserint*), and not at the royal pleasure (*durante bene placito*). As Conway observed, 'fear of

[1] R.A. Fagel 244.

the Duke [of York] makes them every day fetter the Crown'.
Birch, indeed, specifically stated that 'though we have no
reason to misdoubt the King, yet we tremble to think what
we may come under', and Clarges that 'this is the time to
take care against our coming under a bad Prince. . . . Still he
apprehends the Marian days [of Catholic persecution]. . . .'[1]
No doubt there were those among the extremists who wanted
restrictions on the royal power whoever was King, but it was
fear of what would happen when James succeeded that gave
them their hold over the great body of moderate opinion in
the House. The same fears even led to long debates on a dis-
puted election in which Samuel Pepys the diarist was concerned. Pepys was known to be a loyal servant of James's in
naval matters, and the House was appropriately concerned
when he was accused of being a secret Roman Catholic on
the ground that he had an altar and crucifix in his house, 'and
should say, "our Religion came out of Henry the eighth's
codpiece"'.[2]

In the House of Lords the attack on James was even more
direct. We have seen that on 24 January various anti-Popery
proposals had been made, including some for the Protestant
education of all children in the royal family, and another
restricting the marriage of members of the royal family to
Protestants only.[3] In the meantime a committee had incor-
porated these proposals into a bill 'for securing the Protestant
religion', and this bill was the subject of keen debate during
February. With reference to a clause preventing members of
the royal family from marrying a Catholic, Carlisle and Halifax, on 10 February, went so far as to propose that the penalty
for a breach of this clause should be exclusion from the succession. It is true that Shaftesbury in vehemently defending
this clause, argued that it was intended to look forward, and
not backward to James's recent marriage with Mary of
Modena; but everyone regarded it as an attack on James,
and it is easy now to see in it the first hint of the Exclusion
Bill. Indeed, two observers reported that the discussion actually took place on a motion to exclude all Papists from the
throne. Shaftesbury and his colleagues were unsuccessful in

[1] Grey, ii. 415–17; Conway to Essex, 10 Feb., *Essex Papers*, i. 174.
[2] Grey, ii. 407–13, 420–1, 426–33.   [3] See pp. 178–9 above.

carrying their clause, for the Archbishop of York, the Bishop of Winchester, and others opposed any interference with the succession by divine hereditary right as un-Christian; but even without it, the bill remained a serious restriction on members of the royal family with Catholic sympathies.[1]

All these proceedings to guard against the dangers of a Catholic becoming King of England were seen by the Court as the work of 'a combination betwixt the discontented and turbulent Commons in the south-east corner of our House and some hotspurs in the Upper', who included Shaftesbury, Halifax, Salisbury, Carlisle, Clare, and others who met at Lord Holles's house to concert their actions. At the same time the opposition to Lauderdale in Scotland was developing, and there were 'Republican drifts' to secure control of the government of the City of London.[2]

Where did the agents of William and Du Moulin stand in relation to this combination against the Court? Trenchard and Medley sent to The Hague the fullest reports on all these questions of purely domestic policy.[3] In doing so they left no doubt at all where their sympathies lay. Their attitude was that of the extremists, they made no secret of it in writing to Du Moulin, and they still claimed to be acting in the interests of 'Mistress Ford', their code name for William. It may perhaps be thought that their individual political sympathies went far beyond William's own attitude; on the other hand, it has to be remembered that, young and comparatively inexperienced as he was, his view of English affairs must inevitably be coloured by the reports which Du Moulin gave him. Perhaps the most certain indication where William stood in regard to English politics now that peace had been made, is to be found in the instructions which he gave to his representative van Reede about this time.

Charles II had sent Sir Gabriel Sylvius over to Holland with a letter complimenting William on the peace, and on the fact that the Stadholderate and Captain-Generalship of the United Provinces had now been declared to be hereditary

---

[1] Macpherson, *Original Papers*, i. 72; Kincardine to Lauderdale, 10 Feb., *Lauderdale Papers* (Camden Society), iii. 32–33; *C.S.P. Ven. 1673–5*, pp. 220–1.

[2] Sir Gilbert Talbot to Williamson, 28 Feb., *Letters to Williamson*, ii. 156–8.

[3] R.A. Fagel 244 contains thirteen letters written in the month of February.

in the House of Orange. The first purpose of van Reede's mission was to return this compliment. It also had the practical aim of urging Charles, under the terms of the Treaty of Westminster, to withdraw his contingent from the army of Louis XIV, while at the same time permission was asked for William to raise English levies. In addition, the instructions went on,

> Vous aurez à vous informer le plus exactement qu'il sera possible des sentiments de la nation sur ce qui regarde Monsr. le duc d'York. Et au cas que quelques personnes vous viennent trouver de la part et au nom de Du Moulin, vous leur donnerez favorable audience et pourrez vous servir de leur avis autant que vous les jugerez conformes à mes intérêts et pour le bien de mes affaires. Et dans tout ce qui se passera entre vous et eux, vous aurez un soin particulier de ne les point découvrir et de garder exactement le secret qu'ils demanderont de vous.[1]

It is not quite clear from the above whether the people who were expected to approach van Reede 'in Du Moulin's name' were Trenchard and Medley and their like, or some of the influential people at Court or in Parliament with whom they were in contact, or both. But from these instructions in general it seems reasonable to suppose that William's main concern was with fighting his war against Louis XIV, but that he was at the same time keeping a careful watch on the mounting agitation against the Duke of York; and that the connexions with the English opposition which Du Moulin had built up had proved so useful in the past that William wanted at least to maintain them in being if not to lend active encouragement. In this way he might be in a position to benefit from any turn which the relations between Charles, James, and Parliament might take, he could foster anti-French feeling and he could have a party prepared to safeguard his claim to the succession if, as Du Moulin's agent reported, James was diseased and unlikely to have a son.

Before van Reede arrived in England, however, the parliamentary session had come to an end. One or two observers had seen that, since it was most unlikely that the House of Commons would grant any money in its present mood, a prorogation was to be expected as soon as the news reached

[1] See Korvezee, in *Bijdragen voor vaderlandsche geschiedenis*, vi. 7 (1928), p. 250.

London that the Dutch had ratified the peace treaty. One of them, Conway, wrote that the Court Party were much afraid that Holland would insist on having the treaty ratified by Parliament, which would put them in a very awkward position. Finally, however, Charles decided that he could not wait until news of the ratification arrived. There were rumours of a direct attack on James, perhaps even a charge of treason; a committee was drawing up articles of impeachment against Arlington; the House of Commons was showing signs of a desire to re-open the thorny Irish question, and particularly to discuss the French recruits who were being collected there; the Habeas Corpus Bill and the bill for securing the Protestant religion were making progress. So on 24 February Charles abruptly prorogued Parliament until 10 November, making all these bills void without the necessity to veto them. He had decided that, since he could get no parliamentary supply, he would rely on his Treasurer, Danby, to make ends meet by a policy of rigid economy. It would mean comparative austerity for himself and his courtiers, but it would free him from his turbulent Parliament. 'He had rather be a poor King than no King.' By this time, also, he knew that Louis XIV had recognized the inevitability of the Treaty of Westminster, and could even hope for French subsidies in return for his neutrality.[1]

The leaders of the Country Party were confounded by the prorogation. They were powerless while Parliament was not sitting, and could only hope that Danby's economies would prove unsuccessful. The blow was quite unexpected, for they had thought that Charles needed their money so desperately that he would have to accept their bills, as he had had to give way so many times in the previous twelve months; but this was a serious miscalculation, for since peace had been made the King's need for money was not so urgent. 'I never saw such a consternation as was among the members of both Houses; every man amazed and reproaching one another that they had sat so long upon eggs and could hatch nothing. . . .' Some members even feared for their own safety:

[1] Conway to Essex, 10, 17, 24, 28 Feb., *Essex Papers*, i. 174, 175, 179–80, 180–1; Ruvigny to Pomponne, 23 Feb./5 Mar., 26 Feb./8 Mar., 2/12 Mar.; *C.S.P. Ven. 1673–5*, p. 232; R.A. Fagel 244, especially 'Tho. Allen's' letter of 24 Feb.

This sudden prorogation caused many of the guilty Commons (Lord St. John, Sir Thomas Lee, Sir Robert Thomas, Sir N. Carew, Sir Eliab Harvey, Sacheverell, and many others) who had bespoken a large dinner for that day at the Swan Tavern in King Street, to leave their provisions to Mr. Dod and his wife, and to haste away (some by coach, some by water) into the city, suspecting themselves (I verily conceive without ground) unsecure in the suburbs.

'Nic. Smyth' also reported their discomfiture to Du Moulin:

All men stand amazed, nay the wisest cannot forbear wondering; the consternation is so great that we have not only lost our tongues, but our wits. Last night I was with a very considerable man of the House of Commons, and I found him burning of papers with this saying to me, You know the cause, and in the conclusion when all were burnt, he told me that if he had known that I had been in town, he would not have burnt them for forty pounds, but now, says he, *liberavi animam meam.*

'Nic. Smyth' thought that the letter of 14/24 January had been too precipitately sent:

Had not you sent that parcel of woollen goods [letter] so hastily, but waited for a market, you had done like a wise merchant, and we should have made so great an advantage of the tin which I hoped Mr. Richard [?] would have brought over that Mrs. Ford [William], nor you, nor any of the factory, would have cause to repent it, nay I am confident that she would have grown so wealthy, if these woollen goods had been rightly managed, that she need not to have ventured any more to sea.

As it was, he could see no means of serving 'Mrs. Ford' any further, and hoped shortly to see Du Moulin 'in Mrs. Ford's family' at The Hague.[1]

The last words on this parliamentary session may fittingly be those of 'J. T.', who for the occasion changed his name to 'Tho. Allen'. In his letter of 24 February he says that he had intended to cross over to Holland 'because I find in myself a great desire to see Mistress Ford, not only to give her some account of that real action which she was pleased to order me to bring and prosecute for her in the Common Pleas [Commons]; but also to communicate to her some further and

---

[1] Conway to Essex, 24 Feb., *Essex Papers*, i. 179–80; Sir Gilbert Talbot to Williamson, 28 Feb., *Letters to Williamson*, ii. 156–8; 'Nic. Smyth', letter of 25 Feb., R.A. Fagel 244.

fresh thoughts which I have had touching her cause', but these plans had been disrupted by the surprise of the prorogation. Accompanying his analysis of the reasons for the prorogation are the following reflections, which give a good idea of the man:

Certain it is that such a Session was never lost, but though we cannot enjoy the good Bills prepared as Laws, yet the same will be sweet as a history, therefore it will perhaps be time well spent to collect and digest them, which having proposed I find a taking notion. For I had said to some, Let us rather lose all the Bills, and content ourselves with them as a history, than give money. . . . You cannot but think upon the whole matter, that this sudden, though not altogether unexpected accident, has a little perplexed and disturbed my thoughts, which as soon as I have a little recollected, will centre in a resolution of seeing you speedily. But good God, how fortunate have we been! though not in getting all that we desired, yet more than we could reasonably have expected. But no mortal man (wiser than I am sure I am) can, or shall ever be able to give a reason for anything we do, the fates having decreed that there shall never be any consistency in our actions; so far are the politics from being a science with us, that they are a chaos. We shall learn in time to wonder at nothing like philosophers, no not at the greatest follies. What we intend to foster as our dearest, we first suffer to be blasted, almost as effectually as the fig-tree cursed in the Gospel. Yet I cannot but presage that in time to come wisdom and honesty will be preferred before villainy. But good Lord! what will become of Ireland? of Scotland? nay of England itself? But being very late in the night it will be time for me to break off, for I had almost forgot myself. . . .

So ended the parliamentary session which had forced Charles out of the war and threatened to accomplish more. Before Parliament was allowed to meet again in the spring of 1675, the financial and political skill of Danby had modified the situation to Charles's advantage.

11. *The End of the Fifth Column*

Freed from the embarrassment of a critical Parliament at the cost of economies at Court, Charles was much stronger so long as he reconciled himself to a minor role in foreign affairs. This increased security was reflected in the reception which was given to van Reede in March. Charles was friendly enough in conversation, but he would not withdraw the English troops from France or give permission to recruit troops for the Dutch service: his neutrality remained benevolent to Louis XIV. William had foreseen that this was probable, and had ordered van Reede to try to raise troops secretly by arrangement with Lord Ossory and other sympathizers. Van Reede also held conversations with 'the most prominent persons of quality', and received various indications of their goodwill for William and their desire that he should marry James's elder daughter, Princess Mary, prospective heir to the Crown. It does not appear that he met Trenchard and Medley, for 'J. T.' wrote to his 'dearest friend' that 'Mr. Reede I have not seen, nor know whether I shall or no, for I know not any use he can be of to us, and we can be of none to him, as things stand'. If his conversations with 'the most prominent persons of quality' extended to intrigues, no details of them have survived.[1]

In May van Reede returned to England as one of three Dutch ambassadors. They also included Du Moulin's patron, van Beuningen, who eventually remained as the permanent resident ambassador. The fact that they hired the greater part of Exeter House, Shaftesbury's mansion (which was too big for him after he had lost the Chancellorship), was not calculated to improve Charles's opinion either of him or of them; and he soon suspected the Dutch ambassadors of 'managing practices' with M.P.s, to press Charles to ally with Holland against France.[2] There is no confirmation from the ambassadors' dispatches or elsewhere of any such intrigues, but, whether Charles's suspicions were justified or not, they strengthened his determination to break up such connexions between the Dutch and his discontented subjects before Parliament met again. Everything possible would be done to prevent a repetition of what had happened in the sessions of 1673–4.

We have seen that as far back as January, the government knew that the persons primarily responsible for writing and distributing pamphlets and plotting with members of the

[1] Korvezee, loc. cit.; 'J. T.', letter of 6 Mar. in R.A. Fagel 244; William to Ossory, undated, Japikse, *Corres.*, II. i. 342.

[2] Ruvigny to Louis, 21/31 May, to Pomponne, 25 May/4 June, and *passim* in dispatches of June.

Commons were Du Moulin, William Howard, and Medley. 'J. T.' reported to Du Moulin on 10 February, with some irony, that

Your friend William I doubt has been too busy in affairs that little concern him, so that I doubt he will be under some displeasure of His Majesty at his return into England. I am informed the house where he lodges was lately beset. And Col. Blood spent some days and nights lately in inquiring after him among his old friends, to some of whom he said that he had made all this difference between the King and Parliament and had sent all those papers out of Holland, etc. You would do well to give him some good advice if you see him, and desire him to meddle no more in things of that nature. . . .

Colonel Blood, however, was probably mistaken in thinking that Howard had come to England, and in spite of all his underground connexions he was unable to track down any Dutch agents or intercept any communication between London and The Hague. In the spring of 1674, however, the situation altered to the advantage of the English government. Now that peace had been made, Du Moulin and his colleagues began to fall out among themselves. Some of the Englishmen who were in exile at The Hague began to tire of it, and to desire to make their peace with the English government, so that they could return to England and carry on their intrigues there; in some cases also they were alienated by the arrogant demeanour of Du Moulin, who enjoyed great favour with the Prince of Orange, and tended to despise some of the others and treated them as he had treated his colleagues in the Paris embassy five years earlier.

The opportunity of these discontented fifth-columnists came at last at the end of April 1674, though quarrels had broken out earlier. In April Sir Joseph Williamson received instructions recalling him from his fruitless embassy at Cologne: the seizure by Imperial troops of the Francophil William of Fürstenberg, whom the French claimed to be covered by the diplomatic immunity of the congress, served as a pretext for both Louis XIV and Charles II to withdraw their ambassadors and bring the conference to an end. Williamson's obvious route back to England was down the Rhine through Holland, and, especially at Rotterdam, English agents in the Low Countries and English exiles who were

anxious to reingratiate themselves with the authorities flocked
to see him. Williamson seized his opportunity to ferret out as
much as possible of the conspiracy which had made his embassy abortive; and of which he heard that Don Bernardo de
Salinas had boasted that 'if the Peace had not been made as
it was, the whole three kingdoms had been in a flame . . . they
had daily expresses from the principal Parliament men at
that time. [If there were revealed] the names of the parties
that they held correspondence with in the House, he would
wonder.' Williamson also noted 'N.B. Fresno is said to have
distributed great sums'.[1]

Williamson's principal informants were the printer Crouch
and William Carr, who betrayed their colleagues, and Abraham de Wicquefort, of whom more will be said presently.
Crouch's evidence may be taken first. It was the least valuable, for Crouch was only a minor member of the conspiracy
and not in all its secrets. He did not know the real name of
'Smith', and the latter's partner ('Freeman') he identified as
that great bugbear of Restoration governments, the Republican exile Ludlow, who was really safe in Switzerland at this
time. Crouch was, however, able to say that when these conspirators were in England they usually lodged at the chambers
of one Goodenough in the Temple, or at the latter's house at
the corner of Shoe Lane, opposite Baxter's meeting-house.
He reported also that the exiles were optimistic 'to have the
Commonwealth up by Xmas . . . so certain are they of dissensions at the next assembly of Parliament'; and that they had
each received £1,000 for their service to the States-General—
when in Howard's lodgings last Saturday and Sunday, he
had seen 'several bags of money lying there'.

Williamson duly noted down this information, determined
to keep a watch on Goodenough, and made arrangements for
Crouch to stay in Holland to spy on the activities of his former
partners. Crouch was directed to send his reports for the
Secretary of State by way of accommodation addresses at the
sign of the Three Bells in Wapping, or that of the Blue
Anchor in Redriffe; while communication with him would
be solely through the newly appointed English ambassador

[1] This and the following information is taken from Williamson's Journal in
S.P. 105/222 (copied from notes in S.P. 105/231). This extract is dated 4/14 May.

in The Hague, Sir William Temple, who would be 'warned to govern the thing with great secrecy'. We are not told how much he was paid for his information.[1]

With William Carr, Williamson had two interviews, on 30 April and 5 May. It has been seen that Carr had previously offered his services to both sides in turn, but had finally settled down in the autumn of 1673–4, according to the English spies, to make a steady income with Howard by selling passes of immunity for English ships. That source of income came to an end with the peace treaty, and Carr's relations with Du Moulin became steadily worse. He accused him to Williamson of 'persecuting all the English'; perhaps the truth was that Du Moulin distrusted Carr (with some justification), but Carr insisted that Howard also 'is greatly off from Du Moulin . . . and so are all those young men, he having not used them well. They declare if they could be safe, they would for ever abandon Du Moulin.' Perhaps it was once more a case of Du Moulin looking down on some of his fellow conspirators while they felt that he was only their equal. At all events, after Carr's first interview with Williamson, Du Moulin quarrelled bitterly with him in the presence of 'Smith' and 'Freeman', 'principally upon the occasion of his coming to worship us (as Moulin styled it)'.

Carr complained of Du Moulin, but the information which he gave to Williamson related to all the conspirators and there was much about the general political situation as well. He implicated Marvell, identified 'Smith' as Trenchard and 'Freeman' as 'one Metwin or Melain a scrivener', recommended 'a Scotch minister, a notable fellow, a V Monarchy man, subtle, able, venomous,—that were worth the taking off', and stated that the writings of the exiles were no longer corrected by the notorious Dr. Richardson of Leyden, but by the minister at The Hague, one Price 'a great villain, diffames and blasphemes the King strangely'. Williamson's notes of the conversation give a good picture of the little band of exiles at work, though not all the details of Carr's information are equally reliable. He seems to have borne a grudge against Mr. Tucker, an English merchant at Rotterdam, whom he accused of dealing with Howard in the sale of

[1] Williamson's Journal, 6/16 May.

protection passes for English shipping: needless to say, he did not mention that he had himself been involved.

Evidently Williamson felt that it would be safer to trust Tucker than Carr, for it seems that he declined the latter's offers to become an English agent. Carr later repeated his attempts to get into touch with Arlington, Sir William Temple, and Williamson, but he received little for his information in spite of the impudently self-righteous tone that he took: 'receiving no answer I am quiet, and conclude myself very unfortunate, that I am not judged either worthy of employ, or to be paid the moneys I disbursed for the public in the last war, setting aside the often hazard of my life in opposing the implacable enemies of his Lordship and others. . . .'[1]

One possible reason why Williamson decided not to employ Carr was that there was another traitor in the Prince of Orange's service, who might be a much more valuable ally. On 7 May he had an interview with 'Monsr. de W.' A marginal note in his journal in another handwriting says that 'W.' was Count Waldeck (a German prince, one of William's best military commanders, who enjoyed some of his confidence), but context and sequel make it abundantly clear that 'Monsr. de W.' was really Abraham de Wicquefort. Nominally his position in The Hague was that of representative of the German state of Brunswick-Lüneburg, later known as Hanover, but he was also employed in various capacities by the States-General. His knowledge of public affairs enabled him to write a book on ambassadors, and a *Histoire des Provinces-Unies*; it had also enabled him to keep up a valuable secret correspondence with Lionne in Paris, and it now put him in a position to offer information to Williamson.

The notes of the interview between the two men give some valuable indications of past events, such as that 'this last treaty with England and all that led to it passed singly through the Prince's own hands, nobody being acquainted with it, nor meddled with it. Even the Pensioner little or nothing at all, or very little. So Waldeck expressly to W[icquefort].' This throws some light on the problem of how far Du Moulin's actions were authorized by William. There is also much interesting matter on the personal intrigues which were going

[1] Ibid., 30 Apr. and 6 May; Carr to Williamson, 19/29 Oct., S.P. 84/196, f. 201.

on round William, and the information that van Beuningen, on his embassy into England, carried with him 'a blank for the Duchess of York, etc., to consult with the Parliament men. They doubted if to write or not. . . .' It is not clear precisely what was intended here, but Williamson duly made a memorandum to watch van Beuningen's house in London.

There was also some information on Du Moulin's position at The Hague and on William's views about the possibility of a marriage to Princess Mary, to which we shall return; but in Williamson's eyes perhaps even more important than the information which de Wicquefort actually gave was the prospect that he could provide some which would be even more valuable.

[W.] has a friend 8 or 9 hours from The Hague who will be able to tell him the very names etc., of those of the House of Commons that have taken money etc., and are corresponded with. It may cost money, but J. W. [the writer] told him he should be master of all etc. That it's most certain great sums have been given, but several of the Party in the House are yet without reward, and begin to grumble that they are so. In so much that it is possible the next sessions if they be not sweetened, it may turn the whole affair. q. if so many having been in the trick we may not hope that one day they will fall out and tell of one another.

With this exciting prospect Williamson made another memorandum to send a sum of money to 'W.' immediately, while at the same time noting that 'W. proceeds upon the grounds of an honest man in all this, as being persuaded the interest of the States and the Prince [is] to be well with England'! Relying on this goodwill, combined with occasional presents, to provide him with sensational disclosures of the names of Holland's allies in Parliament, Williamson returned to England; and, once back in London, he presumably also arranged for a watch to be kept on Goodenough's house, to waylay 'Freeman', 'Smith', and other Dutch agents when they appeared.

In neither respect were Williamson's hopes fulfilled. There is no evidence that de Wicquefort ever provided him with the list of names which was so eagerly awaited. In the following year he was arrested by the Dutch authorities, copies of letters from Williamson which were in his possession were seized, he was tried and sentenced to a term of imprisonment for corresponding with foreign powers. Howard was under the impression that it was through de Wicquefort handing over letters of his to Williamson that the English government learned of his activities: but this is almost certainly wrong. The correspondence between Williamson and de Wicquefort leaves the impression that de Wicquefort had promised more than he could or would perform, and that all through the summer of 1674 he was extracting as much money as possible from England in return for as little information as possible, always maintaining Williamson's hopes but doing nothing to justify them. He certainly supplied Williamson with a few copies of Dutch official diplomatic documents, but in spite of Williamson's reminders there is no sign of any list of names or details about the Dutch 'fifth column', such as he had promised to provide through his friend near The Hague.[1]

Equally through Crouch and Goodenough, Williamson's efforts to track down his opponents were only partially successful. From March onwards Medley, Trenchard, and Williams had been in Holland, no doubt being congratulated on their good work and receiving instructions for the future. It was not until the end of June that 'J. Thompson', to give 'J. T.'s' latest alias, and 'Mr. Worthington' (Williams) returned to London, having settled a definite code of names for use in a new series of reports to Du Moulin. Evidently it was thought that, although a Dutch embassy including van Beuningen was now in London, Du Moulin's agents could move about in more secrecy and could continue to assist Dutch policy in some ways; and some of their reports on the political situation, and especially on affairs in Scotland, survive, written during July. On Monday, 27 July, however, the government's net at last closed on Goodenough. He was arrested, taken before Secretary Coventry, confronted with the printer Crouch, and accused of 'intelligence with one Freeman, alias Medley, and one Smith alias Trencher'. We do not know what Goodenough said, but on the 31st he was

---

[1] See Williamson's letters, *C.S.P.D.* *1673–5*, pp. 264, 266, 275, 284, 288, 293, 299, 306, 320, 325, 356; Burnet, ii. 63. For de Wicquefort's trial see D. Everwijn, *A. van Wicquefort en zijn Proces* (Leyden, 1857); and cf. also the article by M. Lane in *E.H.R.* xxx. (1915).

sent to the Tower, and the following week the master of one of the small vessels used to carry the conspirators backwards and forwards was also arrested. Inquiries were also made 'after a fellow (named George) who it seems hired his vessel for the said transportation, upon divers pretences, which it seems took not, information being had beforehand'; and on 1 3 August six or seven of the Secretary of State's messengers laid siege to the house of Mrs. Venner (Medley's mother-in-law), inquiring after her daughter and the same mysterious George. Again they failed to find the people for whom they were looking, but it is not surprising that Du Moulin's friend and ally, in reporting this, also said 'I shall go out of town next week'. London was now getting altogether too hot to hold them, and it was time to take refuge in Holland, out of the way.[1]

There was still time for one last entertaining anecdote to be reported, an alleged description of a meeting at Bath between the Marchioness of Worcester and the King's French mistress, the Duchess of Portsmouth, who claimed the same rooms:

And the ladies meeting there at the rooms, a very sore conflict arose, which proceeding from words to blows gave a fine entertainment to the beholders. The Marchioness told her she had better blood in her veins than e'er a French bitch in the world, and that the English nobility would not be affronted by her, calling her tall bitch. There might you have seen their towers [head-dresses] and hair flying about the room, as the miserable spoils of so fierce a rencounter. The Marchioness beat her upon the face, got her down, and kicked her, and finally forced her out of doors. The Marquis stood by as a spectator all the while, not suffering any to part them, for some attempting it, he laid his hand on his sword, declaring a resolution to run him through, whosoever he should be, that should touch his Lady, who bid the said Portsmouth go to Windsor and tell the King what she had said and done.[2]

Solacing themselves with such stories of anti-French sentiments as this, Du Moulin's friends withdrew to Holland, taking 'George' with them. Medley arrived at The Hague on 4/14 September to inquire what provision 'the Quartermaster' (Du Moulin) had made for him, now that Charles

[1] R.A. Fagel 244, letters of 2 July (N.S.), 30 June, 14, 28, 31 July, 7, 14 Aug.
[2] Ibid., letter of 7 Aug.

was so incensed against him. We catch one last glimpse of him there:

> In absence of His Highness [William], I went to wait upon the Pensionary Fagel, to give him an account of my circumstances, but was not able to obtain any audience, nor got any other answer than that he had no time, nor did he make any appointment, so that although I have attended these several times I have not been able to speak with him, so that I am resolved rather than to endure the grievance of fruitless waiting, to put it to adventure. And I do not doubt but the time will come, when they may stand in need of the good opinion of the people of England. . . .[1]

What provision was finally made for him, we do not know, for this description of Medley, resentful of his treatment at the Pensionary's hands, is almost the last trace we have of him before he fades into obscurity, one of the many English exiles waiting in Holland for better days.

Thus Charles's ministers had scotched the conspiracy, but had failed to lay hands on the principal conspirators or to discover which members of the House of Commons had co-operated with them. When Sir William Temple became ambassador at The Hague, he asked William directly who were the discontented Englishmen with whom he had corresponded during the war; but William cautiously made it a point of honour not to betray his friends—after all he might need them again.[2] One other possible source of information remained, namely William Howard.

Having achieved his aim of breaking the Anglo-French alliance, and at the same time secured his own advantage by drawing an income from passes estimated at several hundred pounds, Howard had no reason to remain in Holland any longer. He had no intention of remaining indefinitely in exile there. On his behalf Du Moulin drafted a letter from William to Charles asking for a pardon for him so that he should not be the only person not to benefit from a peace for which he had worked with so much zeal. If this letter was sent, it was, however, unsuccessful: a pardon would have to be earned, and Howard began to meditate means of getting back into favour by disclosing sufficient information for this purpose. In March 1674 there were rumours that 'Mr. Wm.

Howard here talks of travelling for Italy and seeing your excellency [Williamson] at Cologne, but not before he hath milked dry, and received what he can get. He is a man of a very quick conceit, but greedy to the uttermost point. He had done well to have used his abilities, only for his king and country. . . .'[1]

It does not appear that this journey to Cologne was ever made, but in May Carr reported that Howard was 'greatly off from Du Moulin', and it was only a matter of time before he came to terms with the English government. We do not know how an agreement was reached, but Howard returned to England in October 1674, was examined in the Tower, and had an interview with the King in person on the 24th. Unfortunately it has not been possible to trace any 'confession' by Howard, and so we do not know just how much he chose to confess to secure permission to return to intrigue in England. Evidently it did not enable Charles to take action against any of his political opponents for treason: perhaps Howard only confirmed what was already known of the conspiracy, and then retired, soon to inherit the barony of Escrick and to plan fresh intrigues with Shaftesbury and the leaders of the Country Party. Probably the only result of what he confessed was to make Charles more determined to get Du Moulin removed from William's service.[2]

III. *The End of Du Moulin*

During the winter of 1673–4 Du Moulin had been at the height of his influence and favour with his master. For his contribution to the Treaty of Westminster he received tangible financial reward which Don Bernardo de Salinas's secretary put as high as 'pension of 5,000 guilders per annum from the States, for the good service he has done them with his pen'. In reporting this, Bulstrode (Williamson's correspondent at Brussels) also said that Du Moulin was to travel with William as his secretary on the campaign of 1674, 'and would be made William's principal secretary', and that 'Don

---

[1] Japikse, *Corres.*, II. i. 340–1; Tucker to Williamson, 22 Mar. 1674, S.P. 84/196, f. 34.
[2] Macpherson, *Original Papers*, i. 74; Ruvigny to Louis XIV, 24 Oct./3 Nov.; T. P. Courtenay, *Memoirs of Sir William Temple* (1836), i. 343.

Bernardo has been a principal cause of his preferment'. From another source Williamson heard that Salinas was urging that he should be appointed Dutch minister at Brussels; from de Wicquefort he heard that Du Moulin was supported by van Beuningen, and from Carr that he was also favoured by Waldeck 'in hopes to be master of the Prince's secrets, having a mind to govern and finding he [Waldeck] cannot be master of old Zulichem nor of the Master of Requests, who is a good man'.[1]

These reports also indicated that Du Moulin's political opinions, and his bitter opposition to English foreign policy, remained unchanged. Williamson noted down that he was opposing the payment of the indemnity due to Charles by the Treaty of Westminster on the ground that Charles was breaking the treaty by allowing French recruiting in his dominions: he was even said to argue 'that the Fleet in passing [down the Channel] should have called in in England, and demanded the execution of that article', and was reported to be so sure that his advice would be taken that he offered to lay Sylvius a wager that the money would not be paid.[2]

Naturally it became an object of English policy to secure the removal of this dangerous enemy, whom Charles regarded as one of the principal *fripons* who had led his young nephew astray. De Wicquefort advised that he should be declared a traitor and his surrender demanded by the Treaty of Westminster, 'only the Prince must be warned of it, prayed and prayed again to quit him first'.[3] Sir William Temple was the ambassador chosen to bring William to a better frame of mind and a better sense of his duty to his uncle. The idea was that Temple's part in the Triple Alliance of 1668 would make him *persona grata* to the Dutch, but his early experiences were not very favourable. Making his way into Flanders to find William with his armies, Temple was delayed at Brussels for lack of an escort, while Du Moulin travelled to and fro between William's camp and Brussels with guards, half of whom would have contented Temple. In point of fact, this was not due to malevolence on anyone's part, for the

---

[1] Bulstrode to Williamson, 23 Mar./2 Apr. 1674, S.P. 77/44, f. 147; Williamson's Journal, 30 Apr. (Carr) and 7/17 May (de Wicquefort), S.P. 105/222.
[2] Journal, 7/17 May.   [3] Ibid.

truth was that Du Moulin was the bearer of urgent messages after a sudden move by the French army; but it was not a very encouraging beginning for the embassy, showing the confidence which was placed in such 'an inveterate enemy against the Court of England'.[1]

Du Moulin was indeed a confidential secretary of William's throughout the campaign of 1674, of which he wrote a description which was later published.[2] But his duties after the Treaty of Westminster were by no means all secretarial and scholarly; he had irons in the fire not only in England but also in France and in Scotland.

Having been so successful in creating difficulties at home for Charles II, which hampered the English war effort, it seemed possible to make a similar attempt to embarrass Louis XIV. There were, of course, no constitutional discontents in France of which advantage could be taken, but Huguenot revolts had hindered French foreign policy for the past hundred years: perhaps another one might be equally efficacious. It might not be difficult to arrange, since Louis's religious policy was becoming increasingly intolerant and the restrictions on the Edict of Nantes increasingly oppressive. Here, as in the English opposition, was a suitable weapon for Dutch foreign policy and a cause with which Du Moulin personally sympathized; in his eyes one of the objects of his Paris embassy in 1669 had been to secure better treatment for his fellow Huguenots. So, when early in 1674 there arrived in Holland first a representative of Louis de Rohan (a famous name in the Huguenot wars) asking for help for a rising in the west of France, and then a Huguenot noble from Languedoc, the Comte de Sardan, who claimed to represent four provinces in the south of France, it seemed a golden opportunity. De Sardan, who was probably connected with de Rohan, was introduced by Du Moulin and van Beuningen to William, and so impressed him with the possibility of a rising breaking out if it had a little support, that on 21 April 1674 a treaty was signed, promising Dutch assistance in men, ships, and money, while the Huguenots would provide 12,000 to 15,000 men. The Dutch fleet, no longer having

1 Temple, i. 186–7; Japikse, *Corres.*, II. i. 426–7.
2 *Relation de ce qui s'est passé... dans la campagne de 1674* (Leyden, 1747).

the English fleet to contend with, was dispatched to operate off the west coast of France to encourage the Huguenot areas there; and for the benefit of the Huguenots in Languedoc and the south-east, a special agent was appointed in François Riomal, a Huguenot exile who held a commission in the Dutch army.

Riomal travelled to Brussels with Du Moulin, and thence, changing his name to Herman de Soulager, travelled south to Genoa, where he was to remain for the time being, until Spain's adhesion to the treaty was received. On Spanish agreement, indeed, William had made the whole treaty to depend; and to obtain it de Sardan travelled to Madrid to begin some very slow negotiations. In the meantime Riomal waited patiently at Genoa, and began to send a series of cipher reports back to accommodation addresses in Holland, some for William direct, and others for Du Moulin. It seemed the beginning of another promising conspiracy. But unfortunately Spanish approval for the treaty was late in coming, and de Sardan had overrated the desire of the Huguenots for revolt; so that Riomal's reports to William and Du Moulin became steadily more depressed and pessimistic in tone until hope faded entirely. There was to be no equivalent to the Treaty of Westminster with Louis XIV.[1]

Scotland also afforded many possibilities for a skilful intriguer, and since the end of the English parliamentary session in February Du Moulin's correspondents in London had shown considerable interest in the development of opposition to Lauderdale. Shortly before his flight from England 'J. T.' had expressed the opinion that Scottish affairs were approaching a crisis, which 'gives us a fit opportunity of putting things to a push, as you finally expressed your desires to me': he thought that money would be the best way of assisting Lauderdale's opponents, and urged 'Mr. Miller', otherwise Du Moulin, to give detailed instructions on what was to be done. This letter was written on 14 July 1674. At the beginning of November the French ambassador in London reported to Louis that a Scot had been arrested, who had in his possession instructions in Du Moulin's handwriting.

[1] Japikse, *Prins Willem III*, ii. 15–18; Krämer, *Bijdr. Vad. Geschichte*, 3ᵉ series, vi. 133 et seq. and vii. 41 et seq. based on documents in R.A. Fagel 254.

This Scot was William Carstares, who, according to Burnet, was sent from Holland at this time 'with a paper of instructions, that were drawn so darkly, that no wonder if they gave a jealousy of some ill designs then on foot'. Burnet says that the Prince of Orange, when asked about it, declared that these instructions were only concerned with recruiting troops for the Dutch service in Flanders, and this may be true, but the mention of money to be paid, men to be raised, and compliments to be made to the Duke of Hamilton (leader of the opposition to Lauderdale) all seemed very suspicious. Lauderdale was given the task of interrogating Carstares, and, says Burnet, took advantage of it to influence Charles against his enemies; and he told Ruvigny that the Scot had confessed that the Prince of Orange was keeping up relations with Shaftesbury and Halifax. It would be dangerous, however, to accept without corroboration this statement or Lauderdale's addition that Arlington was also in these intrigues. For Arlington was now about to go on a special embassy to The Hague, one of the objects of which was to urge William to dismiss Du Moulin. The confessions of Howard and Carstares (if that tough Scottish conspirator did in fact confess) showed once more how necessary it was to get rid of so dangerous an organizer of conspiracies.[1]

Du Moulin had long foreseen that such a demand would be made of William, and that it would be in the Prince's interest to yield to it: he had been invaluable in forcing Charles to make peace, but was now a serious bar to normal friendly relations with Charles, who, however much William distrusted him, was now the greatest neutral power. Du Moulin saw that he must not expect permanent employment with William, and accordingly in the summer of 1674 he began to look for a retreat in the governorship of Surinam, that same South American colony which had caused so much friction between England and Holland. He could expect William's support in this application, but unfortunately the appointment to the governorship of Surinam was under the control of the authorities of the province of Zeeland, where

[1] R.A. Fagel 244, *passim* Feb.–July 1674; Ruvigny to Louis XIV, 9/19 Nov. 1674; Burnet, ii. 65; 'A Copy of Mr. Carstairs' Examination, Oct. 3, 1674', MSS. Carte 222, f. 192.

the influence of Arlington's brother-in-law, Odyck, was paramount. Difficulties were made, which led to Du Moulin writing for assistance to an old patron, van Beuningen (now the Dutch ambassador in London), in a letter which, whatever its effect, throws some light on his character. It is something of a justification of the policy which he had advocated with regard to England, and which he still continued to advocate. Evidently considerable care was taken over its composition and there are several copies surviving in Du Moulin's papers, so that it may have been a kind of 'open letter' intended for other people besides van Beuningen. Perhaps it was partly intended as a reply to some people who were urging William to give up his relations with the English opposition, since there was a possibility of the English Court pursuing a policy more favourable to him.[1]

Du Moulin begins by pointing out that events had shown that his previous analyses of English policy had been accurate, and not simply the passionate outbursts of an embittered exile; and the same loyalty to William urged him to maintain his attitude to the English Court until he saw evidence of a real change there. The friendship of the English Court, if Charles's prepossessions could be removed, would be valuable, but only if it was genuine. Events had shown how little effect repeated friendly approaches to Charles had had, and how a different policy had brought about the change to a peace treaty to the benefit of Europe; as long as Dutch policy had been based on trying to convert a deluded Court, the English had held out for severe peace conditions, but when firmer measures had been taken (or in other words, when encouragement had been given to the Country Party) Charles could hardly get the Treaty of Westminster signed and ratified quickly enough. Further, 'la terreur a produit la paix, il faut que la terreur la conserve, et lors qu'on ne sera plus craint, on ne sera plus écouté'. The friendship of the English people had been the sheet-anchor which had saved Holland; if the anchor were cut, shipwreck would be almost inevitable. The complaints which the English Court was making about Dutch relations with 'the English people' were the best evidence how invaluable a weapon this connexion was. There

[1] Letter of 13/23 Aug. 1674, in R.A. Fagel 274.

was no evidence that the Treaty of Westminster represented a real change of heart in the English Court; its foreign policy had only been changed because it was powerless to do anything else, and at the same time as it was trying to break Dutch friendship with 'the nation', the Court was working for a general peace treaty favourable to France. Du Moulin's general conclusion was that van Beuningen's policy should be to 'combler la Cour de civilités sans les guérir de leurs soupçons, et conserver l'affection du peuple sans qu'on le puisse accuser de cabaler'.

Du Moulin then went on to apologize for his outspokenness, saying that dissimulation was not one of his qualities, and that he hated it too much to use it in so important a matter. This served as a transition to the more personal part of the letter. He confessed himself not surprised at Charles's bad opinion of him (which van Beuningen had evidently described in a previous letter), but said that it was too flattering since William was well able to take his own decisions. In any case, where the interests of Charles and William conflicted, the irritation of the English Court and its persecution would have little effect on him: 'Le témoignage de ma conscience fera toujours tout mon bonheur, et les épreuves par où j'ai passé depuis diverses années m'ont rendu assez philosophe pour ne plus chercher de félicité hors de moi-même; *hic murus aheneus erit*, etc.'

However, as true philosophy did not forbid its votaries to flee from persecution and to seek some place where they might enjoy a state of 'ataraxy' in peace, he had long thought of retiring to America, and in particular to the governorship of Surinam. There the complaints of the English Court could not pursue him; there he would be able to enjoy the two pleasures of the Prince of poets, which had always been the objects of his love—*dulces musae et dei agrestes*; and perhaps also he would be able to render service to Holland for which posterity would be grateful, 'le soin des colonies étant un des plus dignes d'un honnête homme, quoique des moins éclatants'. He was convinced that in justice the States-General and William would take care of him, and see him honourably settled after the way in which God had blessed his efforts for them; and he flattered himself that van Beuningen would not deny him his support. In the meantime 'je travaillerai à faire connaître à Son Altesse que mon éloignement lui sera plus avantageux que mon service ne lui est utile, et quoique l'honneur d'être auprès de sa personne soit préférable à tout autre emploi, je me soumettrai sans murmure à ce à quoi ma destinée semble m'appeler, et je tiendrai mon bonheur sans égal si je puis me voir un jour dans quelque port où je n'aie plus de tempête à craindre'.

This remarkable picture of Du Moulin reading Virgil in a rustic retirement on the shores of Dutch Guiana, and combining 'ataraxy' with the development of a colony, was not destined to be realized. Even his powerful patrons could not get him the appointment he wanted; and his mood of submission to the inevitable was soon to be tested, for in November Arlington arrived in The Hague with the definite object (among others) of securing his removal.

Since the Treaty of Westminster Arlington's fortunes had been on the decline. In September 1674 it had been arranged that he should resign his Secretaryship of State to Sir Joseph Williamson, and take instead the post of Lord Chamberlain. In some ways this exchange of a post which had given him twelve years' hard work, and latterly the constant risk of parliamentary attack, for an honorary post at Court was probably not unwelcome to him. But at the same time his influence with Charles was steadily decreasing, partly because he was suspected of intrigues with the Country Party in order to save himself in January 1674, partly because he had now, like Clarendon in 1667, outlived his usefulness. Above all, Arlington's influence declined as that of his rival, Danby, grew; for Danby's financial skill was making him indispensable to Charles. By the autumn of 1674 Arlington badly needed some new means of making himself useful to Charles if he was to retain any power at all, and he decided that the best way of recovering his influence would be by being instrumental in bringing together Charles and William of Orange. If he could get William to abandon Du Moulin and his intrigues with members of the Country Party, perhaps even get him to say who his English allies had been, and then arrange a marriage between William and James's daughter, Princess Mary, to cement a new and closer connexion between William and his uncle, then his stock would be bound to rise again. Representing to Charles that he was well fitted to reach this understanding with William on account of his family connexions in Holland, he received Charles's approval for a special diplomatic mission (much to the disgust of James, Ruvigny, Lauderdale, and Danby, who all distrusted the mission exceedingly). On his mission he took with him his brother-in-law Ossory, who had married into the same Dutch family (the Beverweerts), and was a friend of William's, also desirous of a marriage between William and Mary.

Hearing that this mission was about to visit him, William turned to his authority on English affairs, Du Moulin, to ask what change in English policy it portended, and Du Moulin responded by drawing up a last memorial on the English political situation at this time.[1] This memorial of the autumn of 1674 is an interesting pendant to the two written two years earlier when Du Moulin first entered into William's service. Like them, it is long, closely reasoned, and difficult to summarize briefly.

He began by laying it down that it was clear to all with the slightest knowledge of English affairs that the French alliance, the Stop of the Exchequer, the Declaration of Indulgence, the attack on Holland, and the raising of a standing army during the war were all aimed at making Charles absolute; and in the hope that Louis XIV would assist them to vanquish the people's rights and privileges, Charles's ministers had been prepared to see Louis master of the greater part of Europe. Du Moulin's contention was that 'the Court' had since made some slight changes in policy and in personnel, but that its fundamental aims remained the same. The Declaration of Indulgence had been revoked, the standing army had been dismissed, and peace had been made with Holland, only when 'the Court' had been forced to do so. Buckingham had been disgraced at Parliament's request and because the other ministers distrusted him; Shaftesbury had been dismissed because he had changed his mind and formed connexions with the Country Party; Arlington had declined in favour because, though he agreed with 'the Court's' policy

[1] R.A. Fagel 251.

in every way, he was timid and irresolute in carrying it out
when faced by parliamentary attack and prepared to do anything to save himself; so that the ministerial changes which
had taken place did not mean that the fundamental policy
had been changed, but were rather manœuvres to allow it to
be continued. Lauderdale, indeed, was more absolutist than
ever, in England as well as Scotland, and therefore more in
favour, particularly with the Duke of York to whom he paid
his court, but also with Charles, who had protected him
against parliamentary attack in both kingdoms. Danby, too,
Du Moulin mistakenly argued, had attached himself to the
Duke of York and Lauderdale, and in any case, as his office
of Lord Treasurer was 'the most advantageous' in the kingdom, its holder would almost inevitably attach himself to the
dominant faction in order to keep it. It was also noted that
Lauderdale, Danby, and the Duke of York were now all
declared enemies of Arlington's.

At this point Du Moulin added that he could say much
about the Duke of York, but as this matter was a little delicate,
and in any case well known to those most concerned, it would
be sufficient to say that James would, humanly speaking, never
change his views in regard to Holland (the words 'will always
be the most violent and implacable enemy that Holland can
have' are deleted in the original draft), and a sincere reconciliation was impossible. In general, a change in the policy of the
English Court might well be wished for but was not very likely;
the Court's despotic aims inside England were so intimately
bound up with the French connexion, that this connexion
could only be broken if the Court's absolutist plans were
furthered in some other way or forcibly changed. More ex-
plicitly, a change could only come if either there was a
miraculous voluntary reconciliation between King, ministers,
and nation, or the Court was forced to call a Parliament
which would compel the adoption of a new policy and an
alliance with the coalition against France.

Since this was the only way in which there could be a
change in English policy useful to Holland, the only way in
which Arlington could be of service to William would be in
persuading Charles to call Parliament, and then joining with
those members who were best intentioned. It was unlikely,

however, that Arlington would want to do this, or be in any way inclined to oppose the King and his favourites, who could ruin him by taking his Irish lands and the lucrative control of the Posts. Arlington must therefore be treated with great circumspection, and not trusted until the sincerity of his intentions was beyond doubt. Even if Arlington was keen enough on revenge on his enemies to risk ruin by opposing 'the favourites' (Du Moulin added scornfully of his old enemy) his ability was too mediocre for it to be prudent to put him in charge of a matter of such importance; others more skilful would be needed to guide him and keep him on the right path.

Du Moulin concluded by providing a criterion by which all English policy might be judged. The Duke of York was as it were the pulse of the English Court, indicating good or ill health as his favour fell and rose. In general, the memorial bears obvious affinities to the aims and preoccupations of the Country Party, and it is clear that Du Moulin would have liked William to continue in peace-time the connexions with it which had been so successful during the war. William did not accept all of this analysis of the situation, but it was not without its effect on him during the talks which followed with Arlington. It should be mentioned that the memorial is undated, and some of the remarks about Arlington suggest that it may have been drawn up after Arlington had arrived and made some general offer to serve William's interests.

In his aim of inducing William to dismiss Du Moulin, Arlington was successful, for finally the Prince reluctantly agreed, no doubt thinking that it was not worth while to retain him at the price of altogether alienating Charles. The last draft of a letter of William's in Du Moulin's handwriting is dated 17/27 November. A week later Bulstrode reported from Brussels a confidential report that Du Moulin had been disgraced and was about to seek to enter the service of the Spanish governor there. Later reports tended rather to modify this news; the suspicion arose that while this dangerous enemy had been officially dismissed, he was still available for William to consult in private; and finally it appeared, in answer to further pressure from Arlington, that William would not ruin Du Moulin entirely after the services he had rendered, but would send him out of the way to Africa [*sic*] where no one could suspect his conduct. Still, though William refused to abandon his old servant altogether, he no longer acted as William's confidential secretary.[1]

This, however, was the limit of Arlington's success. He could find out nothing more about William's relations with the English opposition. William frankly admitted that he had used every possible means of forcing Charles to make peace, but maintained that since the Treaty of Westminster had been signed he had given up all his intelligences in England. When taxed with the instructions which Carstares carried in Du Moulin's handwriting, he said at first that he knew nothing about it, and made a note to ask Du Moulin; and later, according to Burnet, said that it concerned only the recruiting of volunteer troops. In answer to Arlington's exhortations to him to name those Englishmen with whom he had co-operated during the war, William made it a point of honour to keep their secret. In this connexion Ruvigny maintained that William should frankly have confessed everything, and asked for pardon for himself and his supporters: refusal to name them was to adhere to a crime of *lèse-majesté* and to protect subjects against their sovereign—and besides, he argued, it was a convincing proof that William intended to adopt the same methods again. But this talk of *lèse-majesté*, characteristic of the servants of Louis XIV, had no effect on Englishmen or Dutchmen.[2]

The projected marriage with Princess Mary, which Arlington and Ossory had hoped for, also found no favour with William. Openly he said that Mary was too young (she was only twelve), but there were more serious reasons. He was afraid that the marriage would make him too dependent on his uncles, that it would restrict his diplomacy in Europe, and that it would identify him with an unpopular Court in England. Moreover, Du Moulin's reports and his own experience led him to distrust any offer brought by Arlington. He bitterly resented Arlington's patronizing manner, and

[1] Bulstrode to Williamson, 24 Nov./4 Dec., S.P. 77/44, f. 274; Ruvigny to Louis, 3/13 Dec. and 7/17 Jan. 1675.
[2] Ruvigny, loc. cit., and dispatch of 31 Dec./10 Jan. 1674/5; Arlington to Charles, 14/24, 17/27 Nov., Add. MSS. 32094, ff. 325-31.

complained of it to Temple, 'that it was not only in the discourses of it, as if he [Arlington] pretended to deal with a
child, that he could by his wit make believe what he pleased,
but in the manner he said all upon that subject, it was as if
he had taken himself for the Prince of Orange, and him for
my Lord Arlington. . . .'[1]

Both Charles and Arlington paid the penalty of treating
William as a callow, inexperienced young man who would
make a natural protégé. Arlington now had to return home
and confess the failure of his last scheme to retain Charles's
favour.

His mission had been a dismal disappointment from which
his old servant Du Moulin derived great satisfaction. As
Temple told Danby (assuring him how futile the embassy
had been),

little Moulin, that was inquisitive enough upon the first arrival of
those lords, has said often and publicly since that it was too much
honour for him that so great persons should make such a winter journey for nothing but to destroy poor Moulin. And yet in that very
point I do not see that they had very great success neither, or that he
is not likely to be provided for better than either he deserves or could
have pretended to in any other country. . . .[2]

Indeed, in February 1675 rumours reached Arlington that,
after all, Du Moulin was secretly plotting on William's
behalf to stir up trouble for Charles when Parliament met in
April. Again he made a disastrous error in his approach to
William; he wrote a letter, at once protesting against the
favour said to be shown to Du Moulin, and going on to
threaten that there were discontents in Holland too, and 'si
on les touchait, on les pourrait faire saigner encore'.

William went straight round to read this letter to Sir
William Temple. He had already been declaring to Temple,
'would to God none about the King had worse intentions to
his service, than I have; but if he will not believe me, what
can I do?' He now called on Temple, read the letter 'with a
good deal of emotion', and, comparing it with the threat to
van Reede in September 1672, to make William 'served as

1 Temple, i. 213.
2 9/19 Feb. 1675 in A. Browning, *Danby*, ii. 456–7.

M. de Witt was' (a threat which he apparently attributed here to Arlington),

he swore in a rage, that he could not bear this language from my Lord Arlington . . . under profession of friendship, and of dealing plainly with him, he saw very well that he did him all the mischief he could . . . he wished he might die on the place, if he, or any man he knew here, had the least thoughts of making any intrigues with the Parliament . . . or if ever he had thought or done anything in the war itself, that deserved any such language as this.

As Temple said, a great deal of passion was vented, combined with numerous professions of William's innocence and his friendly disposition to Charles; all of which Temple duly reported in a letter to Charles in the hope that it would finally destroy the credit of his enemy Arlington. Certainly this outburst, on the part of a prince who is usually described as cold and calculating, sounds genuine; and if so it follows that William had given up his relations with the opposition and considered that he had not done anything in the war, which could be construed as encouraging rebellion. If Du Moulin was still intriguing (of which there is no evidence), his intrigues at this time were unauthorized.[1]

In his anger against Arlington, William went so far as to say that through his brother-in-law Odyck, he was deliberately preventing Du Moulin from getting his appointment out of harm's way in Surinam, because as long as that terrible conspirator was still in Holland, Arlington could continue to misrepresent William to Charles. Certainly the *Gecommitteerde Raden* of Zeeland continued to put difficulties in the way of Du Moulin's appointment to the governorship. Letters from William in his support failed to overcome these obstructions, and he stayed on in The Hague, without official employment. For some reason he quarrelled with Captain Brodnax, his old colleague in the distribution of the *Appeal*; Brodnax 'caned him' and as a result spent some time in prison to expiate his offence. By now Du Moulin had fallen out with many of his former rank-and-file associates, but still enjoyed some protection from the authorities.[2]

---

[1] Temple to Charles II, 15/25 Mar., in *Works*, iv. 92–96.
[2] Japikse, *Corres.*, II. ii. 21–23; W. Carr to Williamson, 5/15 Apr. and 27 Apr./ 7 May, S.P. 84/198, f. 227 and 199, f. 6.

During the summer of 1675 the Zeelanders continued to refuse to appoint him. Accordingly at the end of July he paid a fortnight's visit to William's camp, where (apart from glorifying the passion of revenge and saying to members of William's staff that he had never failed to gratify it against people of whatever rank), he induced William to find him another temporary post. Until the States of Zeeland could be persuaded to give him his governorship, he was to be sent as William's representative to the army of the Imperial general Montecuculi, to report what took place there. Care was taken that Pensionary Fagel should inform Sir William Temple, to forestall any English objections to the appointment.[1]

It is hardly to be imagined that he had abandoned his old interest in English affairs, but there is only one indication of the form which this interest took in the winter of 1675–6. This is to be found in a long letter addressed to an unknown peer which was intercepted by the English government. It consists of three pages of derisive sneers at 'the officers of the Royal Regiment of Fops, whereof your worship is adjutant', in which the Court Party is satirized at length. The letter's contents are not particularly important, but the mere fact of the existence of such a letter gives food for thought. Surely it is not the only letter of its kind—though no other letter of this period, either from or to Du Moulin, has survived, so far as is known. Evidently some mysterious intervention in English politics was still being undertaken.[2]

Whatever it was, it did not continue for very long, for all Du Moulin's activities were soon to be cut short by death. On 24 February/6 March 1676 his commission as governor of Surinam was at last conferred upon him, but he never saw the shores of the South American colony for which he had schemed, nor did he enjoy for very long the pension of 1,600 gulden which was voted to him shortly afterwards. His health had not been good even in 1674, and it was probably the disease which was soon to carry him off that prevented him from embarking for his new post. We catch

[1] Huygens den zoon, *Journaal,* in *Werken van het Historisch Genootschap* (Utrecht, 1881), nieuwe serie, iv, pp. 49, 50, 55; R. Meredith to Williamson, 20/30 Aug., in S.P. 84/199, f. 109.
[2] Letter of 31 Dec./10 Jan., 1675/6, *C.S.P.D. 1675–6,* pp. 589–90.

a last glimpse of a complaint made against him by another colleague, William 'Freeman';[1] and then we come to the final reports of his last days and death of 'a consumption, as his friends gave out', in June 1676.

It seems that on Thursday, 8/18 June, Du Moulin met Sir William Temple's chaplain, the Rev. Mr. Barrow, in the Voorhout at The Hague, and, as William Carr hastened to report,

told him, that he had something that lay heavy on his conscience against which he had long struggled, but now believing that he could not many days live, he was desirous to discharge his conscience, telling Mr. Barrow some particulars, as that he had wronged several great men in England, and in particular Sir William Temple, and others he named. But Mr. Barrow being called away to prayers, Du Moulin took his leave, only desiring Mr. Barrow to come to him, at such time as he should send his man for him. On Monday following he sent his man for Mr. Barrow but he was out of the way. The next day being Tuesday, Du Moulin took a vomit which wrought so violently that he broke some veins, so that bleeding at mouth, ears and nose, he died, strangled in his blood. Several people visited his body some little time after his death, who do affirm that he was as black as a coal, and stunk so that they could not endure the chamber. Some report he poisoned himself. All his books, papers and other things were seized on by one mynheer Halewyn, one of the judges of the High Court of Holland, who had order from Pensr. Fagel to bury him. There was 5 coaches at his funeral. . . .[2]

So the Huguenot exile died, and was buried in the Kloosterkerk at The Hague on 16/26 June 1676. There is no clue to the precise nature of the injustice to Temple of which he repented, or of the confession which he might have made at the last, had not the Rev. Mr. Barrow been unfortunately 'out of the way'. The historian has, however, the opportunity of consulting many of Du Moulin's papers, since William, on hearing of the death of 'poor Du Moulin', wrote immediately to Fagel,[3] that, since the dead man had had papers of great

---

[1] J. H. Hora Siccama, *Aantekeningen . . . op de Journalen van Huygens den zoon, W. Hist. Gen.*, 3 serie xxxv. (Amsterdam, 1915), p. 479; Japikse, *Corres.*, II. ii. 79–80.

[2] Carr to Williamson, undated, S.P. 84/201, f. 362, cf. Temple, i. 257–8; Huygens den zoon, *Journaal*, pp. 107–8; van der Meulen, *Registers der graven in de Kloosterkerk*, p. 54.

[3] William to Fagel, 14/24 June, Japikse, *Corres.*, II. ii. 114.

importance in his possession, he should see to it that these did not fall into wrong hands; and Fagel accordingly sent Halewijn to take charge of them. They are now preserved amongst Fagel's papers in the Rijksarchief. And yet—it is odd that no document written later than November 1674 should survive among them, particularly in view of the letter which we have previously noted as being intercepted by the English authorities; and in addition, Williamson's correspondent, in reporting his death, said that he had secured from a servant 'a libel intended to be printed against the next sessions of Parliament'. Did any of his papers fall into 'wrong hands' after all? From Huygens we learn that his servants robbed him on his deathbed: his death took place on the 13th, William wrote to secure his papers on the 14th, and Halewijn may have seized them on the 15th. There *might* have been an opportunity for one of the 'several people' who 'visited his body some little time after his death' to examine the papers first. In any event, however, no papers have since come to light except through Fagel's collection.

Du Moulin's death was a very minor event in the annals of 1676. It passed almost unnoticed at the time, and has since been totally ignored by historians, to whom his career has been at most of passing interest. Yet William had some respect and some compassion for 'poor Du Moulin', and Williamson's correspondent thought his death at least worth reporting in some detail to London. It was the passing of someone who had played a part of some importance in the relations between the two countries at an important European crisis. When Williamson had passed through Holland in the spring of 1674 he had indeed been told that Howard and Du Moulin boasted that they had been worth 40,000 men to the States-General of the United Provinces. It remains briefly to consider the general results of their work (and that of their colleagues) on England and on Europe.

CONCLUSION

URING the two years spent by Du Moulin in the service of William of Orange there had been a transformation in the political scene. When he had fled from England to Holland in August 1672 the Dutch had seemed to be at the mercy of Louis XIV's army: it appeared to be only a matter of time before they accepted the terms dictated by the forces which occupied the heart of their country. Two years later Louis had had to abandon almost all his pretensions. In the late autumn of 1673 Luxembourg had abandoned Utrecht: after the signing of the Treaty of Westminster it was not long before orders were issued for a complete withdrawal from the French conquests in the United Provinces. Arnhem, Nijmegen, and other towns which had had French garrisons were evacuated, and by the end of May 1674 only Maastricht remained in Louis's possession. He had had to confess his failure to subdue the Dutch under the most favourable conditions possible.

Thus William had won the first round in his thirty years' struggle with Louis XIV: he had achieved survival for his country. This was primarily due to the determination which he had inspired in his people, to the inundations which were an insuperable physical obstacle to the French army, and to the diplomatic policy which built up a European coalition to strike back at France; but the pressure which he was able to bring on England, culminating in the Treaty of Westminster, was also an essential factor. Without the hope that England might be induced to make a separate peace, the will to resist of many Dutchmen would have been gravely weakened. Moreover, if the Dutch had had to shoulder over a long period the burden of providing for a sea war against England in addition to the land war against the French, their resources would soon have been overstrained; for quite apart from the problem of fitting out a fleet on a scale greater than that needed for De Ruyter's subsequent expeditions to the Mediterranean, the mere fact of a war with England, irrespective of any battles, meant a grievous interruption to the carrying trade on which their financial strength depended.

Though the English fleet had been able to achieve nothing, therefore, England's departure from the war at the Treaty of Westminster marked an important event in it. William could now proceed to the next stage, of trying to prevent Louis from making further conquests, mainly at the expense of Spain, by leading the coalition against him. In this stage, too, England's attitude was of vital importance, for it turned out that while England remained neutral (and usually benevolent to France) the coalition could restrain Louis to some extent, but could not prevent Louis from taking Franche-Comté, still less win back any of his gains. The European significance of the Revolution of 1688–9 was that it inaugurated a third stage, with England now the centre of the coalition against France, until the Grand Alliance rounded off the work which William had begun in 1672.

Similarly in English domestic politics the events of 1673–4 were the beginning of a process which culminated in 1688–9. The Treaty of Westminster represented the abandonment by Charles of the policy, domestic as well as foreign, laid down in the Secret Treaty of Dover and based on French assistance. Whatever the 'Catholic clauses' had meant in 1670, they meant nothing for Charles in 1674, as he abandoned his policy of indulgence in favour of a return to the traditional alliance with the Anglican Church, and even acceptance of the Test Act, while the open friendship with Louis XIV was given up. Here, too, however, the initial success of the Country Party was followed by a period of frustration such as William had to face abroad: they were unable to make much further headway. Charles secretly received more subsidies from Louis in return for his neutrality; in the person of James the 'Catholic Design' still lived, and all the attempts, foreshadowed in 1673–4, to exclude him from the succession failed; and eventually the 'Glorious Revolution' was needed to foil his plans, and to complete the work which had been begun fifteen years earlier.

Both internationally and internally, therefore, the successful agitation against Charles II's policy in 1673–4 marked the first essential stage in important developments. If, then, the activities of Du Moulin and his collaborators were of decisive importance in this agitation, their reported claim that they had been worth forty thousand men to the States-General[1] had some justification. No doubt they shared the common human failing (particularly common among men of their type) of exaggerating their own achievements. It is possible to speculate that Charles might have been obliged to change his policy in any case, without interference from William and his agents: Du Moulin did not create the constitutional discontents which he exploited. But when this has been said, it remains true that the pamphlets which he wrote and distributed did much to turn this discontent against the French alliance, which the House of Commons had shown no disposition to question in the session of early 1673. It is probably fair to conclude that he did more than any other man to spread distrust of the French alliance in men's minds and to turn this distrust to William's advantage. That contemporaries thought so is clear, not only from the esteem which William, van Beuningen, Don Bernardo de Salinas, and other patrons had for him, but from the hatred of his enemies, from the tone of the references to 'Dutch libels' in letters written to Williamson, and from the efforts made to persuade William to dismiss him, and even to prevent him from becoming governor of Surinam.

If it be true that the sincerest form of flattery is imitation, then the best testimony to the effect of the 'political warfare' waged by Du Moulin's 'fifth column' is to be found in the efforts to copy it. It was not merely that Charles adopted some of the methods of his opponents, in his letter of 7/17 November 1673 and in commissioning Evelyn to write a reply to the Dutch 'manifest' in January 1674; the French ambassador, Ruvigny, was so much impressed by the success of the Dutch methods that he too tried to build up a party in the Commons, and to put the French side of the case before them, and recommended his master that money used to publish pamphlets would be well spent. In March 1674 a French pamphlet on the arrest of Fürstenburg did in fact appear.[2] During the following years, rumours of attempts by French, Dutch, and Spanish ambassadors to cultivate a clientele in the House are numerous, and it is not certain that when

---

[1] Noted by Williamson in his Journal, 6/16 May, S.P. 105/222.
[2] Ruvigny to Pomponne, 30 Mar./9 Apr.

efforts to convince degenerated into plain bribery, they were more successful.

In general, the success of *England's Appeal* and other 'libels' was probably a powerful stimulus to political pamphleteering. Of course, there had been many pamphlets before 1673, but none so obviously effective in bringing about political results; and it is probably no accident that within a few years the *Growth of Popery* (its author once probably connected with Du Moulin) was only the best-known work of many in a period when pamphleteering was organized for party purposes under Shaftesbury. And it was not only the leaders of the English parties who had learned its value. When, in the critical days of November, 1688, copies of William's Declaration were spread about in London, William was employing the same technique which had stood him in such good stead fifteen years earlier.[1]

[1] Macaulay (ed. Firth, 1913–15), iii. 1118.

BIBLIOGRAPHY

THE following are the main sources which have been consulted and the abbreviations which have been employed in the footnotes.

A. MANUSCRIPT SOURCES

R.A. Fagel. The Fagel papers in the Rijksarchief at The Hague. Folders 244 and following contain Du Moulin's papers, seized by William's order as described in Chapter X. Some letters drafted by Du Moulin as William's secretary are reprinted in Japikse, *Corres.* (see below), as also are a few letters now in the Koninklijk Huisarchief at The Hague.

R.A. St.-Gen. The Rijksarchief also contains dispatches from Boreel and the Dutch deputies in England in 1672, written to the States-General.

S.P. Of the State Papers in the Public Record Office, the State Papers Foreign for Holland (S.P. 84), France (S.P. 78), Flanders (S.P. 77), the German States (S.P. 81), and Denmark (S.P. 75) have been consulted: also S.P. 105 for Williamson's papers and journal at Cologne, and S.P. Car. II, the State Papers Domestic.

For. Ent. Bk. Foreign Entry Book 177 in the Public Record Office contains Williamson's notes of discussions at the Committee of Foreign Affairs in 1672–3.

The dispatches of the French ambassadors in London have been used in the transcripts in the Public Record Office. Add. MSS. 34341–4 in the British Museum contain letters from Flanders to Sir R. Southwell.

B. PRIMARY PRINTED SOURCES

Aitzema. L. v. Aitzema, *Saken van Staet en Oorlogh* (The Hague, 1669–71), continued by L. Sylvius, *Historia onzes tijds* (Amsterdam, 1685–99).

Burnet. G. Burnet, *History of My Own Time*, ed. Airy (1902).

C.J. Journals of the House of Commons.

Clarke. J. S. Clarke, *Life of James II* (1816).

C.S.P.D. Calendar of State Papers Domestic.

C.S.P.Ven. Calendar of State Papers Venetian.

Dering. *Parliamentary Journal of Sir E. Dering, 1670–3*, ed. B. D. Henning (1940).

Essex Papers. Essex Papers, ed. O. Airy and C. E. Pike (Camden Society, 1890–1913).

Grey. A. Grey, *Debates of the House of Commons, 1667–94*, vol. ii (1763).

Hop and Vivien. C. Hop and N. Vivien, *Notulen gehouden ter Staten-Vergadering van Holland, 1671–5*, ed. N. Japikse (Amsterdam, 1903).

Huygens den zoon. *Journaal van Constantijn Huygens, den zoon.* Printed in *Werken van het Historisch Genootschap*, 2ᵉ serie, iv. (Utrecht, 1881).

Japikse, *Corres.* N. Japikse, *Correspondentie van Willem III en van Hans Willem Bentinck* (Rijks geschiedkundige publicatien. The Hague, 1927–35).

Letters to Williamson. *Letters Addressed from London to Sir Joseph Williamson*, ed. W. D. Christie (Camden Society, 1874).
L.J. *Journals of the House of Lords.*
Temple. Sir W. Temple, *Works* (ed. 1754).
Wicquefort. A. de Wicquefort, *Histoire des Provinces Unies des Pays-Bas, depuis... la paix de Munster* (Amsterdam, 1861–74).

C. PAMPHLETS

England's Appeal from the Private Cabal at Whitehall to the Great Council of the nation, the Lords and Commons in Parliament assembled (1673). (In *State Tracts* . . . *printed in the reign of Charles II* (1689) and other collections.)
Relation of the most material matters handled in Parliament relating to religion, property and the liberty of the subject (1673). (Also in *State Tracts*.)
The Letter sent by the States-General (15/25 October, 1673) . . . *to His Majesty, together with His Majesty's Answer to the said Letter* (7/17 November 1673).
A Letter from the States-General . . . *to the King of Great Britain. Dated 9/19 December, 1673.*

D. MODERN SECONDARY AUTHORITIES

Barbour. V. Barbour, *The Earl of Arlington* (Washington, 1914).
Brown. L. F. Brown, *The First Earl of Shaftesbury* (New York, 1933).
Browning. A. Browning, *Thomas Earl of Danby* (1944–51).
Christie. W. D. Christie, *The First Earl of Shaftesbury* (1871).
Feiling, *Foreign Policy*. K. G. Feiling, *British Foreign Policy, 1660–72* (1930).
Foxcroft. H. C. Foxcroft, *Life and Letters of Halifax* (1898).
Geyl. P. Geyl, *Oranje en Stuart* (Utrecht, 1939).
Japikse, *Prins Willem III*. N. Japikse, *Prins Willem III* (Amsterdam, 1930–3).
Klopp. O. Klopp, *Der Fall des Hauses Stuart*, vols. i–ii (Vienna, 1875).
Korvezee. Elizabeth H. Korvezee, 'Zendingen van Frederik van Reede naar Engeland . . . 1672–4', article in *Bijdragen voor vaderlandsche geschiedenis*, 6e ser. vii (1928).
Krämer. F. J. L. Krämer, article in ibid., 3e ser. vi and vii (1892–3).
Mignet. F. A. M. Mignet, *Négotiations relatives à la succession d'Espagne sous Louis XIV* (Paris, 1835–42).
Pribram. A. F. Pribram, *Franz Paul, Freiherr von Lisola* (Leipzig, 1894).
Schotel. G. D. J. Schotel, 'Briefwisseling tusschen Karel II . . . en Willem III . . . in 1672', in *Bijdragen voor vaderlandsche geschiedenis*, N.S. iv (1866).
Trevelyan. Mary C. Trevelyan, *William III and the Defence of Holland* (1930).
Wagenaar. J. Wagenaar, *Vaderlandsche Historie*, vol. xiv (Amsterdam, 1756).

INDEX